BOOKS BY JAMES L. CREIGHTON

Getting Well Again
(Co-author with O. Carl Simonton and
Stephanie Matthews Simonton)

Don't Go Away Mad: How to Make Peace with Your Partner

PROFESSIONAL BOOKS

Cyber Meeting: How to Link People
and Technology in Your Organization

The Public Participation Manual

Guide to Social Assessment:
A Framework for Assessing Social Change
(Co-author with Kristi Branch,
James Thomson and Douglas Hopper)

How Loving Couples Fight

How Loving Couples Fight

Twelve Essential Tools

For Working Through the Hurt

By James L. Creighton, Ph.D.

Published by Aslan Publishing
Fairfield, Connecticut USA

Published by Aslan Publishing
2490 Black Rock Turnpike #342, Fairfield CT 06432 USA
Phone: 203-372-0300 • Fax: 203-374-4766
Email: info@aslanpublishing.com • Website: www.aslanpublishing.com
For a free catalog of our other titles, or to order more copies of this book call 800-786-5427.

Library of Congress Cataloging-in-Publication Data

Creighton, James L.
    How loving couples fight : twelve essential tools for working
through the hurt / by James Creighton.
      p. cm.
      Rev. ed. of: Don't go away mad. 1991.
      Includes bibliographical references.
      ISBN 0-944031-71-4 (pbk. : alk. paper)
      1. Interpersonal conflict. 2. Marital conflict. 3. Intimacy
(Psychology) 4. Interpersonal communication. 5. Problem solving.
I. Creighton, James L. Don't go away mad. II. Title.
[BF637.I48C74 1998]
158.2--DC21   98-19882
                            CIP

Newly revised edition
Originally published in hardback by Doubleday as "Don't Go Away Mad"
Copyright © 1990, 1998 James L. Creighton

P.O. Box 1030, Los Gatos, CA 95031
Email: jim@CandCinc.com

Cover design: Linda Hauck, Hauck and Associates
Cover illustration: Lynn Bell, Monroe Street Studios
Cover photo: Phoenix Photography
Keyboarding: Vivian Bradbury, San Serif
Book design: Sara L. Greenfield, Greenfield Graphics
Book illustration: Brad Huck, Purrfect Images
Printed in USA by Baker Johnson, Inc., Dexter, Michigan

10   9   8   7   6   5   4   3   2   1

Aslan Publishing — Our Mission

Aslan Publishing offers readers a window to the soul via well-crafted and practical self-help books, inspirational books and modern-day parables. Our mission is to publish books that uplift the mind, body and spirit.

Living one's spirituality in business, relationships, and personal growth is the underlying purpose of our publishing company, and the meaning behind our name Aslan Publishing. We see the word "Aslan" as a metaphor for living spiritually in a physical world.

Aslan means "lion" in several Middle Eastern languages. The most famous "Aslan" is a lion in *The Chronicles of Narnia* by C.S. Lewis. In these stories, Aslan is the Messiah, the One who appears at critical points in the story in order to point human beings in the right direction. Aslan doesn't preach, he acts. His actions are an inherent expression of who he is.

We hope to point the way toward joyful, satisfying and healthy relationships with oneself and others. Our purpose is to make a real difference in the everyday lives of our readers.

Barbara & Harold Levine, Publishers

To my wife, Maggie

I may have written the book,
but everything in it we lived together.

Acknowledgment

This book draws on everything I have done in my professional life, and thus all the people along the way. But some are owed a special debt of gratitude for their contribution to this book.

This book has been dedicated to my wife, and with good reason. We have learned the skills in this book together, working out our own painful issues, and discovering our own joys. For me, she is in every page of the book, whether mentioned or not. So are our children: Katy Gallagher, William Brown, Priscilla Lutts, Alan Ashby, and Timothy Brown (who has passed away). Whether they intended to or not, each of them has helped me move away from romantic or academic theory about communication and conflict and find practical application.

This is a new edition of a book that was published in hardback edition by Doubleday under the title, "Don't Go Away Mad." Several times the book was slated for paperback publication, then each time something intervened. The book got "lost," a publisher got fired, another publisher went bankrupt. It seemed the fates had ordained that the book never come out in paperback.

For this reason I am particularly indebted to Barbara and Hal Levine, the new publishers of Aslan, for finally making publication of this book a reality. Barbara, herself a successful author, and Hal have taken on the revitalization of Aslan as their personal mission. As one of the beneficiaries, I am very grateful. Others who contributed to the editing, book design and presentation include Judy Tompkins, Marcia Yudkin, Vivian Bradbury, Linda Hauck, and Sara Greenfield. One good thing about all the delays is that, in my opinion at least, the new edition is better organized, easier to read, and more direct. Special gratitude is due my dear friend Mike Lash, who buoyed my flagging spirits when I had just about given up on ever having the book appear in paperback.

I was also blessed with supportive and caring people during the preparation of the hardback edition published by Doubleday. Sandra Dijkstra, literary agent, encouraged and goaded me into finally producing a proposal that communicated the whole vision. Hal Zina Bennett, himself a well-known author, worked with me throughout the preparation of the book, straightening out my struggling syntax, simplifying unnecessarily complex statements, finding organization in confused ramblings. One of the delights of writing this book has been that I started out to find someone to help me in the writing, and have found someone I believe to be a true and important friend. Casey Fuetsch and Jill Roberts of Doubleday significantly shaped the final version of the book, but with a constant concern for the substance of the material. I am grateful.

Early in my career I had the pleasure of working for several years with Dr. Thomas E. Gordon, the founder of Parent Effectiveness Training. Dr. Gordon's work inspired much of my own work with couples and organizations over the past twenty years, and this book itself. I

A c k n o w l e d g m e n t

am indebted not only to Tom Gordon but also to the late Gene Merrill, who introduced me to Tom. Gene was first my boss, then mentor, then partner.

Special thanks go also to Dr. Ron Jones, whose support and insightfulness as a counselor have been so important for my wife and me, and who demonstrated the same penetrating insight in his review of the manuscript.

I also wish to extend my gratitude to the many couples with whom I have worked over the years, letting me share their lives. Finally, I want to express my appreciation to the many researchers, consultants, and teachers who have and are continuing to create the new science of conflict resolution.

Foreword

My marriage ended over fifteen years ago, so I'm an unusual choice to write a foreword for a book about how to stay together. Nevertheless, this book touched my life.

I can't speak for my ex-wife, but for me, the end of our marriage was an event that I never expected in my wildest dreams. When it happened, the breakup of our family was devastating for me and painful and bewildering for each of my three teenaged sons and my four-year-old daughter.

Why did my marriage fail? I turned this question over in my mind repeatedly for years after the divorce. We had been married for twenty years, and although we had our arguments from time to time and our share of differences, I honestly thought we had a healthy marriage. Yet I couldn't help but wonder about the number of issues that my wife brought up during the six months or so leading up to the divorce, problems that we had argued about years before and that I thought were put aside and forgotten for good.

Some time after the divorce I saw a copy of the hardback version of this book by Jim Creighton. As I read the book I began to see clearly how the seeds of discord were sown from the earliest days of my marriage, seeds that quietly grew larger in the hearts and minds of both me and my wife.

I think of this book as a map. In my case it is a map of how my marriage went sour and finally failed. But it can also serve as a map of how to build a strong and lasting foundation for a marriage or any other type of human relationship. I feel certain that had my wife and I worked to incorporate Creighton's recommendations for listening and dealing with conflict, we would still be a united family. As it is, the book helped me and my children recoup what we could from the separation and build love and harmony into our relationships.

I was so moved by the book that I even arranged for a group of us to teach the main principles of the book at an adult education course at my church. We also taught the communication skills to a group of counselors working with prisoners to make a successful transition from jail to a productive life.

Recently there's been a lot of talk about "emotional intelligence," but not too much discussion about how people learn to be emotionally intelligent. The skills and concepts in this book are the basics of emotional intelligence. Creighton's suggestions for how to listen and how to deal with conflict are golden. They can bring much sunlight to all our relationships.

Michael Lash
Prison Ministry Coordinator
St. James Episcopal Church
Potomac, MD

Contents

TOOL #8

TOOL #9

TOOL #10

Introduction

This book first appeared in hardback in 1990, under a different title. I heard from a number of people who had used the skills in this book in their relationships and I was thrilled at some of the different ways people were applying them. One family therapist assigned couples a chapter a week, and then would work with them to ensure they knew how to use the skills in the chapter and could handle the emotional issues that came up when they did use them. A dear friend used the book to train church counselors working with people who were in prison, and his pastor was so impressed that he did a series of sermons using materials from the book. Some couples systematically worked through the entire book together, while others found particular skills helpful and concentrated on them.

From these responses it is clear that the ideal way to work on these skills is as a couple, reading the book together, discussing the concepts, and then practicing the skills together. Start by concentrating on the material which seems most crucial or interesting to you right now. It may take months before you are really applying all your learning to your relationship. But the time and effort you invest will not only enrich your closest relationships; you will find these skills invaluable in the future, personally and professionally.

Because it is easiest to make the needed changes as a couple working together, the letters I received that were the hardest to handle came from individuals who were in pain because of their fights, but whose loved one was not interested in the book or would not even acknowledge there was a problem. This is such a lonely place to be in. It is so easy to feel hopeless.

But if you wait for your loved one to change, you are giving away your power. That person becomes your explanation for why your life cannot be better, and your resentment will only fuel more fights. You have simply got to start by changing what you can change yourself. There are many skills in this book you can use without waiting for anyone else. You can learn new skills for listening so your loved one does not have to escalate emotionally to feel understood. You can communicate feelings without blaming and attacking your loved one. You can identify problems without setting up power struggles. You can put limits on your own behavior even if your loved one does not. It is harder than if you were working together. But if you start fighting differently, it will change how your partner fights as well. Some of the most rewarding letters came from people who had started out making the changes all alone, but later reported that their loved one had joined them in a common effort to change how they resolved conflicts.

When you are first learning, the main difficulty you face is developing skills. But after you have learned them, you are faced with the new challenge of being willing to apply them. Once I have learned, for example, how to communicate my feelings without blaming and accusing, I still have to be willing not to blame and accuse. And there are times when I want nothing more than to blame and accuse. Of course when I do fall prey to these impulses, the results are predictably disastrous, and I end up needing all the skills I possess to dig myself out of the mess.

Like most people, you may be tempted to try to instantly master everything described here, which frequently leads to abandoning the endeavor as just too formidable. Some of the skills you will be learning, such as Active Listening, may take months of practice before you are confident you can use them in any situation. Even after that there will be times when you are so upset you will not want to use them, even if you should. No matter how old you are, you already have years invested in handling fights in the ways that created the problem. Breaking a habit is hard. Do not expect this will be any different. But it is worth the effort.

In many places throughout this book I have referred to the transition from painful fights to loving solutions as a "journey" or "adventure." If you have ever gone on a real adventure you may remember there were times you were scorched in the sun, soaked and miserable in the rain, attacked by mosquitoes, and often just plain bored. Somehow when you look back on the adventure only the memories of exciting times and the satisfaction of conquering the challenges are the ones that remain.

The journey to make your intimate relationships more fulfilling will be no different. There will be times when you will stop and wonder why you ever began, when you will feel caught in between, with neither the protection afforded by the old behaviors nor the promised intimacy of the new. I can only assure you that the rewards are out there and will ultimately prove to be worth every moment of doubt and struggle you experience along the way. I still visit all those places of doubt and fear along that route, and they are all part what finally makes my life easier and my relationships richer.

I would like to think that our need to be close to others, to share our lives, serves some larger purpose. I sometimes have this fantasy that God or Life or whatever you want to call it, created Earth as a kind of school. But there were so many distractions and pleasures that there was a danger people would not learn anything. So to encourage people to grow, mature, heal their emotional wounds, and become happier and more productive, each person was given an innate need for closeness and intimacy with others. It is the ideal motivator to ensure that no matter what hazards are confronted along the way, we will keep changing and growing. As much as we might wish we did not need this closeness, it is this need for closeness which ultimately transforms us into all that we can be as individuals and valued spouses and friends. It is this need for intimacy and closeness that makes us fight, and makes the fights worthwhile.

PART I

THE GROUND RULES

OF LOVING CONFLICT

Take Responsibility for

the Outcome of Conflicts

Most of us receive years of formal training in reading, writing, and social skills needed in adulthood. But few of us receive even a single hour of systematic training in conflict resolution. So it is little wonder that we end up in fights, and that when we do fight we hurt the people we love, and sometimes even destroy our relationships.

When we are in emotional conflicts with the people most important to us we often say and do things in anger that we later deeply regret. We come away from our fights with secret hurts that build up inside, causing us to question ourselves or the relationship. In time, if these secret hurts are not resolved, we may even become convinced that "relationships are just impossible" or that "one or the other of us simply is not fit to live with."

Such battles come as a severe shock to many of us. I know that when I married, more than thirty years ago, I certainly could not imagine that having fights would ever be a problem for us.

There are all kinds of reasons why people think they are different and will not get into fights. Some assume that if they love each other enough that there will never be fights. It is a shock to find that we are far more likely to fight with the people we love, and when we do fight, we are far more likely to say and do things we could not imagine ourselves doing. It is as if love brings things to the surface we did not even know were inside us. We would always have thought of ourselves as pretty relaxed, comfortable people, the person who smooths things over. But here we are screaming, calling names, and plotting revenge.

Some people thought they would not fight because they had been in therapy, joined growth groups, or practiced a spiritual discipline. I started out believing this. I had coped with a painful childhood by undergoing therapy, trained in psychology, and not only participated in but actually helped pioneer the use of personal growth techniques. Certainly I did not expect to find myself in horrible fights. But here I was, behaving in ways that violated my own standards and left me feeling guilty and a fraud.

Some people thought their relationship was made in heaven. They assumed they were so "right" together that they would live happily ever after, without any strain, no fuss, no muss. I suspect that such relationships only exist in the movies, where couples have a script to follow, and they only have to keep it up for an hour and a half. I remember reading that Cary Grant, the suave, sophisticated ladies' man on the screen, had many troubled personal relationships and was acutely aware of this difference between the image on the screen and reality. He once commented that whenever his relationships turned bitter and painful he found himself wishing that in real life he had the charm and sophistication of Cary Grant.

After consulting with people in conflict for more that two decades, I am convinced that there is truth in those words from the old country-western song: "You Always Hurt the One You Love!" But the more we care the more vulnerable we become, so we also experience anger, despair, rage, jealousy, and even hate. The price of intimacy is that we care deeply, and whenever we care deeply there will be plenty of opportunity for conflict. What can we do to avoid hurting others and being hurt?

Society offers many myths about handling these inevitable conflicts. The trouble is that most myths are more destructive than helpful. For example, conventional wisdom says that we should simply avoid expressing ourselves when conflicts arise. But our own life experiences, not to mention nearly a century of psychological research, makes it abundantly clear that avoidance creates far more problems than it solves.

Another extremely common myth is that "nice people don't fight," under any circumstances. A part of nearly everyone, even those of us with professional training, stubbornly clings to this falsehood.

But perhaps the most damaging myth says that when two people fight a lot, they have a shaky relationship. This pressures us to avoid conflicts, and thus also avoid confronting issues around which emotions need to be shared.

Over the past several years researchers have uncovered information that clearly challenges each of these myths. What stands out in these findings is that in the most successful relationships, the partners neither avoid conflict nor look upon it as particularly threatening. On the contrary, they accept it as normal and healthy. They are able to face disagreements openly and with a sense of security because they have learned how to fight. They have learned responses that actually build and strengthen relationships, rather than weakening them or tearing them down.

Many of us picture fights as the result of personality traits or psychological problems: Sue gets into lots of fights because she is "a hostile person." Bob is just "immature," so that when you tell him anything, he turns it into a major crisis. Pete is a "controlling so-and-so." In other words, we talk as if fights are caused by something inherent in personalities. The underlying message is, "If you were just a different person, we wouldn't get into so many fights."

This thinking creates a significant problem. If we believe that fights are caused by personality traits, then we also must believe that the personalities have to change before the conflict can be resolved. No wonder we fall into despair. Every conflict brings up the specter of a superhuman task—that of changing our own or our partner's personality. And given the enormity of the task, the chances are that nothing whatsoever will get resolved.

Looking Beneath the Surface of Our Conflicts

We learn how to fight just as we learn how to drive or dance or cook. We have all been taught how to express our thoughts and feelings and how to react to other people when they express theirs. We have learned what is fair and unfair. We have learned what "justifies" getting into fights in the first place, and we have learned how to provoke other people.

In most cases the learning process is anything but a conscious one. As a result, each of us has hidden rules that govern our behavior. We follow these rules automatically, often not even aware that we are doing so. However, by bringing these hidden rules to light and examining them closely, we can choose the rules that work well for us and discard those that do not.

I was raised in a family where open conflict between adults just was not acceptable. My parents put great energy into "handling" situations, controlling and manipulating them so that conflict never came to the surface. Whenever a disagreement "raised its ugly head," everyone became embarrassed and uncomfortable. I still have child-hood memories of sitting around a silent dinner table, tense and be-wildered. I remember wondering why my parents were fidgeting in their chairs and looking down into their plates. But I never felt free to ask questions about it. Somehow I knew that despite all their best efforts, a conflict had crept into our lives, shaming us all.

By contrast, my wife was raised in a family that taught her to express herself openly. There was permission to be in conflict with-out having to suffer from the shame of feeling she was doing some-thing wrong.

Even though both of us had extensive backgrounds in psychol-ogy and personal development at the time we married, when the chips were down, we both reverted back to old family roles. The rules of our fights with each other mirrored the rules of our parents. Maggie expressed herself openly and vehemently. Meanwhile, I ran around trying to "handle the situation" so that conflicts did not occur.

Whenever our conflicts escalated into fights, I felt like a total fail-ure. Even when a fight turned out to be constructive, bringing the two of us closer, I still had the uneasy feeling that I should have been able to do something to prevent the fight from occurring at all.

Another part of my "fight pattern" was to get through the fight as quickly as possible, no matter what it took. This often backfired. It succeeded only in making my wife feel that I was not willing to listen to her feelings. Consequently, the fight often increased in both vol-ume and duration.

In spite of all our practice in conflict resolution, my wife and I still get into fights. But our fights become painful only when one or both of us revert back to our old family roles. Then we have to consciously say to ourselves, and sometimes to each other, "This isn't working. Let's get back to what we know works." When we apply our knowledge of conflict resolution, we usually find that what we had thought were "impossible problems" almost always dissolve.

Virtually all couples fight. But most of us were not taught how to fight. So we do not just fight, we fight badly. I certainly was not taught to fight. I was taught how to avoid. Other people were taught how to attack. Neither is the answer. To break the cycle of hurt and sorrow, we have to learn new ways of dealing with the inevitable disputes that arise in any relationship. There are skills involved in having a "good" fight, a fight that clarifies issues without hurting the relationship. The good news is that such skills do exist.

Learning to resolve conflicts before they turn into painful fights requires that we not only learn new skills but that we break old habits. If you have ever tried to refine a tennis stroke or golf swing or broken a smoking or eating habit, you know it is not easy. However, let me remind you that none of these required a change in your personality. Rather, you had only to increase your awareness of your habit and consciously learn a new behavior. After that, you practiced until it became "natural" for you. Through exactly the same process, you will develop skills for resolving conflicts in your life.

How You Fight Can Make the Difference

You probably remember some fights that ended with deeper understanding and love. These fights were truly constructive, bringing the two of you closer together. What was it about those fights which made them positive, while others seem only painful and destructive? Why do some couples handle conflicts with seeming aplomb, while others tear apart their relationship over what appears to be the same issues?

It is usually not what we fight about so much as how we fight that determines whether our efforts drive a wedge between us or bring us closer together. How we fight is a critical factor in the outcome of any conflict.

In many ways, conflicts between loved ones are similar to conflicts in any public setting. When we want to know how to run a public meeting, we may turn to Robert's Rules of Order or similar guidelines. Robert's Rules provides us with a step-by-step description of how to open a meeting, how to present the agenda, how to set limits on participants' speeches, how to close the meeting, etc. Of course, in most personal conflicts, there's no set of printed rules. Instead, we fall back on hidden fight rules, behaviors we've picked up that we apply quite unconsciously in the heat of battle.

Later in this book you'll learn how to identify and change the process by which a fight gets worse and worse. Given a little emotional distance from the battle, it may be easy to look back and pick out some key signals of escalation. But when we are fully engaged in an escalating conflict and every action seems necessary and justified by the other person's behavior, the perspective shifts. We had no intention of getting into a screaming match, but our loved one said such a horrible thing that we just could not let it pass. After all, we are supposed to stand up for ourselves. Right? Our reaction triggers their reaction, and soon we are engaged in mortal combat, pitted against someone we care about very deeply.

Taking Responsibility is the First Step

Escalation occurs when we abdicate responsibility for our behavior, justifying our behavior as getting even for the other person's behavior. It means "nobody's in charge around here" because neither person is making choices to protect the relationship. Accepting responsibility is not about deciding who is to blame. Trying to place the blame is almost a surefire guarantee of making the fight worse. Placing blame just creates more resentment, more tit-for-tat.

I got some insight into what accepting responsibility was about during the early years of my career. I had a consulting client who was internationally renowned in his field. He enjoyed the kind of celebrity and prestige that I could only hope I would achieve during my own career. There was a great deal about the man I admired.

Instead, our relationship ended in a way that was very painful to me. After months of valuing what I had to offer he seemed to turn on me, even ridiculing me in front of others. This was a new experience for me, and I found myself carrying a great load of resentment for many months. I would have bad dreams about it, and even wake up experiencing waves of anger.

These feelings did not begin to change until one day I asked myself: "Even though I am convinced that what he did to me was far more grievous, in what ways did I let him down? What could he have expected of me that I did not provide?" Soon I was able to develop a list of things I could have done differently. As I would have predicted, in my own mind none of them justified the rejection I experienced. But I could begin to see how he could have felt let down and unsupported by me. That day my resentment began to lift. I still felt hurt, but I no longer needed to grind away about the injustice and unfairness of the situation.

I had engaged in the first crucial step in accepting responsibility: I had looked at what I could do differently, rather than what the other person needed to do. Accepting personal responsibility is doing what you can do to make the relationship work better, whether or not your loved one changes.

You will not improve your relationships by moving from a position of "it's all your fault" to "it's all my fault." If it were possible to objectively assess whose fault it is that you get into painful fights, the answer would almost always be that you both contribute to making the fight becoming painful. On occasion, one person may be more provocative than the other. But fights don't occur unless both people escalate. Who caused the fight? Both people did.

What can you do about it? No matter how much you may feel hurt or rejected by your loved one's behavior, the only behavior you can change is your own. No matter how much you are convinced that it is your loved one's behavior that is making your fights bad, the starting point is "What am I doing that contributes to making our fights painful, and how can I change that behavior?" It does not matter what percentage of the blame you should bear. If you want to make things different, you have got to change those behaviors over which you have control.

Your loved one may be a "screamer" who shouts and yells when you get into a fight. To you this behavior may be so outrageous that anything you do seems minuscule in comparison. That may be true. But you cannot stop the screaming. You can only stop what you are doing that makes the fights get worse.

Accepting responsibility is not the same thing as blaming yourself. What does it mean to "take responsibility?" It means that you:

- Identify those behaviors that cause problems to escalate into fights
- Learn new skills and behaviors for communication and problem solving that will not contribute to escalation
- Set limits for your own actions based on the kind of person you want to be, and what you want for the relationship, not your loved one's reaction

Is it not better if both people commit to take responsibility for their actions? Certainly. Working together to change how you fight is, by itself, a way of strengthening the "we" in your relationship.

But the essence of "taking responsibility" is that you do it for yourself, because of what you want in the relationship. If it is reciprocated, that is an added bonus. But if you make your changes only if your loved one changes too, you will quickly find yourself back in the blame game, justifying whatever you do based on what the other person does. That starts the climb up the ladder of escalation all over again.

When you develop an attitude of responsibility, strengthening your relationship becomes your goal, replacing other objectives such as winning fights, proving a point or asserting your power over others. This is not to suggest that there will not be times when you will be so upset that you will revert to defensive, adversarial or hurtful behavior. To do so is only human. But as you become increasingly aware of the impact of what you say and do, you will also become better and better at setting limits on your own behavior, even when you are most upset.

Tool #2

Accept Conflict As a Normal Part

# of Human Relationships

When you are hurting, the last thing you want is some "expert" telling you that conflict can be positive or a "natural" part of being human. When you are hurting, it is hard to believe that the source of your pain could possibly have any redeeming value whatsoever. And when you are afraid that conflict may destroy a relationship, emotionally damage your children, or lead to physical violence, than you just want the conflict to stop, to go away. You want peace at any cost, and you cannot even imagine how conflict could be a good thing.

We have all had fights where nothing of value seemed to be gained. Maybe there were even wounds which took many months to heal, if they healed at all. However, there is an important message that must not get lost in all this. That message is deceptively simple: It is not the subject of the conflict itself but the ways we respond that will determine whether it is beneficial or destructive.

As with most things in life, our beliefs can become self-fulfilling prophecies. If we believe that any disagreement is bad, we will act accordingly, generating negative feelings whenever disagreement arises. And thus we find ourselves lost in a jungle of negative behaviors that almost guarantee that our conflicts will be disastrous, seeming to offer proof that our original belief or "prophecy" was correct.

Old Patterns Die Hard

In the early years of my marriage, I am quite certain that my wife's and my method of dealing with conflict was comparable to what I have seen again and again in my consulting practice. The process goes something like this:

When Michelle expresses her feelings, Doug withdraws emotionally, tries to minimize her feelings, and avoids her—doing everything he can to keep from having to deal with her. He is convinced that acknowledging his wife's emotions can only lead to a worse fight. Michelle, who is accustomed to expressing herself openly, becomes resentful of Doug's efforts to appease and control her instead of listening to her. She simply doesn't feel that he is listening to her or valuing her feelings—which he isn't, no matter how much he wants to believe he is. (He is concerned about her feelings only insofar as he is frightened by them.) Thus, she pushes all the harder to get him to listen. Her voice becomes louder and more demanding. If he still doesn't respond, she escalates her efforts, perhaps by becoming accusatory.

Feeling attacked and hurt, Doug is convinced that there is nothing to do but match Michelle's accusations in kind. At this point, their conflict turns into a war. And he suddenly feels that this is solid proof that his original fears had been totally justified: i.e., if you don't do a good job of appeasing, of keeping the other person's emotions under control, conflict inevitably leads to war. Doug the appeaser is thus convinced, though wrongly, that his only salvation lies in learning how to get better at controlling Michelle's feelings. Little does he realize that by doing this he is only fanning the flames.

In the above interaction, not only does Michelle experience the natural anger of being put off, but Doug is also communicating that there is something wrong with her for having feelings. His attitude is that if she would just stop having all those feelings, the two of them would not be having so many conflicts. His not-so-hidden message to her is often: You are a bad person for having all these feelings. You are the cause of our conflicts.

Feeling controlled and unfairly judged, most people who receive this kind of message will become quite defensive, arguing that they have every right to their feelings, and the cycle whirls on like an out-of-control merry-go-round. Doug contributes to the mad spinning by the way he responds to Michelle's feelings. She contributes to it by the way she reacts to him. An so, around and around they go, each feeling completely "justified" in their behavior because of something they see as the other person's responsibility.

Our beliefs about conflict shape our behavior during fights. Convinced that conflict is dangerous and a sign of failure, we react to its first signs just as we would any other situation where we perceive ourselves at risk, with all the weapons at our disposal. We become defensive, reactive, accusatory—all the things that escalate conflicts into crises.

But let us look at this from another angle. We know that our belief systems can operate as self-fulfilling prophecies. So what would happen if, instead of believing conflict was negative, we turned that around and thought of it in a more positive way? If you felt that conflict was normal, that it could turn out well, is it possible that it would turn out that way? This is exactly what happens. If you go into the conflict feeling relaxed, comfortable, possibly even stimulated, and anticipating a good outcome, you are less likely to engage in behaviors which cause your loved ones to feel threatened, in danger or under attack.

As long as we believe that conflict is bad, our reflex will be to suppress or avoid any sign of disagreement. On the opposite end of the scale, if we perceive conflict as offering something of value, then we will be more likely to take the time to understand how it works, what can be done with it, and which skills could make it even more productive.

Old Training Grounds Revisited

Most of us receive years of formal training in reading, writing, and social skills needed in adulthood. But, few of us receive even a single hour of systematic training in conflict resolution. Where then do we learn whatever skills we do have? We learn them from our families. As we are growing up, we witness many conflicts between our parents, our siblings, and between ourselves and our parents. And every conflict of this kind becomes a model, an object lesson in how to deal with conflict.

The trouble is that these models can be very limited. Many of us were raised in families where conflict was considered embarrassing at best, sinful at worst. For others every conflict turned into open warfare, with the volume turned up to a deafening level. In some families, parents keep conflicts hidden from the children, as though disagreement were something dirty or smutty. In others, children get very mixed messages; they are told to "stand up for themselves"— but only when the cause is acceptable to the people in authority. This gives children the message that they are only permitted to disagree when the people in power approve. But the people in power—parents, grandparents, and teachers—are never in agreement with each other over what justifies standing up for yourself.

2   Accept Conflict As Normal

Thousands of people grow up associating conflict with drunken brawls, sometimes leading to physical violence. Others live in families where even the simplest discussions turn into screaming matches, with neighbors and even the police sometimes getting involved. Still others have parents who for many years seemed to solve problems adequately, then suddenly the relationship broke up for reasons a child could never understand, leaving the child confused and fearful.

Many of us had parents who did a good job most of the time, but we can still remember an incident or two when something very painful occurred, leaving us with vague, unexplained fears. Or we believe our families were ideal and we spend our lives attempting to live up to that ideal, an undertaking that places an unreasonable burden on any relationship. Others expend great effort trying to make certain they do not "make the same mistakes" their parents made, unable to understand that their efforts bind them to their parents rather than liberating them.

But our families did not provide our only role models. There was also television and the movies. More often than not, the world flashing onto the screen was divided between good guys and bad guys— hardly ideal training for the ambiguities of real-life conflicts. Television and movie dramas were either "Pollyanna-ish" (as in "Leave It to Beaver" or "The Brady Bunch") or pathological (as in "Dallas" or "Falcon Crest"). Problems were solved either with a little more love and understanding or with fisticuffs and a gun.

In the Pollyanna versions, good people never get divorced, never hurt each other, never feel ambivalent, never scream, and never do any of the less noble and unloving things we find ourselves doing every day. In the pathological versions, the characters always seem either subhuman or superhuman, never expressing the emotions we all feel and must deal with in our daily lives. (Jealousy or lust is about as close as they ever get to love.) We end up with very limited role models, ranging from heroes whose superpowers are unattainable, to freaklike thugs who seem to be from another planet.

Our family and our cultural models feel natural and comfortable to us. There is a sense of rightness to them that is almost like an absolute truth. However, when you enter into a close relationship with someone from another family, you have to begin coming to terms with the fact that they, too, have learned a set of rules for coping with conflict. Although different from your rules, their rules feel just as natural and right to them as yours do to you. The problem is that inevitably some of their rules will be at odds with yours.

Key Beliefs about Conflict

There are four popular beliefs about conflict which get in the way of resolution. They so permeate our culture that few people escape their influence. Often they cause us to doubt the value of our relationships or ourselves. By discussing these four key beliefs, we can put some of those doubts to rest.

• Love conquers all.

This is the official Hollywood version of marriage. If we love each other enough, we can surmount all problems. Our love can overcome anything. This is a bit like saying that if you just loved tennis enough, you could play like a Wimbledon champ—not acknowledging the years of training and practice it takes to become adept at the sport. Just as in tennis, we need to develop basic skills if we wish to become effective at conflict resolution.

The biggest problem with the belief that love conquers all comes when you turn that slogan around. In the heat of an argument, it is all too easy to think: "If we're having problems, it must mean that we just don't love each other enough." Sadly, the relationship gets invalidated for the wrong reasons. The couple is not lacking love; they are lacking communication skills.

• Harmony is normal and conflict is abnormal.

Many of us assume that the natural state of a healthy and happy relationship is total harmony, peace, bliss, and happiness. We view marriage as a kind of machine that should operate without much attention. But every now and then conflict raises its ugly head, and we must strain and struggle to get back to our "natural" harmonious state.

As long as we labor under this myth, we are destined to think that anyone who brings conflict into the relationship is bad, a disrupter of the natural order, a tempter or temptress whose selfish actions threaten our eviction from the Garden of Eden. Even though the status quo of the relationship may now be stifling, we try to ignore all the resentments, worries or doubts that are circling in the air like vultures. In the end, we risk triggering one of the deadliest responses for any relationship: We try to buy peace at any cost.

• People who get into fights do so because they are innately argumentative, defensive, or hostile.

In this view, conflict is the result of a flaw in the person's personality. The implication is that if you get into fights a lot, it is because either you or the person you are with has a faulty personality. One or the other of you is a bad person. There is no hope.

It never occurs to the person clinging to this belief that the outcome has much more to do with skills than with "who we are." In their view, there is little you can do but get out of the relationship. Find someone with a better personality so that you will not have any more conflicts. This belief condemns a person to a life of always seeking the flawless person, never realizing that the answer is much simpler, a matter of learning.

- **Conflict is inherently bad, a symptom that something is wrong with the relationship, a sign of failure.**

Within this belief system, conflict is viewed as something to be avoided, like fire, mad dogs, and lightning. People who move out of this trap do so by first making peace with the idea that conflict is a fact of life. If conflict is normal, then it follows that skills for resolving conflict could make life easier and more comfortable. They need only find out how to do it well.

The Positive Value of Conflict

As painful as conflict may be, it makes at least five positive contributions to relationships:

- **Conflict identifies problems which need to be solved.**

The first and most obvious value of conflict is that it identifies the source of dissatisfaction, irritation, or anger for one or both people.

- **Conflict is a way of creating evolutionary change in relationships, thereby eliminating the need for violent upheaval.**

Change is an integral part of everyone's life: ideas change, and what we want from our relationships changes. The demands placed upon us by our jobs, our families, our friends, and our spouses change around us, and the relationships must somehow accommodate change. When the necessary adjustments can be made in small steps, then a relationship can sustain considerable modification without threatening its stability.

But if one or both parties deny or resist conflict, then the relationship becomes static or like the dry limbs of a dying tree that are unable to bend in the wind. Without the ability to respond, recognize the conflict, and find solutions, the only alternative is "revolution," which usually means ending the relationship.

Recognizing conflict and responding to it in a positive way can prevent stagnation. This recognition allows one or both parties involved to adjust the balance of power and revitalize the basic values upon which the relationship is built.

• Conflict helps us define who we are.

Back in the sixties when I was in college, I was startled one night when a friend came into my dorm room bawling, "Jim, I can't rebel. My parents are more liberal than I am in everything!" What suddenly occurred to me was that the central issue in adolescence was not one of conservative versus liberal or restrictive versus permissive. At least where human beings are concerned, the successful transition from adolescence to adulthood is a process of discovering the boundaries between parents and children. Adolescent rebellion is really a process of determining where "I" stop and "you" begin. Most adolescents solve this problem by testing their parents. Their parents' reaction, even their negative reactions, actually help adolescents establish their own sense of individuality, answering the question "How are we different (or the same)?"

Similar issues exist in most close relationships. We seek out the closeness because on a deep emotional level we experience completeness, a sense of being more fully ourselves, when communication is open and intimate. But this very sense of connectedness can be a threat to our sense of individual identity. We may feel unbearably dependent on the people we love the most and come to resent that dependency. When this occurs, we may find our separate identity by rebelling against the other person, which helps us get a sense of our distinct individuality.

This process of "finding our outer edges," our boundaries, is particularly important in extremely intimate relationships such as those between parent and child or husband and wife. One or both parties may initiate conflict because they feel threatened by the closeness, and thus fear losing their individual identity. Establishing ego boundaries is essential to the health of both individuals and the relationship.

- **Conflict is a way of discharging some of the animosity or resentment which is generated by the limiting aspects of a relationship.**

Even the best and healthiest relationships place some restrictions on the individuals involved. We may have to give up doing things the way we would do them if we were living alone. As a bachelor of twenty, I might have been quite comfortable letting the dirty dishes pile up for several days. When I was thirty, with a wife and children, that habit would have made meal time impossible, aggravating everyone.

When we are in a relationship, we cannot ignore the other person's needs and ways of doing things. We put limits on our behavior in order not to hurt the other person, and hope they do the same. We schedule our time with the other person in mind. We coordinate when and where we are going to take vacations. We even make dietary changes in many cases. Although accommodation to another person's needs can become excessive and unhealthy, some amount of accommodation is inherent in every healthy relationship. And even though we do not always want to admit it, this creates frustration and resentment.

People who act without concern for others find it almost impossible to establish loving bonds. If we want intimacy, we have to accept that there are limits we need to consider, and these limits can feel restricting.

Fighting provides a safety valve for expressing some of the inherent tension that results from these restrictions before it threatens the relationship. When we have no way to express these feelings, we become increasingly aware of our frustration and resentment, and less aware of how much we care for the other person. By discharging the inherent tension, we become aware once again of the feelings of love and caring which were there all along.

• Conflict can be stimulating and challenging.

When conflicts are expressed at levels that do not pose a threat, they can be exciting, stimulating, and even fun. In fact, there are certain people who become "conflict junkies," never feeling quite as alive, quite as fully functioning or involved as when they are in a good fight and the adrenaline is flowing. For many couples, conflict offers new, more exciting involvement with each other following long periods of relative calm.

Conflict is not inherently good or bad; it can be either or both. The important question is whether the ways you are handling conflict in your relationship permit the positive aspects of conflict to emerge. That depends on you and your loved one. There is not something inherent in conflict that makes it painful; it is what is done with the conflict.

From Discussion to War

Conflicts can be expressed in a wide range of ways, from calm, rational problem-solving discussions to major, go-for-the-jugular wars, as in Edward Albee's play, *Who's Afraid of Virginia Woolf?*, in which the couple's entire relationship turned into a contest to see who could inflict and endure the greatest pain. Sometimes what begins as a straightforward discussion turns into full-fledged war. Perhaps the easiest way to describe this process is to imagine a ladder with four rungs. Each rung takes you to a higher level, where the hurt inflicted becomes increasingly destructive. Each step has its own clues to clearly detect when escalation is occurring.

The First Rung: Problem-solving Discussion

In a problem-solving discussion, neither of us feels threatened. Instead, we feel that we are a team. Working together with the conviction that we can solve "our" problem, a spirit of cooperation prevails. We experience openness of communication, and feel we are safe in disclosing our vulnerabilities and our problems. But sometimes, something is said that makes one or both people feel threatened, prompting one or both partners to take a step to the next rung up the ladder.

The Second Rung: Argument

The free flow of communication slows down or is completely blocked, and we begin to shift our goals from problem solving to building a strong case for our own point of view. We begin marshaling arguments to work in our own favor, perhaps withholding information about our own motives or vulnerabilities. We may begin feeling competitive, as if it were now more important to "win" the argument than to find solutions.

As the argument progresses, moving toward a fight, we no longer see the other person as a teammate; he or she has become our adversary. The shift is frequently reflected in voice changes (perhaps a higher tone, louder, more accusative or demanding, etc.) and physical postures (perhaps pacing, tense shoulder and back muscles, arms folded tightly across the chest like a shield, finger pointing or fist shaking, etc.) The overriding feeling is that this is a contest to be won or lost.

The Third Rung: The Fight

What moves us from an argument to a fight is that one of us feels hurt and we are afraid of getting hurt even worse. We feel justified in pulling out all the stops and going for blood because the other person, owing to their behavior, "deserves to be hurt just as much as they've hurt me." The goal of the interaction is no longer to resolve the original issue, but to inflict injury. We bring up grievances from the past to justify our positions. Neither of us is willing to share information about our vulnerabilities. Our perceptions of each other are distorted, and will become even more so as the fight progresses.

The Fourth Rung: War

The fight becomes a war when, fueled by strong emotion, we shift our goal to emotional annihilation or forcing the other person into submission. The goal of solving a problem has long been left behind. At this point, we no longer see each other as whole people but as exaggerated stereotypes. At worst, the "other guy" has become totally evil. At best, that person has no redeeming qualities whatsoever and we can't imagine how we ever got involved with them.

In a war, every action and word is interpreted as the discharge of a weapon, a thrust or counterthrust, a clashing of swords in the ongoing battle. Even efforts on one person's part to reduce the level of the conflict, to take it down a rung or two on the escalation ladder, may be perceived by the other person as tactical maneuvers or manipulations. Warped by our high-adrenaline states, our perceptions become so focused on winning the war that we cannot even imagine the other person as a peacemaker.

One or both of us may actively seek allies or "authorities" to back up our arguments, usually from our group of family members and friends. We will stop at nothing to mobilize support from others or to get confirmation of the evil nature of the other party.

Trying to determine the exact point at which a discussion turns into an argument or an argument turns into a fight or a fight turns into a war is usually an exercise in futility. Identifying where the escalation started is important only to someone trying to attach blame.

Recognizing Escalation

Although it may not be important to determine who "struck the first blow," it can be helpful to identify changes in our own feelings or behaviors that indicate that we are escalating. There are signals that alert us to these changes:

Seeing the other person as an opponent or adversary

As long as we are engaged in problem solving, we perceive the other person as an ally, jointly contributing to our search for a solution. But as we move away from this cooperative effort, we begin to feel competitive. At first the competitive feelings just make us edgy, uncomfortable, and perhaps even confused. Then our behavior becomes adversarial and the prevailing experience is that the other person is clearly not "on our side."

Quite the opposite! We feel that they are clearly standing in our way or taking a position against us. As the fight turns into a war, we may feel not only that our ideas are being attacked but that "my character is under attack." We may even begin perceiving our "opponent" as having nothing but ill-will for us, and we for them. We are usually completely immersed in our own emotions at this point. In the heat of battle, we depersonalize the other person and in our minds we see them as simply "the enemy."

Lost awareness of love or caring for the other person

As the other person becomes an opponent, adversary, or enemy in our mind, we momentarily lose touch with our bond of love for them. For the moment, the part of ourselves that cares very deeply is hidden. It burrows deep, out of harm's way. Without thinking, we concentrate solely on aspects of that person's character that disturb us. Eventually we end up totally out of touch with how we generally feel about them and we may engage in behavior that is totally inappropriate. Having buried our tender and caring feelings, we completely lose sight of the fact that this is a person we love, respect, and need in our lives.

Denial of responsibility

The farther up the ladder we go, the more we tend to justify our own behavior as a reaction to what the other person is doing. We have the feeling that since they hurt us, we have the right to hurt them. We find ourselves engaging in a kind of "tit for tat," "eye for an eye, tooth for a tooth" behavior, with each successive round becoming more accusatory and more adversarial.

Reduced self-disclosure

At the bottom of the ladder, when we are feeling good about each other, we are willing to share our deepest feelings, such as fears, weaknesses, and vulnerabilities associated with the conflict. For example, if both people share their concerns openly, both people feel moved and they try to respond to the other person's feelings. But if both people feel threatened, they often begin hiding their deeper personal concerns, expressing only feelings of anger, accusing and blaming each other in the process. Self-disclosure or expressing our deepest vulnerabilities seems increasingly dangerous as we move to the higher rungs of the escalation ladder. We fear that we are in the other person's hands and must not give them information that could be used against us.

Reduced willingness to change

As we see the other person more and more as an adversary, we become less and less willing to change. It is as though a little voice is warning us, "Whatever you do, don't cooperate with the enemy." We may even get to the point that we will not consider doing anything to respond to the other person's problems or needs.

Openness of communication

All communication, even about factual information, becomes increasingly restricted as we move up the ladder. We begin using all information as a way of shoring up our own position, of proving that "I'm right and you're wrong." On the highest rungs of the escalation ladder, one or both people may cut off all direct communication. At its worst, one or both people may seek allies from among their family members and friends.

Perceptual distortion

When we are feeling cooperative, as in the problem-solving state of a conflict, we see other people fairly clearly and stay in touch with our concern for their well-being. As we move up the escalation ladder, our perceptions of the other person actually change; in our minds, this person whom we ordinarily love and care about takes on the proportions of an ogre. At the very least they become an adversary, and finally an enemy. Although their behavior may have become less than exemplary, the other person has not really changed that much. What has changed is our own perception of them. At the highest levels of escalation it becomes very difficult, if not impossible, to find anything even remotely good about them. Their every action seems only further proof of their evil intent.

Joseph Campbell, the psychologist who became known to the world in Bill Moyer's *The Power of Myth* television series, used to say that there were three parties in any relationship: "me," "you," and "we." In a fight, both "me" and "you" get so involved in defending ourselves that they are in danger of destroying "we."

Think about what happens in a bad fight: You start seeing each other as an adversary. You lose touch with your feelings of love or caring for each other. You start blaming your own behavior on each other. You are less willing to share your deeper feelings. You withhold information and dig in, becoming even more rigid. You begin to see each other in an exaggerated, stereotyped way. In every way, it is "we" that suffers.

The cardinal principle that underlies everything else in this book is: **Protect your relationship even while in conflict.** The simple truth is that you are going to have more arguments, and probably more fights. The real question is not "whether" you will fight, but "how well." "Fighting well" means fighting in such a way that protects the long-term relationship, even though you are very unhappy with each other right now.

We fight precisely because we care. If the other person did not matter to us, a dispute would not rouse the antagonism that would produce a fight. One or both people would just walk away from the situation because it was not worth the effort.

But we lose touch with that sense of caring during a fight. We forget there is a home base to protect. That is why we have to make a commitment to ourselves, and to the relationship, during the times when we are not in conflict. The time to make agreements to protect the relationship is when you are in touch with how much you care, how much the relationship means to both of you.

Understanding Anger

One of the ways we protect ourselves from feeling weak, inadequate, guilty, or powerless is to lash out at whoever or whatever seems to trigger those feelings in us. When a little boy plays in the street and almost gets hit by a car, the parents may feel horrified and protective of the child during the time he is in danger. But after they are certain the child is safe, they may turn their fears into anger toward the child, punishing him or scolding him for being so "careless."

Similarly, when we feel trapped and powerless, enmeshed in bureaucratic rules at work or elsewhere, we may want to lash out at the authority figures enforcing those rules. Or when we arrive at a hotel in a strange city, tired and hungry, only to find the hotel has misplaced our room reservation, we are likely to get very upset with the receptionist at the front desk. The anger is directed at whoever we believe is causing us to feel weak, vulnerable, afraid or powerless at that moment. But the anger is really the secondary feeling. The softer, weaker feeling comes first; only then do we get angry at whatever or whoever we see as causing those feelings. When a couple is going through a very vulnerable life transition, it is easier to be angry at each other than to admit that we feel insecure and vulnerable.

Often anger is only remotely related to the present time and present situation. The anger may also mask fear or anxiety that can go as far back as when we were infants. Each and every one of us has experienced a childhood with wounds, pains, and reminders of our inadequacies and vulnerabilities. Each of us has secret hurts, grievances, and explanations for why other people got a better deal in life than we did.

Whatever the injuries, the wounded inner child continues to be an important aspect of our adult personality. Most of the time we hide this part from the rest of the world, except where we feel relatively safe: in our most intimate relationships. Indeed, part of enjoying close relationships is the relative safety we feel there, giving us the freedom to reveal the inner child.

Often in the beginning of therapy and personal growth groups there is a rather amusing moment that comes soon after everyone has shared their most vulnerable feelings. There is a sense of how comic it is that all these grown-ups are really wounded children in disguise, running around trying to pretend they have their adult lives completely together.

We know how small children can react when they feel emotionally attacked. Sometimes they become hysterical, and the only thing a parent can do is hold the child until he calms down. However, when we adults feel hurt, our inner child is not always that accessible or willing to receive this kind of comforting. Instead, we reach for our sophisticated "emotional weapons," which can do real harm to the people we love.

Not all anger is a defense nor is it intended to inflict injury on others. On the contrary, sometimes a clean, clear expression of anger is the only thing that will change a seemingly impossible situation. But using anger to protect ourselves from having to admit to the deeper feelings can be destructive, indeed, putting increased emotional distance between our loved ones and ourselves. We may use anger destructively either by directly attacking those we love, blaming them for what we feel or by bottling up our anger and turning off all emotional involvement.

To break out of the destructive anger impasse, check inside. What you are feeling angry about may have a different source from the one that seems most obvious. For example, a wife tells her husband that she wishes he would lose some weight. The fact is that he would like to lose some weight, too, but instead of sharing this he gets angry at her, accusing her of always nagging him. After the initial blowup, he checks inside and realizes that what he is really angry about is not her criticism, but the fact that he has tried to lose weight and cannot. He is feeling helpless about controlling his weight and he feels angry that he cannot manage this aspect of his life better.

Sharing our inner selves is the key to intimacy. Anger expressed in a defensive or attacking way only invites anger from the other person. Sharing our vulnerability, that is, expressing the concerns of our inner world, is an invitation for the other person to share their vulnerability with us. When both people let down their guards, they create a sense of union and trust, the basic ingredients of intimacy for which we all yearn. In doing so we are saying, "Here I am. This is who I am, and I don't have to hide my fears and insecurities any-more. It's okay to be me with you."

People who are good at conflict resolution stay as aware of what they are communicating about the relationship as they are about the more obvious issues of the fight. They never lose sight of the fact that what they say or do will have either a positive or negative impact on the relationship. They protect their relationship even while in conflict.

Tool #3

Understand the Reality and

Importance of Feelings

Carolyn and George have been married for more than twenty-five years. Nine months ago Judith, the youngest of their three children, left for college, several hundred miles away. The year before, Barbara, their oldest child, finished college and got her first job in another state. Mark, their middle child, is in the Marines.

While the children were growing up, Carolyn stayed at home. But with the last child leaving for college, she is experiencing a profound sense of loss. She is acutely aware that her years as a full-time mother have ended. She is uncertain about what she wants to do with the rest of her life. She only knows that during this period of uncertainty she wants to be with her closest friends. Many of these friends have children the same age as hers and they have lived through the same challenges and the same joys that she has. They also know what she is going through. At least for now, her sense of security is closely tied to the home where she raised her children. She feels that she needs a strong sense of rootedness in what is comfortable and familiar.

For George, her husband, the children leaving home has a very different meaning. With the last child leaving for college, he feels liberated. He really hasn't enjoyed being a father these last few years. Mostly the kids came to him when they wanted money or had a problem. The rest of the time, he suspects, they wanted to have as little to do with their parents as possible. He also feels bad that Mark, who George thought was the most creative of his children, dropped out of school and joined the military.

George looks forward to his "retirement" from parenthood. He sees the children leaving as a new opening. It provides the opportunity for Carolyn and him to spend more time together, perhaps to travel. He wants to buy a condo and sell the family home to lower expenses and reduce responsibility. The old house has increased in value tremendously. Even after buying a comfortable condo, there would be plenty of money left over for travel.

George thinks his children getting out on their own should be a cause for celebration. But that has certainly not been the case. Lately George and Carolyn have been fighting. He tries to listen when his wife talks to him about getting a job or going back to school. But all of her talk just sounds like something new to tie him down, which just depresses George and he becomes sullen.

When George makes suggestions, Carolyn gets irritated and falls into a brooding silence. When he told her that he wanted to sell the family home and move into a condo, she became almost hysterical. Tearfully, she argued that they needed the big house so that the kids could have the security of knowing they would have a place to come back to. George's response was that this was ridiculous. Carolyn got defensive and told him that this was just more proof of her husband's lack of emotional involvement with the kids. She became accusative, suggesting that maybe if he had been more involved with the kids, Mark would never have dropped out of school to join the military.

This was too much for George. She knew how sensitive he was about Mark's decision. He yelled at Carolyn, telling her that she needed a therapist, not a husband, whereupon he stomped out of the house.

They have had several fights like this, leaving both of them feeling wounded and sad. What makes the fights even more painful is that they both know they love each other very much. But lately whenever they try to talk about their feelings it turns into a fight. So they have begun avoiding such talks. As a result, the time they spend together has become strained and awkward, and even with all their efforts to avoid feelings, arguments over minor differences seem to spark off full-fledged screaming matches.

If love alone were enough, George and Carolyn would be able to work out their problems, and they may yet. But right now they are in pain, and the grief they are experiencing is threatening their relationship. Both of them have begun to think that maybe with the children out of the house, it is time to consider a divorce.

The Unique Challenge of Close Relationships

As outsiders looking in, it is easy to sympathize with both George and Carolyn. They are confronted with the kind of conflict typical of most intimate relationships. The intensity of their feelings is very strong. The issues they are facing run deep. They are both trying to answer the questions, "What am I going to do with the rest of my life? Have our lives, until now, been a success or a failure?"

They are at a point where they simply do not feel that the other person "makes sense." George cannot understand why Carolyn does not feel liberated by the children leaving home, or how she could believe that it is a good idea to keep the big house which drains their finances and is a burden to keep up. He cannot understand why his wife would want to go back to school and get a job when they could have time and freedom to do whatever they pleased.

Carolyn, on the other hand, cannot understand how George could be so unconcerned about the children. She cannot imagine a loving parent feeling relieved to have their kids go out the door. Her husband's feelings are so alien to her that she is beginning to question how she could ever have stayed married to him all these years.

George and Carolyn are in highly reactive states of mind. Anything that even touches on the conflict or upon their feelings about each other causes a blow-up which turns into a shouting match. Neither George or Carolyn understands why, but they just cannot talk anymore without screaming. They are not stupid or insensitive people. Both of them recognize that the things they are feeling are way out of proportion somehow. But they cannot seem to act any other way. Ordinarily they have a little more tolerance, a little more insulation on the nerves. Both of them can handle much bigger challenges in relationships outside the home, but with each other there is no room for error. Every little thing seems to escalate into a painful battle.

In close relationships the real issue, in virtually every conflict, is emotions. If we are to address our conflicts realistically, we must understand the unique logic of the emotional world. Emotions operate by their own rules.

Our Emotional Kaleidoscopes

As a child, I was fascinated by kaleidoscopes. They allowed me to see objects filtered through the shifting patterns of colored glass. The most exciting thing was to see how many different ways the same object looked as the kaleidoscope was rotated.

The emotional realm is much like a kaleidoscope. When we first enter into a relationship, we view the other person through a beautiful, rosy pattern, seeing only the strengths and positive virtues of that person and those things that make us seem alike. When we feel as if we are under attack, however, this inner kaleidoscope often lets in only black-and-white perceptions. We may see only the negative characteristics of a person, distorting who they are and greatly limiting how we relate to them.

It is not always easy to remember that this kaleidoscope is inside us, not outside. If it shifts in such a way that we see an experience as hurtful, perhaps it was our lens, not that external world, that created that feeling. Another small shift of the lens, and the pieces may fall into place in an entirely different way, producing still another feeling.

This is not to say that you should minimize your feelings or pass them off as being unimportant because you have created them. Unless we do value our own feelings, we end up with what psychoanalyst Karen Horney called "the tyranny of the shoulds." We become so pulled and tugged by competing versions of what we "should" be feeling that we lose all contact with our inner selves. When we're fully grounded in our own feelings, we know they are our emotional truth, and accept that we ourselves have created a given feeling or interpretation. We accept responsibility for projecting certain feelings onto other people or onto a situation, without negating the "reality" of our own feelings.

Feelings may be based on accurate observations of the external world or completely off-base. Sometimes we can find a partial basis for our feelings; sometimes there is no basis whatsoever. At other times our interpretations may be very clear and accurate perceptions of what's out there, though these perceptions are still shaped by our own internal processes.

Aaron Beck, in *Love Is Never Enough*, summarized some of the ways our internal processes skew our interpretations of events. His list of "cognitive distortions" includes:

TUNNEL VISION: Seeing only what fits our attitude or state of mind at the moment, and ignoring the rest. Example: Seeing only negative traits and ignoring positive traits in a person you are angry with.

SELECTIVE ABSTRACTION: Taking a statement or event out of context to arrive at an erroneous interpretation. Example: Taking one remark out of a long story and using it as evidence that the entire story was an intentional put-down of you.

ARBITRARY INFERENCE: Making an unfavorable judgment even though there is no basis for it. Example: Cathy assumes that her boyfriend's silence when she brings up the topic means he is unhappy about her weight.

OVERGENERALIZATION: Making absolute statements based on the evidence of a few incidents to claim that a certain behavior is typical or constant. Example: "He never cleans up after himself." "She always cuts me off."

POLARIZED THINKING: Responding as if there were only either/or choices. Example: "I must either do exactly as you want or get a divorce."

MAGNIFICATION: Exaggerating the qualities of another person—either good or bad—or exaggerating the severity of an event, turning it into a catastrophe. Example: Predicting bankruptcy when you have really only gone over your budget for a single month, or saying that your whole summer vacation is ruined when you really mean that you will have to cut it short by a day.

BIASED EXPLANATIONS: Finding a negative explanation for what a loved one does. Example: A child is having real trouble in school and the parent's response is, "I know he's doing this just to spite me."

NEGATIVE LABELING: Attaching a label that casts a particularly unfavorable light on a person or behavior. Example: "He's a womanizer." Or, "She's frigid."

PERSONALIZATION: Taking the attitude that the actions of an-other person, or persons, are all aimed at you. Example: "Other motorists on the freeway deliberately drive slowly just to aggravate me."

MIND READING: Believing that we can tell what the other person is thinking. Example: "I know what you're thinking. You're looking for any excuse to get out of the house."

SUBJECTIVE REASONING: Believing that since we feel an emotion strongly, it must be justified. Example: "I just know you can't stand the way I look, my hair just looks miserable. I can't blame you for not loving me." (She feels miserable about the way her hair looks, but expands this to thinking he could not possibly love someone who looked like that.)

Feelings Are Not Caused by Outside Events

Deep down inside, a part of each of us really wants to believe that "every reasonable person feels about things pretty much as I do." We believe there is a controlling relationship between our emotions and the events occurring outside us. Successful conflict resolution depends on our understanding of why this is not so—of why external events do not control our experience of that event.

We think of our emotions as being caused by things that happen outside us. Getting a promotion makes me feel happy. My best friend poking fun at me at a party makes me feel embarrassed or hurt. Getting a speeding ticket makes me feel upset. My child's problems at school make me feel like a failure as a parent.

But the belief that feelings are "caused" by external events is not the whole truth. It is only one piece of the puzzle. The emotions you experience are created by the meanings you attribute to these events. You decide what each event means to you. If a close friend fails to invite you to a party, there are a number of reactions you might have:

You might feel hurt or rejected; you might start searching your own mind for the "reasons" you were left out; you might feel relieved that you were not invited because you feel uncomfortable at parties; you might feel deeply depressed because your experience seems to tell you that not being invited means that nobody really cares about you. Finally, you might have virtually no feeling about it one way or another because you did not expect to be invited.

The point is this: Your feelings were not caused by a missing invitation. You interpreted what it meant not to be invited, and this interpretation dictated your emotional response. In effect, you projected a meaning from your emotional reality to the external world.

In fact, there are moments in life when we have nothing within our emotional reality to attach to an event and give it meaning. We either lack information or we cannot relate it to anything that has happened previously in our lives. I remember a time when our teenage daughter did not return home at the time we had agreed upon. In fact, she was several hours late. I did not know what to make of it and I began running through a long list of possible explanations: she had been in an automobile accident; she was defying our authority; she was okay but forgot to watch the time, etc.

My feelings about her being late changed with each possible interpretation I came up with. I vacillated and churned between fear, anger, and relaxation. While I waited for word from her, I probably cycled through those feelings and many more several times. The problem was that until I had more information about what actually occurred, I did not know how to feel. In the meantime, I kept experiencing all these feelings like a roller-coaster of emotion until our daughter returned home.

Adding to the complexity of emotion that event triggered, my wife was also concerned. At one moment I would be feeling that our daughter was okay; we did not have to worry. At the same time, my wife would be feeling that our daughter had probably been hurt or was in serious trouble. Based on her interpretation she felt worry or even panic, even as my interpretation was that everything was okay. If we had compared notes at the time, my wife could easily have felt that I was being callous and uncaring, while I could easily have felt that she was making mountains out of molehills.

Parents who have faced similar events know only too well how easy it is to get into a conflict at this point. Perhaps to discharge some of their concern, they get into an argument about whose emotional reality is "right." For example, you might be the parent who argues that it is irrational to get worried without knowing for certain that there is really a problem. Your spouse counters that your lack of worry is only a sign that you do not care about the children.

The period between discovering that our daughter is late and finding out why elongates a mental process that happens throughout every moment of our lives: making an observation and then assigning meaning to it. Ordinarily this occurs within a split second and we barely notice the role we play in assigning meanings to events. But now that same process has been spread over hours. If we get caught up in the possibility that our daughter has been in an accident, we go wild with worry. If we decide that she is defying our authority, we become angry. If we consider the possibility that she may have fallen asleep watching television at a friend's house, we may feel peaceful though perhaps annoyed. Only when we know what has happened do we know how to feel.

By looking closely at how we interpret our daughter's late arrival, we can see how the line between the triggering event and our emotional reactions to it is anything but straight and direct. We take a very active part in creating an interpretation.

Your Rules, My Rules

Each of us possesses a whole inner universe, with rules—unique to ourselves—about what life means. These rules are often very complex, because this inner world is created around our unique life experiences. The rules of my inner universe make sense only to me; yours make sense only to you. Emotions are always highly individualized. What makes sense to you only applies to that world which is contained within the boundaries of your skin.

Let us apply these principles to George and Carolyn. We last saw them in deep conflict, unable to relinquish the demand that the other person "make sense." George's reality is that he feels relieved that the kids are out of the house, while Carolyn can't even fathom how he could feel that way. With the kids gone, she feels insecure and frightened—and George cannot imagine why.

The challenge they face—as impossible as it might seem—is to accept that, no matter how they might argue it, the other person feels as he or she does and has a perfect right to continue doing so. Contrary to popular opinion, conflicts do not get resolved by changing each other's reality; rather, resolution begins when we can acknowledge and accept each other's reality. Neither person's emotional reality has to make sense to anyone else in the world. It just is what it is. And until George and Carolyn accept each other's inner world—instead of insisting that the other person change their emotions to accommodate them—they are going to suffer.

It is Irrational to Expect Everybody to be "Rational"

Have you ever been told, in the heat of an argument or a fight, "I'm wasting my time talking to you. You're just not being rational." The hidden assumption is that there is a rational or "right way" to feel, and whoever is making this remark knows what that way is. But when we can finally accept that each of us has a self-contained and autonomous reality, then we can begin to see how futile it is to rush around trying to get other people to be "rational" by our private rules.

I may accept being yelled at as perfectly normal, responding with ease by simply yelling back. However, you might feel crushed and humiliated and be unable to act in any constructive manner. What is the difference between these two reactions? What makes the difference is what the yelling means to each person. Where our emotional lives are concerned, no two people play by exactly the same rules. The only constructive approach is to accept that everyone experiences life in a slightly different way, with different emotions being triggered. There will only be fleeting and occasional moments when our experiences are the same even when we are looking at the same events.

One of the most frequent problems in conflict resolution is the tendency to dismiss people who do not agree with us as lacking the capacity to solve problems. We try to pass these differences off as proof that the other person's rational faculties are seriously deficient. In the process, we discount the other person, leaving them out of any negotiations to solve the conflict.

I particularly noticed this several years ago while I was mediating conflicts between environmentalists and corporations. Discussions often ended with both sides making judgments and accusations about each other: the environmentalists accused the businessmen of being rigid, uncaring, and motivated solely by economics, while the businessmen accused the environmentalists of being unrealistic, naive, and irresponsible about the economic consequences of their proposals. In other words, both sides were accusing each other of being irrational, of simply not having the capacity to solve problems. Efforts to continue discussions were often labeled pointless, putting the lid on further negotiation.

Over time, of course, governmental agencies and corporations began to understand environmental concerns. And the environmentalists began to gain a greater appreciation for the complexities and constraints within which government and the corporate worlds worked. But for a while, there was little point in trying to sit down and talk because neither group accepted the other as rational.

The same barriers can also affect our closest relationships. One or both people in a marriage may set up an initial condition that, in effect, states, "Unless you make complete sense by the rules of my emotional reality, I do not have to deal with your feelings." In other words, if you are "irrational," I will disqualify you as being incapable of participating in any discussion.

Invariably, this stance escalates the conflict. The person who is being told that he or she does not have valid feelings is likely to respond defensively. He or she might raise her voice, or make more sweeping and vehement statements, or become visibly upset. For the person doing the rejecting, the other's defensive statements offer even more "justification" for ignoring their feelings. This situation either continues to escalate or the discussion breaks off, with both people frustrated.

When we insist that emotions be "rational," we are really asking the other person to make their feelings conform to our own rules. And the only way any of us can bend our emotional realities is by denying our own experience. In the final analysis, we must ask ourselves how rational is it to tell another person that it is wrong for them to be upset when they know for a fact that they are upset?

Denying anyone's essential right to his or her own emotional experience sets up impossible stumbling blocks, condemning resolution efforts to almost certain failure. It creates the condition that the price for resolving conflict is that one person must invalidate his or her own life experience. This is unbearable. No one should be asked to deny their own experience, and to demand this is to guarantee either continued escalation of the conflict or a hidden but festering resentment.

What You "Should" Feel Is Irrelevant

My wife and I were both raised in families that subscribed to the "should" approach to feelings. We were told that we should feel happy, grateful, appreciative, even loving. We should not feel anger, hurt, upset. These latter feelings were "bad," and so were given labels with negative connotations, such as "pouting," "acting immature," "feeling sorry for yourself," "showing disrespect," and so on.

A particularly vivid childhood memory epitomizes the "should" approach to feelings for me. When I was about six years old my best friend lived next door. One day his mother bought two pairs of boxing gloves so that he and I could fight. However, she always insisted on supervising these fights. She also had rules governing how we should fight.

The one rule I will never forget was that we should always keep smiling. The minute either of us stopped smiling, she called the fight off and broke us up. You can imaging how much fun that was! I can still recall the terrible frustration of trying to keep smiling while every part of me wanted to blast my friend's head off in retribution for his last punch.

The "should" school of emotion permeates our culture. Even some psychologists whose training includes the study of emotional processes have rules about what people should or should not feel. These rules are different, and hopefully broader, than what our parents taught us. But the underlying assumption remains the same: that there are external standards and rules for measuring the validity of people's feelings.

This tendency to judge other people's feelings is not just something that other people impose on us. Once we have been trained as children we are likely to continue judging ourselves by these standards. In this case, the judge is no longer outside us. We have internalized it. We may put up with a friend, co-worker or relative who judges us because, in a strange way, that person serves an important purpose in our lives, mirroring the judge we hold inside us and giving it an external reality.

Learning to Accept Emotion as Fact

In my early twenties I had a long checklist I ran through anytime I felt angry. My checklist included questions such as, "Am I being fair? Do I have all my facts straight? Have I heard the other person's point of view? Am I being loving or charitable in my interpretation of the other person's behavior?" Looking back on it, it seems that the checklist was endless, stretching into an emotionally deadening task.

One day it dawned on me that if I was already angry, it did not really matter whether I "should" be angry or not. The fact remained that I was, and there was no disputing that. Being angry did not mean that my perceptions were accurate. Nor was my anger any indication that I was or was not being properly charitable or any of the rest of it.

I remember struggling with this insight for a long time. It did not mean that I should express my anger whenever or however I felt. I still had to make choices about expressing myself. My anger did not give me the right to punch out the first person who walked by. But it did mean that at a given moment my anger was a reality and I had a right to it.

Just knowing what I was feeling gave me a stability and groundedness. I found that as long as I was trying to decide how I "should" feel, I was at sea, torn by conflicting ideas, theories, values, with no sense of having any roots or foundation for what I was experiencing.

As a professional mediator, I turn back to these insights time and time again. In very tense conflicts, with large numbers of people involved, it is very easy to feel tugged in as many different directions as there are points of view. I regain stability by dropping all my "shoulds" and experiencing my emotions exactly as they are at that moment. This provides a solid sense of my own center rooted in my direct perceptions, not in theory.

Some people do not need the lesson I had to learn, that "feelings are facts." It never occurs to them it could be otherwise. In my experience, it is men, more than most women, who need this lesson. Our society tends to give women more permission to express themselves emotionally, but even they have been schooled in the "shoulds." The result is that many men and women know every rule about what they should feel, but they know little if anything about what they actually feel. They may find it relatively easy to share their ideas about what they feel, but sharing the actual feelings is much more difficult for them.

Nobody is more of an expert on our feelings than we ourselves. Any arguments over what you should be feeling are pointless; what you are feeling is what counts. Acknowledging our feelings is where effective problem solving begins and ends, and without the ability to accept our different emotional realities, conflict resolution is going to be anything but easy.

My Encounter with Emotions

In the 1960s, "encounter groups" were very much in vogue. People would sit around in a circle, usually guided by a trained psychologist, and express their feelings. The premise was that this provided people with a safe setting for getting in touch with their emotions.

Being a serious student of psychology, I became interested in this process and joined an encounter group. I still vividly recall the first meeting. We were seated in a circle, and after the group leader explained the ground rules, there was a strained silence. Eventually one or two of the more adventurous spoke up. I was one of the first to speak.

I was chattering away with all kinds of ideas about the way things should be. I was filled with valuable insights to share. I paused for a moment and someone interrupted to say, "That's all fine, but what do you feel?"

Picking this up as a cue to go on, I chattered some more about my ideas and insights. But this time I was hit with, "That's all well and good, but what do you feel?"

I was genuinely stumped. I truly did not know what they were asking. And my recollection is that I lapsed into silence—hurt and puzzled by what had occurred.

It took me a long time to see my problem. I was unable to distinguish between my concepts—ideas, opinions, and judgments—and my feelings. Had I been able to express my feelings, I might have said something like, "I'm frightened because I feel as if I'm involved in a game where I don't understand the rules. I'm feeling anxious because I'm afraid people won't like me. I'm feeling lost and rejected because my ideas are what I think is best about me and there doesn't seem to be room for them here. I feel awkward and unsure of myself when I try to express my emotions."

I did not understand that if I could have been open with my feelings, I would have experienced a real breakthrough. As it was, another man in the group was able to express his own feelings about being in the group—which happened to be very similar to mine. The result was that most of the people in the group immediately felt a sense of connection, because we were experiencing similar feelings.

In that instant, we all felt a tremendous sense of intimacy and close-ness. The effect of sharing our emotions, particularly our most vul-nerable ones, was to draw us all closer, acknowledging and embrac-ing our common humanity.

The Productive Way to Understand Feelings

If we are to keep open communication, there is little question that we must express our feelings. But doing so requires us to acknowledge that we are the authors of our own feelings.

Perhaps we would like nothing better than to put the "cause" of our uncomfortable feelings outside us by making others responsible for them. But it is never that simple. The only way to create harmoni-ous relationships is to accept responsibility.

Even external events that most people agree are "troubling" or "fearful" or "devastating" are still interpreted by us. Without the abil-ity to make sense of events around us, we would be unable to apply lessons we learn from day to day. For better or for worse, this ability is also the foundation upon which we build our feelings. Our own inner kaleidoscope is a kaleidoscope of our own making.

As creator of our own feelings, we could assume three possible stances:

1. My feelings cannot be trusted.

2. If I feel it, it is true.

3. I value my feelings greatly, and communicate them openly, but remain constantly aware that they may be based on erroneous or distorted interpretations of behavior and events.

If you take Position 1, that your feelings cannot be trusted, then whose feelings can you trust? You will probably defer to others and have a dull, unenthusiastic attitude toward life, with little or no self-confidence or sense of your own power. The person who takes this position never fully participates in life, and is certainly not a full and equal partner in the relationship.

If you take Position 2, that everything you feel is true and accurate, you will rarely know anything but conflict. It is rare, indeed, for any two people to interpret events in exactly the same way. Each person will experience a different "truth" about virtually every event. The result, then, for the person who takes Position 2 is that he (or she) can never find agreement with anyone. The assumption that you know the truth will invariably evoke an adversarial response from everyone you encounter.

People who communicate emotions clearly operate from the philosophy expressed in Position 3. Such people openly express their feelings while letting other people know that they accept themselves as the authors of those feelings.

It is especially important to remind ourselves to make room for different emotional realities when disagreements heat up. When we can acknowledge that we can have entirely different emotional reactions to the same event, with both of us experiencing our reactions as "true and real," we are more likely to prevent the conflict from escalating.

Two different emotional truths can coexist. But two contradictory judgments cannot. If, instead of communicating my judgments to my wife ("This is a really dumb party!") I communicate my emotions ("I am really bored"), then the potential for a fight is reduced. Moreover, by communicating our feelings instead of our judgments, and recognizing them as such, we learn to value and respect both our own feelings and those of the people we love.

COMMUNICATION TOOLS

HOW LOVING COUPLES FIGHT

Express Feelings, Not Judgments

We have all had the experience of expressing our most sincere feelings only to have our efforts cause a terrible rift with a person we care about deeply. More often than not that breach occurs not because we expressed our feelings, but because we expressed our ideas, beliefs or judgments. It is not always so easy to make the distinction.

In a close personal relationship, judgments, ideas, and beliefs often mask our feelings of rejection, anger, bewilderment or fear. When we can get in touch with these underlying emotions and express them openly and honestly, we leave the other person much more room to respond to our needs. When we express feelings in the form of ideas, the other person may feel that we are criticizing or attacking them and is most likely to respond in an evasive, defensive or even counterattacking manner.

Let us take a moment to clarify this distinction between feelings and judgments, using George and Carolyn from the previous chapter as an example.

Here is a comparison of their feelings and judgments:

CAROLYN'S FEELINGS	CAROLYN'S JUDGMENTS
Great sense of loss; loss of her self-worth without her role as a mother.	The kids will feel abandoned if we sell the house and no longer have rooms for them.
Uncertain, confused, and afraid about what she will do with the rest of her life.	George's sense of relief that the kids are gone is proof he was never really involved with the kids emotionally.
Insecure, needing the reassurance of close friends and familiar places.	George is insensitive to my feelings.

GEORGE'S FEELINGS	GEORGE'S JUDGMENTS
Relieved from responsibility with the kids gone.	This *should* be a happy time.
Constricted by old roles, old friends, and the house. Excited by new possibilities for travel, more time to spend with Carolyn, new ways to be.	We would be happier if we sold the house and got out of here. Carolyn's reasons for wanting to keep the house are silly and impractical.

It may be hard for Carolyn and George to accept each other's feelings. But if you look very closely at the earlier description of George and Carolyn's arguments (see page 37), you will see that George and Carolyn are not talking about feelings. Instead, most of their attention is focused on their judgments.

As relationship conflicts like George and Carolyn's turn away from judgmental arguments and turn toward sharing feelings, some interesting things begin to occur. For example, let us say that George was able to show Carolyn that he did not think her feelings were silly and that he could fully understand why the children leaving home was having such an impact on her. By letting her know that he understood, he would not be saying that he agreed with her; he would simply be saying that he understood and cared.

George's acceptance of his wife's feelings might allow her, over time, to begin sharing some of his excitement about new possibilities. When we feel another's support for our emotional reality, we frequently feel that it is safe to fully acknowledge our feelings and look more closely at them. In Carolyn's case, the feelings she has around the loss of her role as mother need support and understanding; otherwise, she may become increasingly despondent and defensive.

If George did not feel that his sense of relief was being judged, he might begin to admit to his own feelings of loss and sadness at their last child leaving the nest. For the moment, finding no support for his feelings of relief causes him to hang onto them with an iron grip, leaving little or no room for the feeling of loss. But none of this will happen as long as Carolyn and George continue communicating their judgments rather than their emotions.

Why Communicate Feelings?

Let us start by defining what we hope to accomplish by sharing our feelings. What are our goals? When we answer this question, we can talk about whether our style of communication accomplishes these purposes. Here are four key reasons we might want to communicate our feelings:

• We want to feel understood and accepted

The joy of a close relationship is sharing what is important in our lives with someone who cares. Whether we are excited, sad or upset, we want the other person to understand. But how we communicate our feelings can make the difference between that person listening and understanding or having them want to turn away from us or even push us away. We all have our limits as listeners. If we feel under attack, we are not able to be understanding and accepting. If the feelings being shared are the same repetitive litany of woes and complaints that we have heard a thousand times before, it is going to be difficult to maintain interest or continue to care.

• We want to discharge feelings

We may feel that we "must get the feeling out" before we can go on with the relationship. These upset feelings become a barrier to feeling comfortable. We hope that by getting the feelings out, we will somehow be released from them, and we can feel good about each other again.

Think of all the common expressions we use to describe this process: "venting" our feelings or "blowing off steam," as if our emotions were like steam under pressure, which must be released. Sometimes we describe this release as if it were a tropical squall which blows over, leaving the air cleansed and freshened. Implicit in all of these expressions is the concept of catharsis or purging. Not only are the feelings expressed, but the person expressing them can afterward feel much better—relieved of a burden and "more alive."

We probably would not have so many colorful images if there were not some value to catharsis. Yet many couples find that when they share their feelings, issues get blown all out of proportion and the air does not get cleared. Similarly, while listening to a friend you may get the impression that rather than releasing the feelings, you have somehow become witness to a performance. Like an actor reading his lines, your friend is going over an all-too-familiar script of well-worn grievances, which seems to gain a fresh line with each retelling.

In questioning both couples and experts on this issue, I find that just "getting it out" is not enough. To get a complete sense of relief three conditions must be met:

A. Your feelings are shared with the person whose behavior stimulated them.

If your feelings are the result of the way your boss has been treating you, sharing them with your spouse may give you new perspectives for bringing about positive change. But sharing your feelings with your boss is even better.

B. Your listener seriously addresses and attends the issues raised.

The sense of relief occurs when we are convinced that the other person understands the feelings, and cares enough to address the issues directly.

C. Sharing your feelings does not lead to being attacked by the person with whom you shared them.

You will find little relief from sharing your feelings if you are told that you are wrong, bad, stupid, or crazy for having those feelings. This rejection will make you feel like a victim or at least misunderstood. You may then be prone to escalating your efforts, expressing yourself more loudly, more stridently or in an accusatory manner which gets you nowhere.

- ### We want to motivate the other person toward a desired behavior

Not only do we want to be heard; we also want to influence the other person. However, if the other person feels attacked, threatened or "put on the spot," they are not very likely to respond in the way we desire. People are least likely to take risks or open up to us when they feel threatened.

- ### We want to "get" the other person

Although none of us likes to admit it, sometimes we want to hurt the person who hurt us. This is rarely successful. Instead, the other person responds to our attacks with new attacks, and we end up with a whole new crop of wounds. If you are in the business of collecting grievances—and some people clearly are—then this is an effective strategy. However, if you are concerned about protecting your relationship, then "getting" the other person is little more than a cheap thrill. The question to ask yourself is this: "Would I rather hurt this person or be loved by them?" To communicate in ways which foster cooperation and caring, we must care how our communication will affect the other person and the relationship. The goal is to encourage the open expression of feelings, while reducing any sense of attack.

Express Feelings, Not Judgments

If we want people to respond to us in a positive way, we must learn to communicate our emotions rather than our judgments. But this is not always easy. Sometimes, when we are feeling particularly upset, it is easy to blurt out a judgment. In the long run this causes more problems than it solves, although it may seem like an effective way to discharge our emotions.

If someone were to hear, "You were really inconsiderate not to invite me to the dinner for Charlie!" almost anyone would feel at least a little defensive. The emotional thrust is, "You are to blame for my pain." Most of us will react as if the message were really, "You're a bad person." Since none of us likes to be thought of as a "bad person," we might counterattack with, "The dinner party was months ago and you've been holding that against me all this time. I've never known anyone who holds on to grudges the way you do." In other words, "You're a bad person, too."

But let us take a different approach, by communicating the emotion we are experiencing:

"I really felt hurt when you didn't invite me to the dinner."

In this second approach, we give the person much more freedom to respond. They are not being judged as a "bad person." Since they are not boxed in by an accusation, they can focus much more clearly on your emotion. For example, they might respond by saying, "Oh, that makes me feel terrible that you feel that way. You know, I really thought I was doing you a favor not to invite you. I remembered you telling me how much you hated business dinners." Or, "Oh, I'm sorry you feel hurt. I really am. I was in an awful bind. Joe's boss and his wife had to be invited because Joe was entertaining customers from Japan. It was one of the tense business situations that I know you just hate. Frankly, it would have been fun for me having you there. I could have used the moral support."

When feelings instead of judgments are communicated, we are more likely to respond in a caring way. Our own defensive postures are less likely to be triggered and we are much less likely to counter-attack.

There is no guarantee that if you communicate your emotion, a person will not feel defensive. Many of us were taught, very early in our lives, to blame ourselves for other people's anger, worry, and frustration. So when someone says, "I feel hurt, or left out or put down or upset," these messages set off feelings inside us that may be related to experiences far in the past. You may flip into emotions from childhood and no longer hear what the other person is saying, even though blaming you may have been the farthest thing from the other person's mind.

Because of their own interpretations, the other person may still feel defensive when we express our feelings, but we have done everything we can to communicate clearly and without blame. When people are not feeling attacked, there will be less chance of the discussion escalating into a fight.

Clarifying the Difference Between Judgments and Feelings

It sometimes takes practice to distinguish between emotions and judgments. Below you will find alternative ways to say the same thing. As you compare the left- and right-hand columns, imagine yourself as the recipient of these messages. Pay particular attention to your own emotions, asking yourself whether the message you're reading makes you respond to the other person's feelings in a caring way or if you jump to your own defense.

FEELINGS—EMOTIONS	JUDGMENTS—ACCUSATIONS
I'm worried that we're going way over our budget this month. I'm particularly upset about the clothing bill because it's several hundred dollars over what we budgeted.	You're spending altogether too much money. You're going to bankrupt us with the money you're pouring out on clothes.
I really felt embarrassed when you told everyone about my problems fixing things. I felt about two feet tall. Now I'm worried that they'll think I'm an idiot or something.	How dare you make a fool of me in front of my friends! You haven't got an ounce of loyalty in your body. I'd never treat you like that.
I really got mad when you were late. I started feeling really unloved and abandoned.	You're so thoughtless. I waited more than an hour for you, and now dinner is completely ruined. What a miserable thing to do!
I'm worried about John. He seems so isolated from the other kids at school. I sometimes think it would really help him if he could spend some time with you.	John just doesn't seem able to relate to the other kids, and I think it's because you're never around. You never even give him the time of day. You put your career ahead of everyone in this family!

Most people feel defensive upon reading the comments on the right, and less so reading the left-hand column—although we still do not like to hear that something we have said or done resulted in another person feeling hurt, angry, unloved or abandoned.

Whenever you are faced with a conflict, think about the two columns and ask yourself whether the comment you plan to make is an emotion or a judgment. Try replacing accusative or judgmental statements with emotions or feelings.

Connect Feelings to Behaviors, Not Judgments

It is not enough to go around telling other people, "I feel hurt," "I feel sad" or "I feel thrilled." Our feelings are about something—an event, a behavior or even our own inner experiences. But in the process of communicating the subject of our feelings, there is one more chance to slip back into blame and accusation.

Consider the following two comments: "I'm upset that you didn't include the check with the application." "I'm upset that you were so careless and haphazard."

Both of these messages communicate a feeling: the feeling of being upset. But the first one connects the feeling to a description of a behavior, while the second connects the feeling to a judgment of the person. The words "careless" and "haphazard" stand out like flashing neon signs. If we are the recipient of such a comment, any other information fades into the background and we simply feel attacked. The chances are good that we will respond with a defense: "How was I to know you wouldn't look it over before you mailed it?" Or a counterattack: "If you'd given me all the information in the first place, I would have known to send the check."

If we go to the trouble of sending our message as an emotion, we will have wasted our time if, at the last minute, we turn the words into an accusation. Any time blame is communicated or even hinted at, we hear that blame before we hear the rest of the communication.

Judgmental labels such as "thoughtless," "inconsiderate," "careless," and "haphazard" rarely move us toward the solution to a problem or the resolution of a conflict. But they can certainly touch off defensiveness.

Even when people we are judging also judge themselves, they will not necessarily have the same labels as we do. Although you may judge your spouse's behavior as "immature and impulsive," he or she may look upon that same behavior as "spontaneous and uninhibited." As a result, your label and theirs will be at war, and this war will undoubtedly spill out into the relationship.

You can easily and quickly distinguish between judging a behavior and describing it by looking at the chart below. In the left-hand column, the feeling is attached to an action. In the right-hand column, the feeling is attached to a judgment.

DESCRIPTIONS	JUDGMENTS
I'm mad that the toys were left all over the floor.	I'm mad because you never pick anything up. You're so messy.
I'm irritated by the spelling errors in this report.	I'm irritated because you are so careless about your spelling.
I'm worried that the kids may need more attention from you.	I'm worried because you're so uninvolved with the kids.
I'm anxious that we may get behind financially and never be able to catch up.	I'm anxious because we are both such spendthrifts.

It is not easy to keep judgments out of our descriptions of other people's behavior. Particularly in the beginning, it is just hard work. We need to be patient with ourselves. It takes more than care in language; it also takes a change in how we relate to our own and other's behavior. If I persist in judging myself, it is hard not to apply the same judgments to others. The conscious effort to use nonjudgmental language is a good exercise in teaching us how to be less judgmental of ourselves. But for most people this is an ongoing struggle.

Being Careful to Phrase Your Feelings as an "I-Message" Makes the Process Easier

By using an "I-Message" (a term coined by Thomas E. Gordon), you would successfully communicate that you felt hurt and embarrassed, but you have not said, "You're to blame for my feelings." With the "You-Message" you would clearly be blaming the other person for your bad feelings. Be careful, though; sending an I-Message is not just a matter of putting "I'm" or "I feel" in front of the sentence. For example, "I feel that you really put me down and embarrassed me in front of the group" still ends up being a You-Message. It is true you have put the words "I feel" in front of the sentence, but you have not accepted responsibility for your feelings—you are still blaming someone else. Still it is useful to use the term "I-Message" as a reminder to own and be responsible for your feelings rather than blame others.

I-MESSAGE	YOU-MESSAGE
"I felt very hurt and embarrassed when you pointed out my mistake in front of the group."	"You really hurt and embarrassed me in front of the group."

Describe What the Other Person's Behavior Means to You

A client of mine was raised in a family where tickling was an expression of affection. But when he married, he found that his wife became very upset and angry when he tickled her. He knew she became upset, but he did not know why, and he thought she was very unreasonable. Sometimes he would tickle her anyway. Finally she shared her whole story with him. When she was a small child, her older brothers would hold her down and tickle her until she lost control. For her, being tickled brought up feelings of powerlessness, rage, and fear. Once her husband understood the emotional impact on her, he never tickled her again.

His wife might have said, "I really get upset when you tickle me," which would have met all the guidelines we have discussed up to now—but it would not have had much impact on her husband. However, when he heard that behind the upset were devastating feelings, he was deeply moved, and changed his behavior accordingly.

This example illustrates the need to let other people know how their behavior affects you. It is a start to let the other person know you are angry, sad or happy. But this may not make sense to them emotionally until you also tell them how their behavior triggers memories or takes on special significance. Only then will they have a clear picture of why their behavior has such an impact.

FEELING	FEELING + MEANING FOR YOU
I'm feeling upset that we blew our budget again.	I'm really upset that we blew our budget again. It always gives me the feeling that we're slipping farther and farther behind and we'll never catch up. It's really scary, like when my father went bankrupt.
I'm really annoyed when you're late for an appointment.	I'm really annoyed when you're late for an appointment. I guess what it says to me is that you think that my time is less important than yours, and then I start feeling really put down.
I'm upset that you leave the water running.	I'm upset that you leave the water running. We got a surcharge on our water bill this month because we exceeded last summer's water use, and it really makes me feel like a hypocrite when I talk about caring for the environment.

As you can see from the examples, the importance of an emotional communication is enhanced when you understand the specific, personal meaning it has for the other person. But even when you articulate this information, it does not mean that the other person will automatically salute you and say, "Yes sir! I'll never do anything to upset you ever again!"

It is easy to slip into the assumption that because I feel bad, you should change your behavior. But this is not something anybody owes you; the other person's compliance is strictly voluntary. In a relationship where the two partners are constantly altering their behavior to satisfy the other person, they both soon discover that there is not any me left. They become each other's puppet, controlled by each other's needs, and this becomes a breeding ground for resentment and every kind of defensive behavior we have discussed.

On the other hand, if you never allow yourself to be influenced by your loved one's feelings—no matter how much your behavior hurts them—you will probably find it very difficult to maintain the relationship. We modify our behavior because we care. But if we are not changing our behavior voluntarily and freely, we become resentful.

This goes back to the issue of taking responsibility for our feelings. My wife may do something which triggers my childhood feelings of inadequacy, of being a hurt little boy. I may let her know what I am feeling and why. But if she gives in every time I start feeling like a hurt little boy, pretty soon my internalized three-year-old boy is running the relationship. Because my wife cares about me, she wants to know when I am feeling bad, and she may be supportive even when it does require her to temporarily put aside her own needs. But ultimately my hurt little boy, and all the feelings attached to him, are my responsibility, not hers.

So how much influence can we expect to have on each other? The amount is dependent on the tangibility of the impact. What exactly do I mean by tangibility? Most people agree that impact is tangible when it is:

- costing me money.

- harming my possessions.

- consuming too much of my time.

- requiring too much work.

- endangering my livelihood.

Communications trainer Robert Bolton estimates that at least 90 percent of well-constructed, non-blaming messages that describe tangible effects will result in the other person modifying their behavior or at least trying to resolve the problem.

But what happens when a mother says she feels devastated because her adult daughter has sexual relationships without being married? The daughter may feel bad that her mother is upset, but she will continue to make her own choices. In this case, rather than seeing the mother as tangibly affected, the daughter is likely to see the mother's feelings as being caused by the mother's own beliefs, not the daughter's behavior. Here, we are not looking at tangible effects, but at values, ethical standards, and moral judgments. In the same way, if you had lunch with a business associate of the opposite sex, your spouse may feel jealous or threatened. But if you limited all your behavior so that your spouse never felt threatened, you could live your life totally under the control of his or her fears and anxieties.

Because we care about our loved ones, we listen to their feelings—and when we can, we respond. But because we also care about ourselves, we cannot let others' feelings totally control us. It is their job to be responsible for their feelings, and our job to be responsible for ours. Communicating our feelings is one way to take responsibility for ourselves; but that responsibility stops short of insisting that other people alter their behavior to please us or make us more comfortable.

Putting It Together

In this chapter, we have presented five guidelines for effective emotional expression. When I want to communicate a feeling effectively, I use the following simple formula which captures all five guidelines:

Step 1. Begin with a first-person pronoun

"I'm..." Or "I feel..."

Step 2. Add a word describing an emotion

"...Irritated..." Or angry, sad, disappointed, hurt, etc."

Step 3. Describe the precipitating behavior or event

"...That I had to look all over for the car keys..."

Step 4. Name the tangible or emotional impact

"...Because it took so much time I was late for my appointment."

Step 5. Describe what the other person's behavior means to you

"...and I interpreted that as meaning that you didn't think my needs were important."

When You Forget and Start Blaming and Accusing

Although these guidelines will help you express your emotions, there are bound to be times when you forget everything you know and revert back to blaming and accusing.

As psychotherapist Daniel B. Wile suggests, sometimes people just have to send blaming and accusatory messages because of their bottled-up feelings about the issue. Dr. Wile suggests that we remind ourselves that these first "You-Messages" are stepping stones to more productive "I-Messages."

When you find yourself slipping into accusatory "You-Messages," do not judge yourself too harshly for the slip. Look for the feeling which underlies the accusation so that you can start over with an I-Message. Above all, accept responsibility for your own reaction, rather than blaming your loved one for it. By using these guidelines, you can transform the defensiveness back into loving communication.

Conflicts offer rich opportunities for discovering and working through distortions and emotionally loaded perceptions that block us from being more effective in our lives. In our more casual relationships there usually is not enough commitment to motivate us to work together. Auto mechanics, waiters, or even coworkers probably do not care that their behavior evokes painful childhood experiences. But close relationships are different. It matters to us that we resolve the conflict. And that commitment to resolving conflicts in our closest relationships is the basis for perhaps the most valuable laboratory for self-discovery that life has to offer.

"Truth" is so large that no single human can ever know it all. When we care enough to hear the other person's version of the truth, and have the courage to articulate our own, we often discover a larger truth that enriches and expands both of our lives.

Tool #5

Listen So That People Feel Understood

As we saw in the last chapter, communicating feelings in an accusatory manner is one sure way to escalate a conflict into a major fight. Another way is to communicate the message that we're not willing to listen or that we do not value the other person's emotions. Of course, most of us do not usually send such messages intentionally. But when we do, we invariably broaden the emotional gap between ourselves and our loved ones.

There is one simple principle that my clients always find extremely helpful: Resistance breeds resistance. We have all seen this principle at work. Anytime we act in ways that tell others we do not understand them or that we are not listening or that we flatly reject them, their original feeling will get even stronger. Resisting each other's feelings only results in a rapid escalation of the conflict, with both feeling perfectly "justified," convinced, at least for the moment, that our reaction is caused by the other person provoking us.

Sometimes, instead of expressing ourselves more emphatically, we go underground with our feelings. For example, if you express your feelings to your boss—or to some other powerful person—and they reject what you are saying, you may feel very resentful. You may want to defend your feelings but you dare not do so directly.

When we pull back, our feelings do not just mysteriously evaporate; instead, resentment builds, festering away like an infected wound. In a close relationship, of course, this can have direct consequences.

Underground battles are "cold wars," with the participants smoldering quietly, distancing themselves farther and farther from each other every day. Though not a single shot is fired, the casualty lists can be just as great as in more open forms of warfare.

Most of us would not intentionally say or do things to force another person to become angry or resentful. But the things we do that evoke these reactions are often quite subtle, at least in the beginning. Very often this emotionally deadening process begins not with what we say but with how we listen.

Are You Listening or Are You Getting Ready?

Have you ever noticed how people listen during an argument? They wait for comments that they can grab hold of and easily disprove or that give them a good lever for a counterattack. In the process, they do not hear the other person's full message. They hear only the cues they can use in their own defense.

An effective listening exercise illustrates this point: I ask participants in my workshops to split off into pairs. One person takes the role of speaker, the other the role of listener. The speaker then expresses his or her feelings on a subject that he feels strongly about. The listener's job is to do only one thing: listen to what the other person is feeling. Whenever there are natural stopping points or pauses, the listener is to come up with one word which describes that feeling. For example, "You're feeling sad" (or happy, or frustrated or whatever word best describes what that person has just expressed).

Many people simply cannot carry out the designated role as a listener. They find themselves making judgments about the speaker's feelings. Or they have suggestions about what the speaker should do. Those who can listen invariably comment on what hard work it is. For others, there is a moment of insight when they realize that for most of their lives their idea of listening has been to concentrate not on what the speaker was trying to communicate but only their own internal reactions to the speaker. Effective listeners shift their focus from their own reactions to the unique emotional reality expressed in the other person's thoughts and feelings. In effective listening, you fully accept that other people feel as they do. Your job is simply to understand them.

But that is not what usually happens. Most of the time all our effort goes into making people change what they feel. The message we too often communicate is, "It's not okay with me that you feel as you do." This can be seen in the following example:

What Roberta Says	What the Listener Says	What Roberta Hears
I'm so upset that we're not taking a vacation. I was really looking forward to it.	Well, you know very well why we aren't going. I've explained it to you a hundred times. It just doesn't make any sense financially.	I'm going to give you some information so that you won't feel as you do.
I know what you've said. I'm not deaf, you know. But you never listen to me. You just spend all your time repeating yourself like a broken record. You're totally unreasonable.	I'm unreasonable! You're the one holding out for some fantasy vacation we can't afford.	You're unreasonable for having your feeling.

What Roberta Says	What the Listener Says	What Roberta Hears
Well, somehow we find the money to spend on your expensive suits but we can't spend a cent on the vacation I want. We have money when it's for something you want, but not for anything I want. You're just on a big power trip.	Roberta, listen to me. You're being completely unfair. Those are work suits. I need them to make a living for us. Can't you just act like an adult and see my point? We can't afford a vacation this year. We just can't.	It's unfair and childish of to feel this way.

This conversation is typical of so many we have all had. The listener concentrates just long enough to figure out how to respond. The emotional thrust of each of these responses is to tell the other person that they are wrong or unreasonable or unfair or childish, etc. Then, each time Roberta feels thwarted, she ups the ante a bit and slips into an accusatory tone. Feeling the effects of the accusations, the listener's responses become increasingly judgmental, and soon we have an all-out-fight going. It is a fight that never had to happen. Let us take a look at how the same conversation might have gone had the second person been a more effective listener:

ROBERTA: *I'm so upset that we're not taking a vacation. I was really looking forward to it.*

LISTENER: *You're really feeling disappointed.*

ROBERTA: *Yes. Sometimes, I just feel like I'm in a rut, and I was hoping a vacation would get me out of it. I feel as if all I do is go to work, come home, do chores, and go to a movie now and then. There has to be more to life than this!*

LISTENER: *So a lot of the disappointment you're feeling is because you saw the vacation as a way to break the routine.*

ROBERTA: *Yes, that's right. I guess I did. Don't you ever get stuck like that, and just feel there's got to be more to life?*

In this second example, the listener is simply accepting Roberta's feelings. Remember the lesson in previous chapters: People feel as they do. When the listener refrained from trying to change Roberta's feelings, Roberta no longer felt a need to defend them. She was free to move on to other feelings. As a result, the conversation took a surprising turn. Roberta began to describe her feelings about being in a rut, and she and her listener began sharing deeper levels of emotion. Roberta and her listener would probably never have gotten to these deeper feelings in their first conversation.

Attitudes that Get in the Way of Listening

Why is it so hard for us to just accept other people's feelings? Part of it, of course, is that when we hear loved ones' feelings, we often hear criticisms of ourselves. Whether those criticisms are intended or not does not matter. The point is that we are not comfortable with being criticized or described in a negative light, especially by people we are close to.

I have often observed that a listener will respond defensively to a half-dozen words of criticism embedded in a 200-word communication. They will focus on those few words while seeming to hear little, if any, of the remaining message, even though the rest may have contained important information.

It is easy to understand why we might have trouble listening to a loved one's feelings concerning our own behavior. But what about when our loved ones come home from work or school after a particularly difficult day and sit down to unburden themselves from all the trials and tribulations of the day? Even though none of what they say is a criticism of us, we find it difficult to respond except to tell them what they might do or "should have done," to avoid the pressures and frustrations they experienced. What dynamics are at work at these times, making it difficult for us to listen to the other person's feelings?

The answer can be found by examining four beliefs which influence us all, both in our everyday communications and in conversations with those we love.

• People want solutions.

Let us say your friend Fran comes to you and says, "I'm at my wit's end with John. He's always making appointments that affect both of us without telling me about them. I usually hear about them at the last minute, and then I have to change my plans to accommodate him."

If you are like most of us, your immediate response will be to start thinking up ways that Fran might better cope with John. We immediately assume that Fran is asking us to help her come up with a solution. So we immediately start generating ideas: Have you tried this, have you tried that, etc. But then something very peculiar happens. The more ideas you come up with, the more Fran seems to have a ready argument why your suggestions will not work. Moreover, she may even start becoming annoyed, and pretty soon you are angry at her for showing such a lack of gratitude for your efforts. It might go something like this:

FRAN: *I don't know what to do about John. He's always setting up appointments without checking with me first.*

LISTENER: *Have you told him it bothers you?*

FRAN: *Well of course I have, but he just keeps doing it anyway.*

LISTENER: *Maybe you need to turn things around and do the same thing to him a few times so that he knows how it feels.*

FRAN: *I've already done that, but it doesn't seem to bother him like it does me. He doesn't seem to care, and it drives me crazy.*

LISTENER: *Well, maybe, you need to refuse to show up when he sets appointments without consulting you.*

FRAN: *That's easy for you to say. But it's hard to do when it's some-one like our loan office, or the IRS or some very important person, where I won't just get even with John but I'll hurt myself in the process.*

The listener gets so involved in trying to help Fran that she can-not pay attention to the feelings Fran is expressing. The result is that Fran ends up feeling that no one is really listening to her or under-stands what she is going through. Likewise, the listener may go away feeling unappreciated for trying to help since, after all, Fran has re-jected everything which has been offered.

Whenever I get into conversations like this, I feel more than a little annoyed with myself. I have suckered myself into the "Yes, but…" game. Anytime you find yourself in the "Yes, but…" game, you can count on the fact that you are not providing the listening that the other person wants.

If you look closely at the conversation between Fran and the lis-tener, you will see that Fran never once solicited advice. The listener interpreted Fran's complaint as a request for advice. A request for advice might have been forthcoming had Fran felt satisfied in having another person listen to her, but in this case it did not happen. In-stead, Fran ended up feeling frustrated, once again, in just "getting it out." Any new perspective on her own feelings, which might have occurred if she had felt understood, never came. So, she was unable to move on.

When we respond to other people by applying our own solutions to their problems, we direct the conversation away from them. In effect, we dictate that their next comment be an evaluation of our suggestion. However, there is an alternative. If we just accept the other person's feelings, we let them stay in charge of where to go next. Let us look at some of the different ways the same conversation might have gone if our friend's feelings had just been accepted:

FRAN: *I don't know what to do about John. He's always setting up appointments without consulting me.*

LISTENER: *You're frustrated that he doesn't consult you, and you're not really sure what to do about it.*

Once she feels that her initial comment has been accepted, Fran can let go of that feeling and the conversation can move on in any of several directions.

DIRECTION 1: That's right, I sometimes think he's still into some big macho thing where men make all the decisions and women are just supposed to go along with it. He does this sort of thing a lot. Sometimes I'm not sure we're going to make it together.

DIRECTION 2: Nothing seems to work. I've even tried reversing the situation, setting up appointments without telling him. But most of the time he just seems grateful I took care of it. It's like it just doesn't mean the same thing to him that it does to me, and he doesn't appreciate that for a woman it's very important to be treated as an equal. I'm beginning to wonder whether I'm too sensitive about always being treated as an equal. Maybe it's how I interpret things, not his behavior.

DIRECTION 3: That's right. Nothing seems to work. Have you ever had that problem with Bill? What do you think I should do?

In the first example, it now appears that the initial problem was only symbolic of a larger conflict Fran is feeling. Talking about ways to get John to consult Fran before making appointments would not have been nearly as helpful as letting Fran talk about her uncertainties concerning the relationship as a whole.

In the second example, Fran is still working on the appointment issue, but she is looking at the possibility that her way of interpreting John's behavior is the real problem. At least that is what she is telling you so far.

In the third example there is a clear-cut request for you to share your feelings and suggestions. When there is a clear request, it is appropriate to offer your suggestions. But it is only at this point that we could count on our suggestions being anything but an impediment to genuine listening. When as listeners we start focusing on solutions, our minds start racing ahead, searching for problem-solving ideas rather than genuinely listening to the other person's feelings.

Keep in mind that even when there has been a clear request for suggestions, you may soon find yourself playing the "Yes, but…" game. That is the time to step back and acknowledge feelings rather than coming up with an endless list of alternate suggestions.

For so many of us, when other people offer suggestions—most of which, let us admit, are fairly obvious—we feel put down. Good intentions or not, we interpret suggestions as judgments of our competence. In some cases, solutions even recreate parent-child relationships, in which the person—who has only wanted to be heard—suddenly feels backed into a corner, having to accept solutions they might not even agree with. Rather than being seen as well intentioned, the proffered solutions become viewed as power trips.

Above all, constantly making suggestions instead of listening to feelings can lead the other person into a growing sense of frustration, a painful impression that "He never really listens to me. He just tells me what to do all the time." And this kind of frustration can deaden what was once even the liveliest relationship.

• It is our responsibility to make people feel better.

Another mistaken belief plays out when we turn into "cheerleaders" of sorts. We become reassuring, sympathizing with them, trying to divert them from their problems, or humoring them. Here is an example of how such a conversation might go:

TED: *Sometimes I just don't think I'm getting anywhere. I read the paper, and people who started out the same time I did are being named vice-president and president of major corporations. Here I am a lowly assistant manager. I'm not sure I'm ever going to make it.*

SUE: *Aw, honey, we all have bad days. Look at how complimentary Mr. Winters was on the job you did with the quarterly report. You'll get the recognition you deserve. Just hang in there.*

TED: *Yeah, he was complimentary, but he hands out compliments to everybody. It doesn't mean anything. I thought I was going to accomplish more in life than this. What it this is as far as I'm ever going to go?*

SUE: *You should be ashamed even talking like that. You have a nice home, and a family who loves you. What's wrong with that?*

TED: *I'm not saying that I don't think you and the kids are great but... Oh, never mind, it was just a bad day.*

At this point, Ted has stopped talking about his feelings. He may not even be aware of what has happened. What started out as an effort to express his discouragement has turned into something else. He now senses that Sue is going to feel very hurt if he gives the impression that he does not think that she and the kids are enough.

Sue has not really listened to him. Instead, she has "handled" his feelings; all her efforts have gone into getting him over his feelings rather than accepting him as he is and responding accordingly.

Along with sympathizing with Ted, Sue has sent him the message that he really should not feel as he does. If he only looked on the bright side, and appreciated his home and family more, he would see that his feelings about not moving up the corporate ladder are unfounded. By the time their conversation is over, Ted feels not only discouraged about his job but also discouraged that he cannot share his true feelings with Sue for fear of hurting her.

Had Ted been able to talk openly about his feelings, which, after all, most human beings have in one form or other during their lives, he and Sue might have had a moment of very deep, intimate sharing. Instead, Ted has gone underground, where he will feel more isolated, more alone than ever. His sense that there is something wrong with him has increased.

It is a very human reflex to want to cure, as quickly as possible, any painful or sad feelings that arise in our lives. But all too often, instead of accepting that our loved ones are hurting, our efforts to "cure" end up blocking their feelings. Instead of accepting that our loved ones are hurting, and respecting their right to have those feelings, we jump in and "handle" the situation. Unfortunately, the original feelings do not go away under these circumstances; they only go underground, to emerge another day, perhaps this time in a slightly different form.

For many years my wife headed an institute, the Cancer Support and Education Center in Menlo Park, California, which helps people with cancer or AIDS to mobilize their own emotional resources and support their recoveries. I worked there with couples who were having communication problems. As you can imagine, with life-threatening diseases hanging over their heads, people bring intense feelings to the relationships. Patients may temporarily feel totally exhausted and defeated. Patients are usually frightened by the specter of dying, whether that prospect is remote or imminent, and their loved ones are often equally frightened.

Moreover, patients' loved ones may have all kinds of conflicting feelings, wanting to be supportive but resenting that they have to put their own lives on hold. There is a swirl of frightening emotions mixed together with very deep and intimate feelings.

For these people the largest barrier is the impulse to rush in and try to make "bad" feelings go away by cajoling, humoring or persuading. The impulse is to do whatever is necessary to avoid feeling frightened, discouraged or hopeless. But we see, time and time again, that it is actually an act of nonacceptance to insist that people quickly get over painful or hurt feelings. We are saying, in effect, "I'll accept you as the warm, lovable person you'll be as soon as I can get you over these feelings. But I cannot accept you as you are." We cannot share feelings with the person who fails to acknowledge and accept our painful or frightened feelings. All these efforts to block feelings simply add to the burden.

When feelings are met with resistance the feelings invariably increase in intensity, even when they go underground. Imagine how isolated people can feel, even when they are together constantly, when they cannot share the feelings that matter to them the most!

Most of us are not facing anything as traumatic as a life-threatening disease. But the same principles that apply in these high-stress situations also apply in our daily lives. We have a need to express our deepest feelings but this need is often in competition with the very human desire to avoid or escape what is painful.

I sometimes like to entertain the possibility that we all might one day be able to accept each others' feelings exactly as they are. I wonder what would happen if it was okay for people to feel whatever they feel and not have others try to change them. It is perhaps the greatest compliment, and the highest expression of love in a relationship, to accept each other's feelings no matter what they are.

Fully accepting each other's emotional reality is far more rewarding than never showing our feelings of hurt, discouragement, or sadness. To avoid or deny difficult feelings leads only to alienation and separation. To accept them is to accept the whole person, not just the part that we find easy or pleasant.

- **If we accept certain feelings, they will stay that way forever.**

For some unknown reason, we all seem to think that if we do not do something to change certain feelings—such as discouragement or depression—those feelings are going to stay that way forever. If we do not talk people out of their bad feelings, somehow they will just get stuck there. Oddly enough, just the reverse is true.

Anytime you extend acceptance to a feeling, a process of transformation begins. This is true whether you accept the feeling in yourself or in another person. If someone is depressed and you just accept that she feels depressed, without trying to convince her it should be otherwise, this acceptance carries an important hidden message: It is okay for you to be and feel whatever you are.

Anytime we put up resistance to another person's feelings, their reaction will probably be to defend their right to have those feelings. When we accept them, there is nothing to defend; as a result, they become more flexible, and the feelings prove to be more transitory. Acceptance may result in the expression of stronger feelings, because we have signaled that it is safe to share. But then, as these feelings are expressed, they also begin to change. It is as though with the freedom to talk openly, that feeling becomes less threatening. Acceptance of feelings often permits people to move from anger and defensiveness to more vulnerable feelings such as inadequacy, fear, and loneliness.

- **The opening problem is the real problem.**

It is very easy to believe that a person's first complaints are the real issues this person wishes to address. But the reality is, wherever feelings are involved, the opening comments may be nothing more than a safe place to start. We are inclined to get caught up in conversations which have little or nothing to do with the real problem. Sending solutions can lead to its own problems. But sending solutions to the wrong issues can compound the confusion even more. It is no wonder that what starts out as casual conversation about a small conflict often turns into a full-blown fight!

As I have shown, when people sense acceptance, they are likely to share deeper, more vulnerable emotions. This gives us a clue to the real purpose of opening comments; most of us use them to "test the water" before going on to more fundamental issues.

People move to deeper, more internal feelings when they feel it is safe. Because of this the definition of the problem continues to change until the core issues have been identified. If you are not listening carefully, you may never even notice the transition from one topic to the next. As a result, you may feel that the speaker is getting off-course and may try to pull the conversation back to the more superficial opening comments.

Starting out with a "safe" problem, then moving to more vulnerable feelings, is common practice. You will probably begin noticing how often it occurs in your life. When you finally do get past the opening comments, sharing the feelings that really matter often turns into a voyage of discovery for both the listener and the speaker.

The key is for the listener to become attentive to shifts in the conversation, and open the gates for deeper understanding of the real issues.

These four beliefs get in the way of listening effectively. With some of these impediments out of the way, we can turn now to talking about what it would mean to listen in a totally accepting way.

Acceptance is Not Agreement

What would it be like if we all learned to listen in a totally accepting way? It would certainly change the way we communicate. But before we can really address that issue, it's necessary to make a clear distinction between acceptance and agreement.

Acceptance means that we acknowledge the other person's feelings. Our own feelings may be very different. But it is a fact that people feel as they do, even though their feelings may be based on ways of viewing life which are totally unique to them—and totally foreign to us. What is the point of resisting it? Accepting feelings is simply accepting the reality of the human condition. People feel what they feel, and we each have a right to our own emotional reality.

Agreement is a different matter altogether. It is not just the acknowledgment of what the other person feels. Agreement is also a statement that as far as you are concerned these feelings are right, proper, good, and justified. The emotional message of agreement is "you're absolutely right to feel as you do."

This difference can be illustrated as follows:

STATEMENT	Response: ACCEPTANCE	Response: AGREEMENT
Sandra: "I'm just fed up with that bank. Nobody should be treated the way they treated me. I'm going to move our accounts right away."	"You've really had it with them."	"You're absolutely right. It's outrageous the way they've treated you."

To listen in an accepting way does not mean that you must be in agreement with the speaker. In fact, perhaps the greatest value of really listening is that it allows us to listen with an open mind in those circumstances where there definitely is not agreement. Because we are not resisting the other person's feelings, genuine differences can still be addressed without turning the exchange of ideas and feelings into a fight. Let us look at the skills that allow us to do that.

The Skill of Active Listening

Active listening is not a new invention. In the past, it has been called by many different names, including Reflective Listening and Mirroring. I have chosen to use Thomas Gordon's term "Active Listening" because it suggests that the listener has an active role in understanding the communication between two or more people.

The key principle employed in Active Listening is to respond by summarizing, in your own words, what you understand the other person is saying, and to check out with him or her whether or not your understanding is accurate. You have already seen some examples, but here is a somewhat more extended example:

MARGARET: *Johnny's been absolutely impossible the last few days. I know it's a horrible thing to say about your own kid, but I just feel like strangling him.*

ACTIVE LISTENING RESPONSE: *You're really frustrated, and at the end of your rope.*

MARGARET: *That's absolutely right. I mean he's been totally exasperating. He's testing me on everything I say or do. I can't say anything to him without him pushing it to the absolute limits. I'm absolutely at a loss about what to do with him.*

ACTIVE LISTENING RESPONSE: *You're puzzled why he always seems to be testing your limits.*

MARGARET: *Yeah, I can't do anything without it being turned into a power struggle. I don't know whether it's adolescence or it's something I'm doing to set it up.*

ACTIVE LISTENING RESPONSE: *You're worried that something you're doing provokes his reaction.*

MARGARET: *Yeah. I know my parents said things when I was a teenager that just drove me crazy. They used to infuriate me, and I'd fight them about everything. I'm afraid I'm beginning to sound just exactly like my parents. After all the complaints I've had about the way my parents raised me, it's a real shock to have the roles reversed.*

ACTIVE LISTENING RESPONSE: *It's disturbing to think you're doing the same things that drove you crazy when you were a kid.*

MARGARET: *That's right. I'm not only having to cope with Johnny, I'm also having to rethink some of my attitudes about my parents.*

I am willing to bet that at least some readers feel that these responses seem stiff, distant, or possibly even patronizing. I have had the same reaction when reading transcripts of real conversations like this, yet I can testify that these responses, said in a genuine and caring way, would be experienced by Margaret as very supportive. Notice the number of "yeahs" and "that's rights," each one indicating that Margaret feels as if the listener understands her.

Because her present feelings are being accepted, Margaret feels free to explore new feelings, and in the process makes the discovery that Johnny's exasperating behavior is not all that is bothering her. She is also worried that she might be doing something to provoke his behavior, and she was troubled by having to rethink some of her judgments about her own childhood. These are all feelings that probably would never have come up if the listener had responded in a less accepting way.

Had Margaret's feelings been met with suggestions for how to cope with Johnny, it is highly probable that we would have had another replay of the old "Yes, but…" game. She might have even taken the listener's suggestions as criticism, touching off a major fight. Certainly it is unlikely that she would have felt comfortable enough to explore her feelings about her own childhood if the listener had not taken this accepting position.

Learning Active Listening is a little like learning a new tennis swing.

To get good at it, you have to actually do it, not just read about it. As in learning new techniques in any sport, repetition and practice are your best teachers.

Active Listening involves breaking old habits, and at first it will seem unnatural, just as a new tennis swing often does. But if you keep doing it, despite its feeling unnatural, you can replace old habits with new ones. If you would like other people to practice with, check with your local colleges and community service organizations. Many of them, across the country, offer communication courses where some version of Active Listening is taught.

Guidelines for Becoming an Effective Active Listener

There are four basic steps for becoming an effective Active Listener:

1. Summarize without judging.

Remember that the main message you want to communicate is acceptance. Focus your attention on summarizing rather than judging what the speaker says. When you respond, choose you words carefully to ensure that what you say is non-judgmental.

For example, Elayne comes to Rob after being chastised by her supervisor for not meeting her sales goal for the quarter. Elayne says, "Nobody else met their goals either. It just isn't fair the way he singled me out and ridiculed me in front of the whole group. I was humiliated." As an Active Listener, Rob might respond, "You're feeling hurt that he singled you out, when no one else met their goals either."

A judgmental response might be, "You're feeling sorry for yourself because you got picked on" or "You're really being defensive about being criticized." The phrases "feeling sorry for yourself" in the first sentence, and the words "defensive" in the second have negative connotations for most people. How many times, as a child, were you told, "Stop feeling sorry for yourself"? Similarly, telling another person that they are being defensive is anything but a non-judgmental statement.

Most of us are so accustomed to judging our own behavior that it is easy to let the same judgments creep in when we are responding to other people. We may scold ourselves or give ourselves advice constantly, with an inner dialogue that we may or may not ever actually verbalize. If we had a way of recording this "self-talk," it might sound something like this: "Oh, that was a stupid move, pulling out into traffic like that. You almost got rear-ended." Or, "I should have stopped by the store for a bottle of milk on my way home. How dumb of me! I knew we were out." When we are responding to others, the same inner voice chatters away, this time with its comments directed at the other person. The effective Active Listener resists the temptation to verbalize this voice.

As you begin practicing Active Listening techniques, you will probably discover, as most people do, that we have excellent vocabularies for judging, but very limited vocabularies for expressing feelings. Somehow, "You're really being defensive" comes to us much more naturally than the phrase, "You're hurt."

The difficult part of becoming an Active Listener may be the development of an emotional vocabulary. We do this by simply listening, in our daily conversations and in the things we read, for words that describe our emotions; words like hurt, happy, relieved, sad, anxious, frightened, tense, worried, etc. Having such words on the tip of your tongue will make it much easier to respond non-judgmentally.

Practice your emotional vocabulary by substituting these feeling words whenever you find yourself judging your own behavior. Become an Active Listener instead of an Inner Judge. Instead of saying, "That was stupid of me to pull out in traffic like that," try substituting a less judgmental phrase, such as, "I feel really scared that I almost got rear-ended just then." By doing this, you will not only gain practice, but also develop a more constructive form of "self-talk" for helping you through difficult moments.

2. Summarize both feelings and ideas.

One of the dangers of Active Listening is that your responses can sound as if you are parroting the other person. The person might even think you are making fun of them. This occurs primarily when the summary statement gives greater emphasis to the idea than to the feelings. For example, suppose your spouse says to you, "I'm going to take Greg's car privileges away from him if he comes in late one more time. He's just gone too far!"

If you focused only on the ideas expressed, your response might sound something like this: "You think we should take his privileges away." This response, with little if any acknowledgment of emotions, might easily evoke the response, "I just said that, didn't I?"

A response which captures both feelings and ideas might sound like this: "You're really fed up, and think we need to do something about it." This second response is more satisfying emotionally. It lets the other person know we acknowledge and understand their feelings. Acknowledgment of feelings will make us feel understood, not mimicked or possibly even belittled.

Active Listening is probably most effective when people's feelings are strong. But we need not limit it to these circumstances. We can also use it to summarize and emphasize agreements or to clarify a particularly lengthy and confusing statement, or to get closure to a lengthy discussion so that people feel free to move on to another topic. For example, after a lengthy discussion of who is going to do what to get ready for a trip, you might summarize your understanding of who does what. Your Active Listening summary will deal primarily with ideas, not feelings, but it is still a good way to pull things together, and check out whether there is agreement.

3. Avoid lead-in phrases.

Some training courses in Active Listening teach people to start each feedback response with lead-in phrases such as, "What I hear you saying (or feeling) is…" or "If I understand you correctly, you're feeling…" The point is to remind the trainees that even their Active Listening responses can be colored by their own interpretations rather than being objective summaries of the other person's feelings. However, in close personal relationships these lead-in phrases can have the effect of distancing the listener from the speaker. From the listener's point of view, it starts to feel very mechanical. In fact, it often has the effect of focusing the conversation more on the listener ("Watch me do my listening thing") than on the person who has the feelings.

Sometimes we use lead-in phrases to buy time while we think up an accurate response. But buying time can be accomplished with silence. Most of us rush to respond as if the world would come to an end if we do not have an instant answer. A pause of seconds can seem like an eternity. But the truth is that such a pause can also communicate that we are being attentive and thoughtful.

It is a good idea always to approach Active Listening with a certain amount of humility. It's always possible to misunderstand what was said. I find that a slight voice inflection at the end of an Active Listening response can subtly ask, "Did I understand you correctly?"

4. Match the speaker's intensity.

We want other people to understand how strongly we feel. "Feeling" words contain careful gradations of intensity. We use words such as "irritated" or "annoyed" when the feeling is moderate. We move up to words such as "upset" or "angry" as our feelings become stronger. And finally, we use words such as "furious" or "outraged" when we are intensely upset.

In Active Listening, choose emotional words which match the intensity being expressed. If someone is absolutely furious and you come back with an Active Listening response such as "You're annoyed that… ," their response is likely to be, "You dumb so-and-so, I'm not annoyed; I'm ready to strangle someone." In other words, "You didn't get my message."

If you choose cautious words to summarize powerful feelings, people may feel that you are patronizing them or that you are trying to calm them down rather than accepting their feelings. All too often there is more than a little truth in this. On the other hand, if the words are too intense, people may think you are trying to make a mountain out of a molehill.

In my experience, more people err on the side of minimizing the intensity of feelings as opposed to exaggerating them. It is all too easy to slip into a role of trying to make people feel better. There is some tendency to try to minimize the emotion in the hope that this will ease the pressure the person is feeling. But people often perceive this as your effort to minimize their feelings. So they are likely to escalate their expression. As they escalate, the listener may start becoming defensive and tempted to counter with his or her own feelings and judgments.

There Are Lots of Right Answers

Some people avoid using Active Listening because they fear they will not come up with the "right" answer or response. So they end up hanging on to their old ways of responding. But in Active Listening, there are many, many "right" responses. Active Listening also permits you to identify "wrong" answers and correct them quickly. Look at the following example, in which Julia has just come back from getting some medical tests:

JULIA: *I don't understand why the doctor hasn't given me more information. Could there be something else wrong? Why is he being so close-mouthed?*

LISTENER: *You're puzzled why he won't give you more information.*

JULIA: *That's only partially it. The big thing is that I'm worried there's something else wrong that he's not telling us about.*

LISTENER: *So you're worried that it's something more serious.*

JULIA: *Right.*

In this conversation, the first Active Listening response was at best partial, concentrating primarily on the ideas expressed, not the feelings. But by staying with the Active Listening it was possible to recoup and acknowledge Julia's fear, thus completing the communication.

A crucial element is to have a genuine interest in what the other person feels. I have seen people who were ineffective as listeners because it always seemed as if they were performing a stage trick rather than having a genuine interest in the other person. I have heard other listeners who were bumbling and halting, yet people just loved to talk with them because they felt these listeners were really trying to understand them. The skill works only if it reflects a true spirit of listening and desire to be helpful.

Active Listening in Close Relationships

As helpful as Active Listening can be, there are some inherent limitations when it is used in close relationships. In a very close relationship, Active Listening can seem mechanical and indifferent or even patronizing. And there are time in close relationships when both people are so upset with each other, or so threatened by each other's feelings, that neither person is effectively able to use Active Listening.

Sometimes Active Listening can be more irritating than helpful. In questioning couples enrolled in training programs, a frequent complaint was that sometimes it felt as if the Active Listener was disengaging him or herself and assuming a false role as a "helper" or "therapist." In the midst of a heated discussion, we want to feel that we are equals. When that balance is thrown off, the situation can become volatile. In a fight, we want the other person just to be themselves, and it is at these times that Active Listening can feel like the other person is playing a role. This problem is greatly exaggerated when the listener feels challenged. At such times our Active Listening can come off as stilted and awkward—and therefore more noticeable to the other person.

Making a Conscious Choice to Listen

If Active Listening is a behavior that we sometimes love and sometimes hate, how are we supposed to tell when we should use it and when we should not? More importantly, what is the alternative?

The best solution is for couples to talk about what they need. You can agree on simple signals, such as "I need you to listen to me," which is understood to mean, "Please use Active Listening." Similarly, there will be times when you need to say, "Please don't use Active Listening. Just listen silently," when the Active Listening seems distracting. These messages need to be understood so that they do not come across as an accusation. If your "I need you to listen to me" comes across as "Why can't you use Active Listening, you miserable crumb!" you clearly are not encouraging the response you desire. On the contrary, you are mostly stimulating anger.

Couples need to talk about how they communicate. But discussions about communication are more productive when both parties involved are calm and feeling good about each other—not in the midst of a fight. Any discussion of communications that takes place while you are upset has a tendency to be colored by the ill will of that moment.

What about those times when you flat-out cannot listen to each other? Let's face it—there are times when the other person is saying things that absolutely are not okay with you. In fact, what they are saying makes you feel very upset, angry or hurt. There are times when your loved one is the last person on earth you want to listen to in a loving and accepting way. Right then, you are just mad. But if your anger is the only thing you are left with, escalation begins, and soon you are making painful recriminations. What is the alternative? What do you do when Active Listening fails? The answer lies in employing the Five-Minute Rule.

The Five-Minute Rule

The mechanics of the Five-Minute Rule are relatively simple. Two people—lovers, partners, parent/child, whoever—agree that either of them can invoke the Five-Minute Rule whenever the conflict starts to escalate.

Once the Five-Minute Rule has been invoked, one person is chosen to go first. If you cannot agree any other way, you can flip a coin. The person chosen then gets five minutes to say whatever she (or he) wants, in whatever way she wants. The listener will not interrupt or comment, and should avoid any disturbing nonverbal communication such as making faces, repeatedly checking the time, or making rude gestures. After five minutes, the roles are reversed, and the other person gets five minutes to speak without interruption.

Many couples discover that without the interruptions and side commentaries, it is hard to fill up five solid minutes. Usually, after about three or four minutes, whatever had to be said has been said, and anything else is repetitious. However, after you have switched roles and listened to the other person for five minutes, you will probably have more to say, and it may be necessary to have another five-minute round.

After one or two rounds employing the Five-Minute Rule, one or both people are usually ready to make some sort of conciliatory gesture. It might take the form of an Active Listening summary of what the other person has said. It might be a feeling message such as, "I really feel bad that you felt so hurt by what I did." It might even be an apology.

Many couples who have take communication training from me have insisted that the Five-Minute Rule saved their marriage. It has certainly been a helpful tool for resolving conflicts in my own life.

Why does the Five-Minute Rule work so well? I think the reason goes back to the principle that when feelings are met with resistance, they persist. In this case, you have five minutes to express yourself with no one telling you what you should or should not be feeling. Also, if you are the listener, even though you may be sitting there for five minutes with clenched teeth, you have nothing to do but hear the other person out. In spite of the fact that you might not like what they are saying, your understanding of the other person's emotional reality will be increased.

The Five-Minute Rule is not a panacea, but it will usually discharge enough of the tension so that you can get away from accusations. And with a little luck it may even bring the two of you back to where you can at least remember the close and loving feelings that make your relationship worthwhile.

All this raises another question: Would it be realistic to make an agreement, as part of the Five-Minute Rule, that we refrain from communicating blame or accusations? As logical as this might seem, the answer is probably no. The essence of the Five-Minute Rule is that it serves as a safety valve for when you are both very upset. Trying too hard to be careful about how you communicate seems to reduce the valuable cathartic (purging) effect.

Remember that the main function of the Five-Minute Rule is to give you the opportunity to express what you are just bursting to say, without interruption. One or both of you may say things that are outrageous. Never forget that when you are extremely angry, your body is in a unique physiological state resulting from hormonal changes. In this reactive state, the things you say are likely to be distorted by the heat of the moment. What you say when you are that angry is an exaggeration of your normal emotions, blocking out the loving and caring emotions that you have for the other person when you are not so upset.

As with any other resolution tool, the agreement that either of you can invoke the Five-Minute Rule has to be made at a time when you are both feeling good about each other. If you wait until you are upset and then propose it without a prior agreement, you are not going to calm down during an argument to discuss whether or not to use it.

Like Active Listening, the Five-Minute Rule helps to heighten awareness of each other's emotions. When emotions are expressed and we feel like they have been acknowledged, they can be released and the conflict can be transformed.

HOW LOVING COUPLES FIGHT

PART III

CONSTRUCTIVE

FIGHT TOOLS

Recognize and Break

---

the Spiral of Escalation

Just because there is a conflict does not mean there is a fight. Every day couples solve problems without ever raising their voices. Yet other conflicts, involving issues which are not visibly more complex, turn into screaming matches that threaten the very foundations of relationships. Whether a conflict becomes a fight does not rest on the size or complexity of the issues involved, nor on the value of what is at risk, but almost solely on the ways people manage themselves.

Take the time to analyze your pattern of fighting. The object is to protect you and your loved ones from behavior that could threaten the foundation of your relationship. The time to do this is when both people feel good about each other, not in the midst of a battle. Once in a fight, we are in no position to discuss patterns of behavior. Attempting to do so could even escalate a fight.

Finding the Balance

Our goal is to know how to reduce escalation. However, even when conflicts escalate into contests, fights, and wars, all is not lost. Even in higher levels, there is the potential for resolution.

As I have said before, the key is to protect the relationship itself—even while in conflict. We do not need to choose between open communication and the protection of the relationship; this is not an either/or proposition. Both are required if we wish to enjoy healthy and fulfilling relationships.

To be effective, you need to take responsibility for the outcome of your conflicts, and know how to put limits on your fights.

As part of Tool #2 on pages 27–29 we explained the four levels of conflict, from problem-solving discussion to argument to fight to war. Note that as people move up the scale from problem solving towards fighting and war, they increasingly blame the other person for the conflict. By the time we reach the fight level, neither person is taking responsibility for their own behavior. Each, in effect, says, "I'm just reacting this way because he (or she) is being so nasty to me." We all know the feeling. We feel that the other person's horrible behavior justifies anything we might do or say.

In its most extreme form the need to attach blame can become compulsive, with neither person wanting to back away. They continue bashing at each other with little or no concern for the possible consequences. If either person was suddenly stopped by an outsider and asked why they were behaving in this way, both would probably answer, in effect, that everything was prompted by the "evil deeds" of the other person. There would be little or no awareness of their own contribution to the fray.

We need to learn how to make choices about our own behavior. There are clear alternatives to merely reacting. Regardless of what the other person is doing or saying, we really can make choices that can keep the conflict focused and constructive.

How do we regain our sense of choice? As with most things in life, it happens as we gain familiarity with the territory. The "Path of Escalation" is the predictable pattern of behavior that a conflict takes. When we understand these patterns, much of the fear and self-doubt that would otherwise emerge is greatly reduced, if not removed. In the process, we move from reactive toward increasingly proactive or choice-centered behavior.

The Predictable Path of Escalation

The sequence of escalation behaviors typically proceeds as follows:

1. Triggering comment or action

One or both people make a comment or take an action that provokes the other person's defensiveness or fear.

2. Proliferation of issues

After a short period of discussion, one or both people start bringing up new issues or expanding the basis for the argument.

3. Formation of adversarial alliances

One or both people begin pulling in other people for support, thus forming alliances. This may be done either directly by asking another person to take sides, or by quoting them, or claiming that these others "agree with me." The "allies" may include what other family members or friends have said (intimated) as "proof" that the speaker is right.

4. Distortion of communication

One or both people begin to communicate through exaggeration, broad sweeping generalizations, character attacks, and prolonged and hostile periods of silence.

5. Rigid and extreme positions

The harder people fight, the more entrenched they become. One or both people become rigid and extreme in their positions through depersonalizing the other, taking the position that, "I'll never give an inch," etc.

6. Focus on hurting each other

Although the conflict may have begun with the goal of solving a problem, as both people increasingly become defensive the goal shifts to hurting or attacking the other person's position as having no validity.

Unless one or both people take responsibility for stopping the escalation, they will race up this path. To illustrate this, here is an example that begins with that most trivial of domestic annoyances, the cap left off the toothpaste.

BILL: *Dammit, Ann, why can't you ever remember to put the cap back on the toothpaste? You know how that drives me crazy!*

ANN: *Oh, quit making such a big deal out of it. I just forgot, that's all.*

BILL: *But you know I can't stand it, and you just keep on doing it. I've asked you again and again to stop doing it.*

ANN: *Look, I don't care whether the cap is on or off. The only reason I'd ever think about it is that it bothers you. You should be thankful that I ever remember at all.*

BILL: *But that's the whole point. You ought to care. You're like a kid expecting Mommy or Daddy to clean up after you all the time. It's not just the toothpaste cap. You also leave your clothes lying around. If I didn't make the bed, it'd never get made. You never take responsibility for keeping this place looking nice.*

ANN: *Looking nice by whose standards, may I ask? You want every-thing done your way. Just because you're rigid and uptight, don't expect me to live my life that way.*

BILL: *Rigid and uptight? Everybody in your family makes jokes about how your room was always a disaster. I've seen the look on your mom's face whenever she comes in here before I've had a chance to clean up.*

ANN: *You leave my mother out of this or you're in deep trouble, buster. I've had enough of your trying to run my life. You're always on my case about everything. I bet it must really fry you, Mr. Control, to realize I'm pulling down ten thousand dollars a year more than you are. In the real world people care more about performance than they do petty little things like toothpaste caps.*

BILL: *You just couldn't wait to rub my face in that, could you, Ms. Executive? Well, you can take your ten grand and put it you know where, 'cause I've had it. I don't want anything more to do with you or your big salary.*

At this point, Bill slams out of the room, while Ann bursts into tears.

To demystify the inner workings of fights, let us look at Bill and Ann's exchanges as they progress from minor complaint to do-mestic crisis.

1. Triggering comment or action

In this case, the triggering action was Ann's leaving the cap off the toothpaste. Most people would agree that this is not an earth-shaking event. But the toothpaste cap was not the real problem. The real problem was what this act meant to Bill. If we were able to tune into Bill's thoughts we might hear, "I've asked her repeatedly to put the cap back on the toothpaste. Why does she keep forgetting? She either wants to annoy me or she doesn't care how I feel." So now we have moved from a question of the cap being left off the toothpaste to Bill feeling unappreciated, ignored, and uncared for.

Bill's drama has been played out solely in his head, but it has caused him to feel rejected, threatened, and thwarted. Even if Ann were to promise never to forget the toothpaste cap again, there would still be a chance of conflict. The real issue is not toothpaste caps but feelings and needs that are being "ignored," and until these feelings are satisfactorily addressed they will continue to be a potential source of conflict.

Notice that Bill starts this interaction with Ann in an accusatory way. By focusing on the toothpaste cap, he fails to express what is really bothering him, his sense of being ignored. To express this, he would have to let Ann know of the symbolic importance of the toothpaste cap. For example, he might say, "I'm really upset that you left the cap off the toothpaste tube. Since I've told you before that it bothers me, I start thinking that it means you don't care about my feelings, and then I start feeling very hurt and angry."

This approach might trigger Ann's defensiveness, but at least they would be talking about the real problem—Bill's feelings of abandonment. Also, this approach gives Ann sufficient information to see that the real issue is not that he is on a power trip but that his feelings are hurt.

Let us turn our attention to Ann. Her initial response to Bill's complaint was not particularly defensive. She simply says that she cannot see why it is "such a big deal." But given Bill's perceptions at that moment, he feels ignored.

Ann could have said, "I'm sorry. I know it really annoys you. I try to remember but I really got rushed this morning." This comment would have let Bill know that she cared about his feelings and was trying to respond to them. This might have been enough acknowledgment for Bill to back off and let the issue drop.

2. Proliferation of issues

Once the cycle of escalation begins, each person strives to find his or her strongest position. One way is to think of additional grievances. Bill is the first to do this when he shifts from the toothpaste cap to Ann's not picking up her clothes or making the bed. He is beginning to "compile evidence" to support his complaint.

A universal characteristic in proliferation is moving from specific complaints about a behavior to greater and greater generalizations. Bill did this when he shifted from his complaint about the toothpaste cap to Ann's general messiness. After this, he went a step further when he accused her of "adolescent" behavior and general irresponsibility.

Ann also switched from her complaint that Bill was making too much out of a little thing, to a complaint that he was always trying to control her and always had to have things his way. Then she went on to claim that he was generally ineffective because he was always concentrating on petty things.

Expanding the issue is one of the driving forces behind escalation. It creates a "can you top this?" competitiveness which feeds on itself. Turning a specific problem ("you left the toothpaste cap off") to an absolute ("you just won't take responsibility" or "everything has to be done your way") not only enrages the other person, but also defines the problem poorly. If the problem is really the toothpaste cap, Bill and Ann might solve the problem by buying toothpaste in the new pump-type dispenser, which has no cap. But there are few available solutions if the problem is defined as "Ann won't take responsibility" or "Bill has to have everything done his own way."

As escalation occurs, our perceptions also become distorted. Making absolute statements may be strategic, but we come to believe these characterizations are true. In the heat of a battle we come to believe that the other person is, in fact, always irresponsible, controlling, thoughtless, inconsiderate, and so on.

Beyond this, we are failing to take responsibility for our active role in making these observations. The judgment that a behavior is negative is solely our own perception. Even if it were true that Ann never put the toothpaste cap back on or that she always left her clothes all over the floor, she does not cause Bill to feel as he does. Another person in the same situation might have very different feelings about picking up after her. For example, such a person might believe that this was a way of feeling useful and valued, and Ann might be very grateful.

So Bill—like the rest of us—finds events in the outside world that seem to "justify" his feelings, but the fact remains that we are all the actual creators of those feelings. Our feelings and perceptions are not universal truths; they are only true for us. We best serve ourselves and others when we focus our attention on having our own feelings recognized rather than on trying to prove that what we perceive is an absolute truth for everyone. Whenever we assert that our own judgment is truth we only compound the problem, setting ourselves an impossible task and challenging the other person to a showdown.

3. Formation of adversarial alliances

By now, both people feel so threatened they may desperately seek ways to increase their sense of power and control by forming alliances or claiming the support of other people. This occurs even when only two people are present. In this case, Bill brings in Ann's family. He is saying, in effect, "It isn't just me who feels this way. Your family feels you're messy and irresponsible too."

There is a kind of ganging-up taking place. This is a dangerous strategy because the other person, feeling under attack, is nearly always going to do something to exert equal or greater power. Until now, Ann has not really been as provocative as Bill. He has been the one to initiate each movement to the next higher level. But now Ann feels justified in dropping her emotional equivalent of an atom bomb—her remarks about making more money than he does.

While Bill is only able to claim that Ann's family supports his position, he might seek out an actual person (usually a close friend or family member) to support him. After the fight, both people may try to draw other family members or friends into taking their side. Once sufficient support has been lined up, the fight will be reopened, but nobody any longer entertains the goal of solving the problem. That is long past. The goal now is to win, and the price is rising like the national debt.

Another version of alliances is to quote an authority. Passages from the Bible, the marriage vows or perhaps a family counselor "prove" that the other person is a sinner, an ingrate, a fool or possibly mentally ill. If the authority is chosen wisely, it is an authority with which the other person cannot disagree. If this happens, the conflict may switch to a slightly different tack, with the two combatants arguing over whose interpretation of the authority is right.

4. Distortion of communication

Bill's stomping out of the room temporarily cuts off communication between himself and Ann. But like most couples, they will probably reestablish communication after they have both had a chance to cool off. They might decide, however, that they have suffered such major hurts that they keep up the fight, indirectly. Instead of addressing anything even resembling real issues, they will resort to sharp digs and negative side comments. Ann might say in a sarcastic tone, "I suppose that's an example of your neatness?" when he accidentally spills a cup of coffee at breakfast the day after their fight. Or Bill might make an equally sarcastic comment to a waiter when Ann changes her order three times: "That's what these high-priced executive women think is their right."

With this withdrawal from direct communication, the potential for resolution gets worse and worse. Neither person is willing to make an overture for fear of appearing to be the one who is giving in. Any overtures are often hidden in emotional barbs, as in, "I don't suppose you'd like to go out to a movie with me?" Or "Guess there's no chance that a neat and tidy person like you would be willing to accept an invitation to go out to dinner with a messy person like me?" When the other person reacts negatively, the person who made the overture may point to it as proof that the other person was unresponsive to making up.

People may develop increasingly distorted perceptions of each other when communication is cut off. This can take the form of simple selective perception, that is, when we focus on a negative aspect of a person's personality. We forget all positive characteristics, at least for the moment.

A more elaborate form of distorted perception is Mirror Imaging, where we project our own feelings to our adversary, but often in an exaggerated form. Mirror Imaging is a bit like visiting the hall of mirrors in the fun house, where we see our own image in hilariously altered ways.

If, for example, I am angry at you, I would see you as being in a rage at me. If I am being scheming and devious, I will see in you as the consummate example of duplicity, justifying every trick or scheme I could possibly imagine. The power of this Mirror Image is that it reveals our weakest and most vulnerable parts. Since it reflects our own feelings, the image that we project upon the other person is a perfect reflection of the thing we fear the most about ourselves.

5. Rigid and extreme positions

Couples who carry the escalation process to this fifth level see each other as the "Adversary" or even the "Enemy." They are locked in a battle which somehow threatens their very existence. To give up or give in is perceived as something akin to dying. This "foxhole mentality" may take a number of different forms.

There may be a desire to root out any parts of ourselves which are conciliatory. A woman leaving a marriage may wonder aloud, "How could I have ever loved that monster?" She may even deride herself for ever being "so stupid" as to be with such a person. When relationships are breaking up, it is not unusual for one person or the other to say, "I now know that I never loved you in the first place," and be completely convinced that this is true. Both people may seek out friends who reinforce the negative image of the person they used to love.

If families or other people are involved, there may even be tests of loyalty or commitment to the cause. A family member who says something nice about the adversary may be cut off as being disloyal. Anyone who appears to be "getting soft" on the enemy will be ostracized.

6. Focus on hurting each other

Bill and Ann go directly to the "war" level when Ann, feeling threatened by Bill's dragging her mother into the argument, belittle's Bill's earning power. This was clearly aimed at hurting him as much as possible.

In this final stage of escalation, our perception of the mean and evil nature of the other person becomes so exaggerated that we feel any behavior aimed at the other person is justified. Because they have hurt us so badly, anything is fair game. There can be almost total abandonment of any sense of moral responsibility for our acts. Eventually, we may be appalled by our own behavior. But at the time of the fight, it certainly feels fully justified. After all, "All's fair in love and war, and this is war!"

Inhibiting Forces

Clearly, no relationship can withstand continued escalation of every conflict. But there are inhibiting forces which help prevent conflicts from swirling into wars. And the most powerful inhibiting force for most couples is the need to preserve the relationship.

Ending a marriage may have far-reaching consequences. Divorce can threaten parent-child relationships, jeopardize economic well-being, and cause the loss of valued associations with other family members and mutual friends. Any of these factors can provide important incentives for resolving conflicts.

Another curb against escalation is the need to get the cooperation of the other person on everyday matters. A married couple or two people living together are forced to make numerous little decisions just to maintain the household. If their communication is cut off over a single issue, it may become impossible to resolve every other issue.

The most effective curb against escalation is the love and caring we have for each other. Even if we feel hurt, we still want the relationship to continue.

Choosing Not to Escalate

The key principle for breaking the spiral of escalation is: *Take responsibility for your own thoughts and feelings. You do not have to let the other person's behavior dictate yours. You do have a choice and can make a commitment to behave within your own ethical or moral limits, regardless of what the other person does.*

Obviously it works best if both partners make the same commitment. You may even agree to signal each other when you sense that escalation is occurring: "Oops, I think we just expanded the issues" or simply, "We're escalating." You can also talk together, after a fight, about what happened and how to prevent future escalation.

A word of caution: When discussing escalation, do not slip into blaming and accusing ("You escalated this conflict when you…"). To break the escalation cycle, you have to concentrate on your own behavior: "I know I made things worse by dragging in that reference to your father." It is usually easier to talk about how things escalated after you are both calm so that this discussion is not just another way of getting at each other. Then you can talk about how you are going to cope with escalation.

If only one person is making the choice to be responsible, it is more difficult to curb the escalation cycle. But it can still be done. The first step is to be aware of what is happening so that you can make a conscious choice. The next step is to break out of "tit for tat" patterns of thinking. Just because the other person attempts to hurt you does not mean you have to respond in kind. The other person may test your resolve to keep the issues focused, but if you hold firm, the fight is much less likely to escalate.

Other important behaviors for breaking the spiral of escalation include the following:

Share your feelings—without blaming or accusing

Avoid blaming and accusing communication by sharing feelings rather than judgments. If you have slipped into being blaming and accusing, it is still possible to say, "I'm sorry, I've started blaming and accusing." Follow up with a statement about how you are feeling: "What's really going on is that I'm feeling deeply threatened (or hurt or whatever)…" This kind of communication invites—notice I said "invites," not "guarantees"—the same kind of non-accusatory communication from the other person. You have to make this move entirely for yourself, however. The other person may not automatically reciprocate. If you believe they "owe" you because you made yourself vulnerable, their failure to respond in kind will fuel the bad feelings you are harboring, and you are likely to use their failure to reciprocate as new ammunition.

When we reveal our vulnerability in order to elicit a particular reaction, we are really engaging in manipulation. That is, we are acting not out of sincerity but to get the other person to do something we want. We are trying to control their behavior, and this invariably lead to frustration, disappointment, and anger—the seeds of escalation. So whatever you do to curb escalation must be done for yourself, out of your own resolve not to threaten your relationship.

Stay focused on the issue—without bringing up new topics

Conflicts usually start with a discussion about a single issue. However, as escalation occurs, the discussion moves into more generalized statements about the other person. For example, a question over who should take the kids to the Little League game expands into a fight about who does the most work around the house.

To break the pattern, both people must make a commitment to catch themselves whenever they feel an urge to respond to one issue by bringing up a larger one. Sometimes this can be accomplished by simply telling yourself, "No, I won't do it! I am going to stay focused on the specific issue that triggered this discussion."

This is not easy. There will be times when, in spite of your best intentions, you are going to slip. But do not beat yourself up. I have been teaching this skill for many years, and I still slip badly at times. When you do slip, do not despair. Stop what you are doing and use your communication skills to try to break the spiral before it goes any further. You might say, "I'm sorry, I started expanding the issue. What is really going on is that I'm feeling frightened and hurt (or whatever)." Remember, getting back to these very basic emotions reminds you and the other person that you are caring people in a valuable relationship.

Express your personal feelings—without using other people or authorities as ammunition

In the heat of the moment we often say, in effect, "I'm not the only one who thinks this about you," and then proceed to drag in one or more people who agree with you. With so many allies we momentarily create a sense of greater power. However, the other person literally feels that you are ganging up on him. It is a threatening position to be in, indeed, even though the "allies" are mostly imaginary.

This is the bottom line: If you are going to drag others into the fight, recognize that doing so is highly provocative. Nine times out of ten it will not help you get your point across. On the contrary, it will escalate the conflict enormously in virtually all cases. In addition, pulling others into your fight by quoting them or just attributing an opinion to them can destroy the relationship between the person you are fighting with and the person you are quoting.

Take responsibility for your own words and actions—avoid "you always" or "you never"

Nobody always does anything. Blanket statements such as, "You're always irresponsible" or "You never carry your share of the load" are patently untrue. The other person may occasionally act irresponsibly. They may even do it frequently. But what is even more important in our discussion here is that such statements are provocative, and they almost guarantee escalation. In addition to being exaggerations, they are blaming, and accusing, and judgmental. If they have any value whatsoever in a conflict, it is to signal you that you are feeling threatened or fearful and you need to take responsibility for your feelings as well as your behavior. It is time to get back to the feelings you are experiencing.

Stay with behaviors—without using labels

Another signal that you are feeling threatened and are escalating the fight is when you start labeling. When you find yourself saying, "You're irresponsible," "You're sexist," "You're power hungry," "You're a woman hater," "You're castrating," "You're off the wall," it is time to pull back. Stop labeling and start focusing on specific behaviors. Say, "I'm really upset that you didn't tell me you'd be late," rather than, "You're just a completely thoughtless person."

Break the pattern of resistance

When we feel resistance to our feelings we express ourselves more intensely. It is a little like knocking on a door when you know someone's home. If you get no answer, you knock a little harder.

In most fights, each person is feeling the other's resistance. Both feel blocked and thwarted, and the frustration just continues to build. The larger the frustration, the greater the temptation to haul out the big guns and blast away at the door of resistance.

To avoid resistance, try Active Listening, in which you summarize your understanding of what the other person is saying, or use the Five-Minute Rule for times when you are too emotionally involved to listen with an attitude of acceptance. These two techniques let you express your feelings without the frustration that comes from constant resistance through interruption and contradiction.

If there is so much resistance that the best thing to do is to break off the fight, do so until both of you have settled down. Instead of the Five-Minute Rule, you might take a five-minute break. If you do break off the fight, agree to resume the discussion at a particular date or time. Without setting up a specific time to resume, withdrawing can feel like just another form of resistance. You run the danger of leaving unresolved issues festering just beneath the surface. There is often value in breaking off intense discussions, but this should not be used as a way of avoiding the issues.

Focus on discussing the problem—without insisting on a solution while you are still upset

When we are upset, we want resolution. We want the whole thing settled right now. In an emotionally tense situation this urgency can contribute to escalation, and since urgency is often interpreted as an effort to control, it can make people feel even more defensive. Unless it is a crisis situation where something dire is about to happen, it is often advisable to finish the fight first. Then work for a solution or make a date to work on it. Fights may help to bring issues to the surface, but the problem-solving session can take place at a later time.

Looking Back and Moving On

These are but a few of the many highly effective actions which help us put limits on escalation. Before going on with your reading, go back and study the four rungs of conflict beginning on page 28 and the predictable path of escalation on page 105.

The next two chapters explore how our behaviors can provoke fights and how we can set up mutual guidelines for curbing destructive behaviors.

HOW LOVING COUPLES FIGHT

Identify and Set Limits on

Crazy-Making Behavior

No one can drive us crazy faster than a loved one. These behaviors might be slightly annoying when a friend does them. But when a loved one does them, they suddenly seem like a personal affront or a conscious effort to provoke us. Especially in the midst of a fight, these "crazy-making" behaviors are likely to escalate the situation, as if someone threw gasoline on a fire.

Like other fight behaviors, crazy-making behaviors are typically unconscious. We learned them from family or friends as a way to cope with feeling hurt, vulnerable or powerless. Sometimes these behaviors involve efforts to control our loved one's behavior. We do not want them to think or feel the way they do because it makes us feel inadequate or insecure. Our unconscious belief is: "If I can just keep him (or her) from saying or feeling those things, then I'll stop hurting or feeling bad." But our loved one reacts to being controlled by increasing the intensity of their feelings, often saying things in ways that are even more hurtful or by breaking off communication.

Other crazy-making behavior has to do with subtle maneuvering to establish "who is in charge around here." The discussion seems to be about one thing, but it is really about each person's power in the relationship. Both people may feel they need more power because they presently feel powerless. Demands for power usually are met by power tactics from our partner, leaving us feeling powerless once again.

The first step in reducing behaviors that inflame each other is to learn to identify them. Because they are unconscious behaviors, we may not even be aware that we are engaging in them—and certainly we are not aware of their destructive impact on the relationship. Let us start with a behavior closely related to blaming and accusing, one that I call "crossing the line."

Crossing the Line

Each of us has invisible boundaries beyond which we do not like other people to cross. One of these has to do with people telling us what we "should" or "ought" to do. Another has to do with people labeling our behavior, attempting to stereotype us, or "pop psyching," that is, trying to psychoanalyze us. For most of us, this is truly "crazy-making." We feel as if our private world is being violated, and when this happens, we can go wild.

Imagine, if you will, a magic line which separates you from your loved one. When you are on your side of the line, you are talking about how their behavior affects you on a practical or emotional level. When you cross over to the other side of the line, you are evaluating or judging their behavior or even trying to tell them who they really are. For example:

YOUR SIDE OF THE LINE	THEIR SIDE OF THE LINE
I'm hurt, angry, sad, etc.	You're inconsiderate, rude, and irresponsible.
It makes extra work for me when you do that.	Don't you think it's about time you started giving other people a little consideration?

We usually have a negative reaction when anyone violates our boundaries. Often this means taking an eye-for-an-eye stance, that is, combating the person who crossed our line by crossing theirs.

To stay on your side of the line, ask yourself, "Am I describing my own feelings about how the other person's behavior affects me or am I judging, labeling, or evaluating the other person's character?" If you have crossed over the line, acknowledge it. You might say, "Let me start over. I'm sorry for analyzing your behavior. I felt embarrassed when…"

When another person has crossed your line, first remind yourself that coming back with similar behavior is only going to escalate the conflict. Sometimes, it is best to simply ignore their comments with the understanding that they are upset and you need not react to, or participate in, crazy-making behavior. But often in a conflict we seem to require words to remind ourselves, as well as tell the other person, where we stand. We might respond by saying, "Wait just a second. I'm having trouble communicating openly. I feel as if I'm being judged. I'd like to get back to…" And then, bring the conversation back to the topic which you feel precipitated the original conflict.

Playing Shrink and Interpreting Each Other's Behavior

"Pop psyching" or "playing shrink" has become a popular pastime. It is a particularly maddening version of crossing the line. People who have been in therapy, people who practice therapy or people who read (or write) books such as this one, are often particularly guilty of "pop psyching" or "playing shrink."

As our knowledge of human behavior increases, it becomes a real temptation to analyze our friends, loved ones, and co-workers. The only problem is that we are not usually invited to be their psychotherapists. Nor do we usually ask our friends, lovers, mates, co-workers or family members to act as our therapists.

Without a request for help, "pop psyching" and "playing shrink" are nothing more than sophisticated forms of crossing the line. This is particularly true if we employ these behaviors in the middle of a fight. Even if you are right, the other person is bound to interpret your amateur psychologizing as an attack—not as a sincere effort to help them. The more sophisticated your perceptions, the bigger the weapon, and the more likely the other person is to react in a negative way. Save your psychologizing for times when you are feeling more like equals. Even then, do so only if you are certain you have an agreement to assume a helping role.

Hitting Below the Belt

We all carry wounds from the past, and these wounds can be so sensitive that we fly into a rage or are devastated whenever anyone even hints at them. Part of getting to know another person is getting to know their wounds. But this knowledge puts us in a peculiar position. When we are fighting, it is all too easy to use this knowledge as a weapon, and once you pull the trigger, you have committed yourself to a truly crazy-making action. Poking around at old wounds can cause pain that can last for hours, days or even years.

Hitting below the belt can do permanent damage to the relationship. Also, as with most other crazy-making behavior, it allows you to feel justified in suspending all limits and launching into a no-holds-barred fight. As a matter of survival, you will hit back with whatever weapons you have, wherever and however you can. This is war.

Here are a few examples of hitting below the belt:

• Kay is very sensitive about the fact that she did not finish high school, while her husband, Mark, has a college degree. Whenever they get into a fight, Mark calls her "dumb" or "stupid" or says things that imply he could not expect someone of her intelligence to understand. This is terribly upsetting to Kay, and she strikes back by ridiculing his sexual performance, which is sporadic and uninspired. Mark is so devastated by this that following such a fight, they often do not have sex for several months.

• Jerry feels that in the past Jennifer has just dismissed his feelings without really caring, so now he begins fights by declaring that if she does not change, he is going to leave the relationship. At first Jennifer felt panicked by this but now it just makes her angry, and she responds, "Fine. So go!" Jennifer's response only serves to reinforce Jerry's feeling that she does not care about him, and he spends a lot of time after a fight thinking he probably should leave, if only to show her that he really means what he says.

• Whenever Diane and Phil get into a fight, she brings up an extramarital affair that he had in the first year of their marriage. Phil feels terribly guilty about the affair, and feels that because of it he has no right to really defend himself. But he starts feeling so crazy when his wife brings up the past that he often just storms out of the house. Phil's walking out drives Diane mad. She is afraid that when he gets angry like this, it means he is going to have another affair behind her back.

What is below the belt for one person may be fair game for another. George Bach, author of *The Intimate Enemy,* observed in his "fight training" classes that some people are so sensitive to low blows that they "keep their belt lines tucked around their ears and cry 'foul' at every attempted blow."

He said that some people need help in lowering their belt lines to more realistic levels, while others need to remove fake belt lines, where they pretend to be very sensitive to issues which do not really bother them that much. Bach concluded that couples need to let each other know where their belt lines are so that they will not unintentionally strike a low blow. Even more important, couples need to know that while they may want to score points during a fight, there are some blows that are so crazy-making that they can actually end the relationship.

Couples who have a history of hitting below the belt need to specifically identify which areas are off-limits, which areas particularly drive them crazy, and how they are going to handle any violations of the limits they set.

As an example, Mark considers any comments about his sexual performance to be hitting below the belt. It would no doubt be advisable to make this subject off-limits as a way for Kay to get back at Mark. Likewise, Mark's knowledge of Kay's sensitivity about her education should also be an off-limit subject for him. However, we need to make a clear distinction between hitting below the belt and addressing issues. Mark and Kay's sexual problems probably should be discussed directly. However, rather than being addressed in a crazy-making way during an argument, they should be addressed at another time with the sincere goal of resolving that issue. So, too, should Kay's lack of self-esteem. The real purpose of declaring certain topics off-limits is not to make open and honest discussion possible, but to limit the use of each other's wounds and vulnerabilities as weapons.

If you are in a relationship where it still is not possible to talk about setting limits, there are two approaches you can take. First, you can continue to be responsible for your own behavior even though someone hits you below the belt. As bad as it might be to receive such a hit, you will create even more discomfort all around by hitting back in a similar way. Remind yourself that you may feel justified in hitting back, but what does that get you? If you both feel justified, but you wipe out the relationship in the process, what have you accomplished?

Second, let the person know how hurt you are by their comment. But once again, in accordance with Tool #4 (Express Feelings, not Judgments), do your best to send feelings rather than blame or accusation. You have the best chance of being heard when you say, "I feel absolutely devastated when you say things like that. It is such a painful area for me. I just feel wiped out and angry when you make comments like that." By contrast, there is little chance of being heard when you say, "You just don't care at all about my feelings, do you? Otherwise, you couldn't even think about making a remark like that. What a cheap shot!"

Dredging Up Grievances from the Past

Earlier I talked about how every time Diane felt hurt she would bring up the subject of Phil's affair. An affair can be a pretty traumatic event in a relationship, but one's knowledge of it can also be used as a weapon. We are all likely to have a collection of past grievances which can be whipped out at a moment's notice: the time you made a fool of yourself at a party; the time you embarrassed me in front of my boss; the time you got drunk and wrecked the car; the time you insulted my friend; the time you said to ignore the kids and one of them got hurt. For most people the list is endless.

All of these are genuine hurts and pains, but all of them can also be used destructively. The more unspeakable or hurtful the other person's behavior was, the less able they are to defend that behavior, and the more crazy-making it can be as a weapon.

One thing you can count on—dredging up old grievances nearly always escalates a conflict. You are not really solving past problems;

even worse, it can mean that you are not resolving present issues. This is likely to increase the backlog of unresolved issues.

Couples who continuously dredge up old grievances can minimize this particular form of crazy-making behavior. First, make an agreement to sit down together in the near future to declare this particular crazy-making behavior off-limits. Also discuss how you will handle violations of any agreement you make. For example, you might agree that if one partner brings up old grievances, the other partner will advise, "Let's stay focused on the subject at hand rather than dredging up old grievances." Or if the person continues to press the subject of the old grievance, you might say, "We need to make a choice here. Are we going to discuss the issue at hand or are we going to discuss the old grievance?" This choice should not be presented as an attack or a challenge but as a real choice which the two of you can make.

Second, in some cases you may discover that there are unresolved feelings about certain issues that you or your partner keep bringing up. If this is the case, schedule a time to sit down and discuss that issue directly and to address those old grievances which are still the cause of worry, concern or anger.

Dumping

Many people store up their grievances, saying little about their frustrations or resentments until a fight starts. Some people deliberately build up their storehouses of grievances as a strategy; others do it because they have difficulty addressing issues when they arise; and still others do it because they feel it is easier to ignore what seem to be small irritations at the time they actually occur. In the heat of a conflict, however, it seems that the dam breaks and suddenly you are both flooded with more complaints and problems than a whole army could handle. Often these grievances are loosely bound around a common theme—inconsiderateness, rudeness, thoughtlessness, mean-ness, etc. But all of this is presented as "evidence" that no criticism they might present could possibly equal the injustices and insults they have suffered. As one person put it, "Dumping isn't a genuine expression of feelings; it's a criminal indictment."

Dumping is crazy-making behavior because it frustrates the re-ceiver, who knows that anytime an issue is raised it may result in a "dump." When you engage in dumping, you communicate only a single message—that you think the other person is a horrible human being. Inevitably the person being dumped on will get defensive, try-ing to outdo the "dumper" with an even bigger and more powerful weapon of his own.

There is not a human being alive who wants to face an avalanche of old grievances anytime they want to work out a problem. Healthy relationships simply cannot thrive in a climate where conflicts can-not be addressed in a constructive manner.

The problem of dumping must get addressed very directly. Agree to a time when you can sit down together and discuss the problem openly. While the goal may be to set limits on dumping, it is helpful for both people to express how they feel when they are being dumped on or how they feel just prior to using this tactic themselves. As with other crazy-making behaviors, make an agreement to declare dump-ing off-limits and discuss how you will handle any violations of this agreement. Agree on certain language to remind one another when dumping starts, "Oops! Dumping." Or simply, "Time out! We're start-ing to dump."

In all forms of crazy-making behavior, it is important to under-stand that we are making a choice. Whenever we choose such behav-ior, we are forgetting to honor and protect the relationship itself. In-stead, we are choosing momentary victories whose price may end up being the very thing we cherish the most.

Hit and Run

"Hit and run" is just what it sounds like: You hit someone with a big emotional blow under circumstances or in a manner which ensures they cannot get back at you. For example, you tell your wife that you have invited your relatives (whom she cannot stand) to stay for a week just as she rushes out the door, late for work. Since your wife cannot stop to deal with it, she must wrestle with the disturbing news all day, with no way to resolve conflicted feelings.

Another form of "hit and run" is one that therapists refer to as "passive aggressive" behavior. It is aggressive behavior in that it is designed to take a poke at the other person, but it is done in a way that the person taking the poke can disclaim any intent to do harm (thus the word "passive"). For example, a lover might make a remark about her partner's sexual impotence, a subject she knows is devastating. Then when there are howls of pain, she says offhandedly, "But you know I was just making a joke. How can you possibly imagine that I would say something which would hurt you, when I know it's such a sensitive topic?" The damage has already been done, but now she hides behind the claim that it was a joke, causing her lover to feel he is being unreasonable for getting so upset.

Significant emotional issues need to be discussed at a time and in a manner when there is a reasonable chance for resolution. Hitting someone with a problem when there is no opportunity to resolve it simply produces outrage, with no benefit except the continuance of ongoing subterranean guerrilla warfare. Hit and run behavior in emotional matters is just as irresponsible as hit and run on the street.

Martyrdom

Martyrdom is a behavior designed to control others by saying such horrible things about yourself that others hesitate to criticize you in any way. If, for example, you complained because someone was late, a "martyr" might respond, "You're right, I'm horrible that way. I just can't get my life together. My husband's left me; my house cleaner was arrested for selling drugs and I found out she was trying to sell them to my kids; the plumbing is all stopped up. I just can't do anything right."

Who could possibly complain after a story like that? But nevertheless, at some level we know that we had legitimate complaints, and a right to express them. As sorry as we may feel for this person—and martyrs are wonderful at creating the circumstances in their lives which reaffirm their martyrdom—it is frustrating and ultimately unsatisfying to have feelings immediately trumped by a litany of greater disasters.

Not every martyr controls by creating disaster. Some control by instantly acknowledging how messed up they are emotionally, that they cannot imagine how you could possibly care for anyone as screwy as they are, and they would understand perfectly if you left them. That thought may be very much on your mind after all that. But the setup is that you will look like such a horrible, uncaring person if you did leave that you probably will not. But you will feel controlled, resentful, and trapped.

We can only hope martyrs will eventually discover that you cannot both control your loved ones and also have closeness. The person being controlled will one day throw off those controls and end the relationship.

Resistance

Barb and Tom are spouses as well as partners in a consulting company. Barb is worried that they may have expanded too fast. But every time she tries to talk to Tom about this, Tom will not listen. He ridicules Barb for worrying so much. He refuses even to consider the possibility that there could be a downturn in the economy. When the economic figures come in below projections, he always argues that the solution is to spend more money on marketing, hiring more people with additional expertise, and so on. Tom's ridiculing of Barb for worrying, his refusal to consider possibilities of an economic downturn, and his stubborn insistence that the solution to all challenges is to spend more and expand their base of expertise are, in this case, all forms of resistance.

When Barb first addressed Tom with her concern, she was not even sure that her concern was justified. She just wanted to talk about it. But now that Tom ridicules her every time she brings up the issue she is more convinced than ever that there is a problem. What is worse, she is beginning to wonder if she made a mistake going into business with Tom. She is beginning to notice that Tom responds with resistance to a lot of problems. When people try to express their concerns, Tom just denies there is a problem, and either criticizes or ridicules the other person for thinking as they do.

Tom is a perfect example of a habitual resister who digs in his heels and insists that things are exactly as he wants them to be. Resisters just will not accept other people's feelings and concerns or give any time to understanding other people's point of view. When, in total frustration, people leave their relationships with the resisters, the resisters deny any responsibility for the estrangement and often express the feeling that they have been horribly betrayed. The resister's stance toward virtually everything in life might be characterized this way: "I don't want things to be that way, so they aren't."

If we resist listening to other people's feelings and concerns, those people tend to push harder, expressing themselves more loudly and more emphatically each time, until they either get satisfaction or they go away forever. Resisters get a lot of hard knocks from life, since they are denying what is really there in favor of what they want to be there. Resistance greatly inhibits both creativity and the expression of feelings. This behavior makes it almost impossible to openly discuss problems and resolve conflicts. Change occurs when we accept things as they are and begin to work out more effective relationships with the people and situations that cause us conflict. In short, we never find solutions until we admit there is a problem—and that is just what resisters do not want to do.

If you are in a personal relationship with a resister, you know how maddening such people can be. In fact, just staying in the relationship is a major undertaking. In all your efforts to effect positive change, you seem to end up banging your head against a brick wall of resistance. Anytime you express a feeling or concern you get put down for even raising the question. You have to care a lot about the relationship to keep going with a resister.

Some people in politics and business use resistance tactically, and are very conscious of what they are doing. In personal relationship, however, many resisters are largely unconscious of it, and their efforts are anything but tactical. Rather, they are reflexive and reactive in their responses, and they use this crazy-making behavior because they are frightened, anxious people seeking any way they can to feel that they have some control in their lives. By resisting other people's feelings, they hope they can avoid having to deal with issues that they find frightening or which make them feel inadequate and helpless. However, if they persist, and fail to learn more effective ways of relating, other people simply give up on them.

People who use resistance need to be reminded that all people have different emotional realities. It is entirely possible for Barb to feel anxious about the expansion of the business, and for Tom to feel comfortable that everything is okay. Just because Barb feels anxious does not mean she is right about the business being overextended; nor does Tom's feeling that they are okay mean that they are not. But if Tom wants to maintain his partnership with Barb, he also needs to acknowledge that Barb is feeling anxious. No relationship can endure where one person resists acknowledging the other person's reality.

If you are now in a relationship with a resister, you undoubtedly already know how tough it is to talk with them. Invariably, such efforts end up with you getting put down for finding their behavior troubling; they can be masters at turning things around so that you are somehow wrong or inadequate for having trouble with them. Do remember that the resister's behavior is based on a deep sense of insecurity, regardless of how authoritative they may seem to be in their resistance. That being the case, any effort to talk about their behavior when one of you is already upset could result in even greater resistance on their part. After all, that behavior is their major defense, and like all of us, they will tend to use it as a shield whenever they feel threatened. Even if you both agree to a time to discuss the issue, you are going to have to make sure that you keep on your side ·of the line. Resistance can be so frustrating that you are likely to slip into blaming, accusing, labeling or playing shrink—and remember, this is just going to intensify their resistance.

If the resister has some awareness that his or her behavior is not working, and also has some willingness to change, you might want to try a very structured form of Active Listening, as we discussed in Tool #5 (Listen So that People Feel Understood). The following structure works well:

- The two people take turns at being listener and speaker. (See instructions for Active Listening in Tool #5, page 90.)

- After each person speaks, the person taking the role of Active Listener summarizes what the speaker has just said.

- They switch positions (with speaker becoming listener, listener becoming speaker) only after the speaker is satisfied with the summary.

This structure may feel awkward and mechanical at first, but it is highly effective in allowing the resister a chance to fully explore, and become comfortable with, an alternative form of behavior.

Defensiveness

Defensiveness is the need to explain or justify our own behavior when it is questioned or criticized. It is usually accompanied by a tremendous urgency to convince the other person that our intentions were good and reasonable, and that we had excellent grounds for our behavior. To illustrate, Beth reacts defensively to her husband, Ken:

KEN: *I don't understand how that bill got paid late. We may not be able to get a mortgage because of the black mark on our credit rating.*

BETH: *Well, it certainly wasn't my fault. I sent it in two days before the deadline, same as always. I can't help it if the post office messed up.*

KEN: *But you did call to tell them that?*

BETH: *Of course I did! I called and they said they go by the date of delivery, not the postmark.*

KEN: *You let me handle it. I never screw up on such things, and this really puts our mortgage in jeopardy.*

BETH: *I do the best I can. I can't do any more than that. What can you expect with the hours I work? I work full time plus do everything at home, and now you blame me because the check didn't get delivered on time. It isn't fair!*

If this conversation were to go on, Beth would have a defensive comeback no matter what Ken might say. Ken did not start out blaming and accusing; he was clearly upset that the check arrived late, and he wanted to discover the problem and make corrections so it did not happen again. But that does not mean he was attempting to find someone to blame. In response to Beth's defensiveness, he does become judgmental ("You should have let me handle it.").

If Beth were to respond to Ken in a completely non-defensive way, things might have gone quite differently. Let us replay the above scenario as if Beth had communicated openly from the start:

KEN: *I don't understand how that bill got paid late. We may not be able to get a mortgage because of the black mark on our credit rating.*

BETH: *You're worried we might not get our mortgage.*

KEN: *Yeah, if our mortgage doesn't get approved, I'm going to have to explain it to my father. I told him we were buying a new house, and if the deal falls through it'll just be more evidence for him that I'm a failure.*

Once Beth acknowledges Ken's feelings, we see that he is not blaming her at all; he just wants to be sure it does not jeopardize the mortgage (a goal Beth probably shares, as well).

Defensiveness is as crazy-making for the defender as it is for the person on the receiving end of such behavior. When we are defensive we treat nearly everything expressed to us as a sign that the other person is trying to blame us. The other person may just want to express a feeling or resolve a problem. But the defensive person always assumes that other people want to prove them wrong.

All of us indulge in defensive behavior from time to time. I certainly do. Every time I talk about this I am reminded, with some embarrassment, of an experience I had very early in my career. I was conducting a workshop at a "growth" center on the East Coast. Most of the participants had expressed their satisfaction with the way I had run the workshop, but the psychologist who ran the center did not. As he drove me to the airport, he tried to describe some of his feelings about my work. I had an answer for every negative observation he came up with. I told him that since he had observed only a small portion of the workshop he could not have a complete picture of what went on. To another of his comments I responded by suggesting he had unreasonable expectations. To still another of his comments I replied that perhaps there was something wrong with his perceptions about the workshop since the participants had all expressed their satisfaction. And so it went. Finally, he blew up at me. He told me that he had not been certain that his observations were well-founded when he first began talking. But since I had been so damn defensive, he was now certain that his concerns were correct.

I had to admit he was right about my defensiveness. Every time he expressed a feeling, I assumed he was blaming me. I spent all my time telling him, in various ways, that he was wrong, unfair, and unreasonable to feel as he did; and he went from being somewhat disappointed in the workshop to being convinced I was a totally defensive person who had no business conducting workshops.

This defensive posture was so unconscious that I had not even realized I was doing it. I was so accustomed to reacting defensively that I am not even sure I knew how to be non-defensive. This is not uncommon. People who were raised in homes where defensive communication predominates are often unaware of the other ways of responding.

In the years since that workshop I have had a lot of time to replay that scene. Hindsight is such a wonderful way to reclaim your lost pride! I might have saved the day if I had simply used some Active Listening, accepting that he was disappointed in my workshop even if others had liked it. I could have said, "You're really disappointed in my workshop?" or even acknowledged some of my own feelings about the workshop, saying, "I wish I'd been more willing to get into the areas you just mentioned."

Being non-defensive means that we do not have to defend ourselves against other people's feelings, even when they are unhappy with us. We do not necessarily need to accept responsibility for other people's feelings. Other people can be disappointed in my without my having to assume that I am a bad person or that I am to blame. Of course, sometimes I am at fault, and then it is completely appropriate to say, "I'm really sorry that I hurt you. I wish I'd thought about how it would affect you. Is there anything I can do to help?" Over the years, as I have wrestled with my clients' as well as my own defensiveness, I have come up with the following beliefs that trigger this particular brand of crazy-making behavior:

- **Feelings are about who is to blame.**

People are likely to act defensively if they assume that other people communicate their feelings in order to establish who is at fault, who the guilty person is. It does not occur to them that much of the time people do not care who is at fault. They simply want to have their feelings acknowledged.

- **When people are upset, they want explanations.**

People often believe that when other people express their feelings—especially when the feeling is dissatisfaction—they are asking for explanations. If you are a defensive person and someone comes to you with a problem which involves you, your first response is that this person wants an explanation of your behavior—why you did or did not do something. Sometimes this is true, but most of the time other people just want to be heard, want you to listen, to have the feeling that you understand them. If you give them that, they may be satisfied, asking for no explanation.

- **If you do not refute the other person's feelings or judgments, they will last forever.**

Some of the urgency we experience when we are most defensive often seems to come from a hidden belief that if we don't dispel the other person's feelings or judgments about us, these feelings or judgments will become eternal indictments against us. There is often the feeling, "I have to get rid of these negative feelings right now because if I don't they're going to hang over my head for the rest of my life!" In reality, feelings and judgments are usually quite transitory. The irony is that when we get defensive, we may leave other people with a permanently negative impression of who we are and what we are about.

- **If that is how people see me, that must be how I am.**

Very often, defensive people judge themselves even more harshly than others judge them. Perhaps they simply cannot tolerate other people's judgments on top of the mountain of criticism they have already heaped on themselves. The way the judgment goes is, "If I hurt Sue, I must be a bad person." To avoid accepting the label "bad person," there is a great sense of urgency to establish why it is unfair or unreasonable or simply crazy for Sue to feel hurt.

All these beliefs are introduced to our consciousness at an early age through everyday interactions with our parents and other significant adults. This is one reason why the sense of threat seems so real. The person who is feeling unfairly judged may actually be acting out conflicts that originally occurred for them in the first few years of their lives. The fear they experience is not adult fear so much as it is the fear of a child who is afraid that parents, who seem all-powerful, will withhold their love. So when the threat we feel is out of proportion to the present situation, we are really reacting to memories of how threatened we felt way back when we first learned whatever crazy-making behavior we are now engaged in.

Nobody likes having other people upset with them or holding negative judgments about them. But defensive behavior usually has the effect of increasing the other person's negative feelings rather than dispelling them. It invariably leaves the person on the receiving end feeling that you are not listening to them and that you are trying to make them wrong. If you did not do anything wrong, then there is nothing to defend. And if you did do something that hurt another person, intentional or not, the least you can do is take the time to hear them out. Listen to their feelings, rather than burdening them with your justifications.

Listen very carefully to your own inner dialogue when you are most defensive; you will probably be surprised by what you hear. Most efforts to justify our own actions are really conversations with our own inner judges, not with the other person who we feel is criticizing us. When we feel defensive, we can remind ourselves of this fact, and perhaps use the criticism as a clue for looking inside to better understand why we are judging ourselves so harshly.

The skill of Active Listening is a model for non-defensive communication. If you are someone who lapses easily into defensive behavior and you haven't been clear on the alternative, the way to be non-defensive is to acknowledge what the other person is feeling without getting into a discussion of who's to blame or whether or not those feelings are "fair." The same guidelines used in dealing with a resister can be used when you or your partner lapse into defensiveness:

- The two people take turns at being listener and speaker.

- After each person speaks, the listener summarizes what the speaker has just said.

- After hearing this summary, the speaker gives feedback on that summary.

- Listener and speaker swap roles.

Blame Fixing

Things that are done, it is needless to speak about… Things that are past, it is needless to blame. —Confucius

The need to affix blame nearly always begins with fear and self-judgment, the same attributes which plague the defensive person. The crazy-making part is that it has nothing to do with problem solving, though it can seduce us into believing that it does. If the argument started over child rearing, money, or sex (the top three, all-time favorites of most couples), and you are arguing about blame, you are not even on the right topic. Blame fixing only leads to more of the same kind of behavior, actually taking you farther and farther from the real issues.

When the goal is protecting the relationship the question is never one of affixing blame; rather, it is how to solve the problems which we are facing. While we are engaged in blame fixing and trying to fix responsibility for the painful past, no one is taking responsibility for the relationship in the present or taking responsibility to create a better future.

Blame fixing can often take on very sophisticated forms, as in the following dialogue between two people who, though well-versed in all the finest tools of communication, still have not looked closely enough at blame fixing:

"Well, if you hadn't expanded the argument, this fight wouldn't have been so bad."

"What do you expect after your opening comment was so accusative? Anyone would fight back after a crack like that."

"Well, at least I didn't try to drag in your mother and father, and the kids!"

"I wouldn't have needed to do that if you'd just done a little Active Listening."

On and on they go. The couple's tools for better communication have simply been converted into more ammunition for fighting their ongoing battle. When they sat down together and addressed how blame fixing was affecting their relationship, they learned some very interesting things.

Both felt that the other's negative feelings posed an imminent threat to their own self-worth. So they felt absolutely compelled to shift blame. They felt that unless they did this, they would have to live with their own negative self-judgments plus the other person's. Their only hope for feeling better about themselves was to somehow make it clear that the other person was at fault. As they explored this logic, however, both people quickly admitted that even affixing blame did not change their own self-judgments.

Nearly everyone who works through blame fixing comes to the realization that the ultimate threat to self-worth is not another person thinking badly of them for a while; rather the real threat is communicating in ways that tear their relationships apart. The most effective way to build self-worth is to be truly effective in getting what we all want from life: love, warmth, intimacy, recognition, a sense of purpose. Blame fixing blocks all of these. It is oriented to the past, rather than to the potent present and all it holds for the future.

For people who have been raised in environments where defensive communication predominates, slipping into blame fixing is natural and automatic. It takes conscious effort to stop it.

It is easier to cure blame fixing if you both work at it. Even when you agree to work on it together, there will be plenty of times you will not be able to resist the urge to blame back, even though you know the outcome is predictable.

But in the final analysis, the only behavior we can change is our own. Waiting for the other person to change only prolongs the pain. Remember that when we resist or deny feelings, they do not go away; they persist and may even grow, until they are quite blown out of proportion. No matter how provocative your loved one has been, blame fixing provides the resistance that keeps the behavior going. Hard though it may be, if you refuse to play the game the other person's behavior will have to change somewhat because it is a two-person game; trying to play it solo is about as satisfying as playing a solitary game of checkers.

How can you respond when another person is trying to fix blame on you? One option is to use Active Listening: "You're really upset because you feel I was unfair (or whatever your behavior was)." Notice that this response, while acknowledging the other person's feelings, is not an agreement that you were being unfair. Notice the distinctions between the two:

AGREEMENT	ACKNOWLEDGMENT
You're right. I really was unfair.	You're really upset because you think I was unfair.

The point is that you want to acknowledge their feeling, without agreeing to the accuracy of their perception.

The other alternative is to express feelings, without blame or accusation. If both of you use the guidelines for communicating feelings (summarized on page 71 in Tool #4), and really stick with them, you will find blame fixing almost impossible.

Blame fixing is the ultimate form of crossing over to the other person's side of the line. Once the blame fixer gets back on their own side of the line, they find that they have to talk about feelings. They feel hurt, sad, left out, rejected, angry or whatever.

Remember, as soon as you start taking responsibility for your feelings instead of trying to make the other person responsible for the event that triggered them, you set the stage for talking about the real issues that can strengthen your relationship and deepen the intimacy you both experience.

Having to be Right

Saturday is Carl and Gwen's night out and they've been talking about what they want to do. One idea is to try out the new restaurant in the neighborhood, then go to see a movie. But the movie is at seven, which means they will have to eat early. Carl thinks the new restaurant starts serving at 5:30 p.m.; Gwen says she thought the restaurant opened at six. But Gwen and Carl's communications get stuck at this point.

CARL: *What is this? I'm the one who saw the restaurant and read the sign on the door. Can't you take my word for anything?*

GWEN: *My God, can't I disagree on a silly little thing without you flying off the handle?*

CARL: *Well, it's not just this; you question everything I say. Why can't you, just once in a while, accept what I say without challenging it?*

At this point the prospects for spending a pleasant Saturday evening together are beginning to look pretty grim. The problem is not a new one. Carl is demanding that Gwen accept him as a final authority, one who is always "right." In his mind, any questioning of his facts is a challenge to him as a person. When he is challenged, being right becomes even more important than the people in his life. He seems to value his being right above love, friendship, personal property or even his own life.

In Carl's case, having to be right is not just something which occurs over important moral issues; rather, it is a driving need to feel that he is right in every interaction. For him and others like him, even the pettiest disagreement can escalate into a war to prove that people who question him are ill-intended, dishonest, distorted, or in some way less than honorable.

Carl's need to be right is a mask, disguising inner feelings of being somehow weak, defective or wrong, feelings that are a holdover from painful childhood experiences. When we are acting from the adult parts of our personalities, we do not lose our sense of personal worth just because we make mistakes now and then. However, a person like Carl can experience feelings of inadequacy and insecurity when the contradictions and disagreements inherent in life's endless challenges evoke doubts about his ability to cope. He answers these perceived threats with a full frontal assault against any and all who raise questions which make him feel insecure. Some individuals, as well as groups and even nations, act as if their survival absolutely depends on always being right.

But even when you understand the basis for this behavior it is still maddening when you have to face it time and time again. There is never room for more than one version of the truth. More than that, simple disagreements are turned into arguments which are at least unpleasant, and can quickly escalate into fights that threaten the relationship.

It would have taken less than a minute for either Carl or Gwen to pick up the phone and find out what time the new restaurant starts serving. But they are not even arguing about that anymore. Instead, the fight is now about each other's character: Carl feels Gwen is always challenging and undermining him; Gwen feels Carl is such a control freak that he cannot even tolerate a silly disagreement. The argument could go on for hours, even days, because the real issue, Carl's lack of self-worth, is not getting addressed.

Carl is probably unaware of his feelings of loss, inadequacy or insecurity. His inner thoughts, if he could clearly express them, might run along these lines:

"I did something neat by discovering the new restaurant. Gwen will appreciate this. It will be fun to check the place out with her."

Then, when she challenges him about the time it will start serving, he thinks:

"What is this? I'm the expert on that restaurant; it was my idea. She's taking away my sense of doing something special."

All Carl knows is that he felt a letdown, a loss or a threat when Gwen questioned the time. While Gwen is genuinely just talking about time, Carl is feeling that she does not appreciate his thoughtfulness. He cannot just let go. He feels that he has already lost, that something has been taken from him and it is Gwen's fault.

Let us say that Carl had responded to Gwen's original question with, "Well, I thought the sign said five-thirty, but let's phone and check." Something very different would have occurred. Not only would the argument have been averted, but he probably would have gotten credit for finding the new restaurant. Ironically, his need to be right gets in the way of his getting the recognition he really wants.

Of course, Gwen also contributed to the argument in our first scenario because she instantly saw Carl's need to be right as an effort to control her. She could easily have said, "You may be right, let's phone and check," and it is unlikely that Carl would have needed to escalate the fight. But reading Carl's behavior as an effort to control her, she becomes resistant, and the heat begins to build. If being "right" is a problem in your life—whether you are the person who needs to be right or the person who has to cope with a partner like that—be particularly sensitive about "owning" your statements: "My memory is that the restaurant opens at five-thirty," leaves room for the other person's memory. However, "It opens at five-thirty" seems more authoritative and invites a challenge.

Similarly, a statement such as "I don't like the couch" is less likely to evoke a struggle over who is "right" than, "That must be the world's ugliest couch!" Even when you are talking about perceptions and judgments, it's helpful to acknowledge them as your perceptions and judgments, rather than as irrefutable truths. Setting yourself up as a final authority is a little like a gunfighter bragging himself up as the "big gun" in the Old West; you are bound to get challenged, and your relationships are going to be short-lived, at best.

Stop Driving Each Other Crazy

Because we are only human after all, we are going to engage in a certain amount of crazy-making behavior. Yet you can learn skills for minimizing the number of times you get stuck. And when you do get stuck, the tools in this book can help you dig out of most messes you might create.

Above all, take responsibility for your own behavior. If you find yourself blaming or becoming defensive, do not use their behavior as an excuse for what you are doing. It only takes one person to de-escalate a conflict. All you need is to set limits on your own behavior. And the amazing thing is, when one person changes his or her behavior, it tends to break up the game. The other person may not move directly to the behavior you hope for, but change will occur.

In the final analysis, we change our own behavior for ourselves, so that we can feel good about ourselves. We no longer need to go through life simply reacting to the environment. We are making choices, and one of those choices is to protect our relationships.

But it is not always easy to change. When I have tried to change one of my behaviors that drives other people crazy, I've sometimes experienced a great deal of emotional resistance and pain. It was as if I needed that behavior, and without it, I felt terribly vulnerable and frightened. When this occurs, it is a clear sign that the behavior serves important emotional needs. Confront the needs. Just because you are frightened and vulnerable is not automatically a reason to avoid change. Bravery is not the absence of fear, but doing what needs to be done even though you are afraid.

Nevertheless I encourage you to be gentle with yourself, and seek out help and support to explore the emotions that are roused by your efforts to change. The first level of support could come from your loved one. Talk about your feelings as you make these changes. Know that changes that would be relatively easy for one person could be difficult for another. You will find talking about your feelings as you change gives you strength to move toward more open, less defensive communication. Eventually it all comes around; you may be the person who needs support at first, but as you continue to make changes as a couple, there will come a time when you will be the one doing the supporting.

Do not hesitate to get outside help if you get stuck. I have done it frequently, and so I have given some guidance in Tool #12 on what kind of outside help is useful, and for what circumstances.

Everything we explored has been aimed at helping you develop ways of reaching mutual agreements. Removing crazy-making behaviors helps create a climate for collaborative problem solving. Working together to identify and change how you communicate not only is tremendously supportive, but also builds trust and confidence in each other, making it possible to reach mutual agreements. And one of the first agreements you will need is a set of rules which keep your fights from escalating to defensiveness and crazy-making behaviors.

Tool #8

Replace Power Games with Fight Rules

Some crazy-making fight tactics create serious inequities in relationships, intensifying adversarial roles and driving a wedge between the two people involved. Let us now explore the elements of "power struggles."

Power Struggles

For many years in my workshops I would draw a big circle next to a little circle on a flip chart. Then I would ask participants to think about relationships in which they felt like the little circle next to someone who was the big circle. The lists usually included: motorist/traffic cop; patient/dentist; client/attorney; subordinate/boss; taxpayer/IRS; and so on. Almost invariably there would be at least one man in the class who would suggest "husband/wife" or a woman who would suggest "wife/husband." This would lead to a discussion of how power is not just the result of the other person's actual authority, that is, their ability to reward and punish; it is also a function of our own perception, how we interpret the other person's role in our life. It is entirely possible that a husband will see his wife holding the greatest power in their relationship at the same time that his wife sees him as having the power.

Our perception of power can be based on many different things. It may be based on a perception of our own inability to assume an assertive position, or it can be based on our perception of how assertive our partner actually is. A husband might say of his wife, "She has more power because she makes more money than I do." The same wife might say of her husband, "He has more power because he is always so calm and rational, even in the most trying of circumstances." Then he might say, "But I see her as powerful because she feels free to express her feelings."

After workshop participants identified relationships in which they felt like the little circle, we'd talk about how they felt when they were in relationships with "big circles," and how they behave toward "big circles." Every group has reported considerable ambivalence about being in relationships with powerful people. On the one hand, powerful people like bosses and experts may promise rewards or information we want. But we also feel uncomfortable, sometimes even resentful, about being dependent on them.

In fact, people reported engaging in all sorts of behavior aimed at "evening-up the score." This behavior might include "cutting the other person down to size;" teaming up with others to reduce the potential threat; and finding other powerful people, as advocates, who could counterbalance the threat. In fact, the perception that another person has more power was enough to trigger "evening-up" behavior, even when that perception was not an accurate assessment. If two people both think the other one holds the power, both people may feel entirely justified in "evening-up," because both people think power could be used against them.

A significant difference of power in a relationship can become a major source of instability. Nobody likes to feel like a subordinate in their relationships. Conflicts are far more likely to be resolved in a mutually acceptable manner when the power of the parties is essentially equal. When there is an imbalance, the person with the greatest amount of power is likely to fight on, thinking she (or he) will soon be able to "win."

Small circles, that is, people with less power, are less likely to work for a mutually satisfactory agreement. They are often afraid that because of their lack of power they will be forced into agreements which are against their interests. They may also feel that they will not have enough power to ensure that an agreement is kept once reached.

The use of power or even the threat of its use, creates an atmosphere in which achieving mutual agreements is very difficult. The usual outcome is creating situations where power will be challenged.

A Panoply of Power Games

We have previously discussed a few of the more common "power games," such as using other people or authorities as ammunition—"Your mom and dad agree with me, too!"—as a way of gathering evidence for our own perceptions; and using our knowledge of the other person's vulnerable points to weaken their position—"You know you've always had trouble controlling your temper." Here are some other prevalent behaviors.

Unilateral decision making

One particularly maddening use of power, guaranteed to generate conflict, is the practice of making unilateral decisions about things which significantly affect both people. This is the ultimate use of power because it says, "You're not even important enough that I have to consult with you." This produces feelings of rage and helplessness which are particularly likely to result in a dramatic escalation of any conflict.

True, each person needs to have areas which are independent of the other. Having to share decision making on everything is both stifling and inefficient. And, of course, many decisions do not require discussion. Some affect only one person. However, even when you have clearly defined rules around decision making in a relationship, perception can be an important factor.

Perceptions about which decisions should be joint decisions and which should be unilateral vary greatly from one family to the next. You might be from a family where everyone sits down and discusses every decision, even down to which kind of soap to buy for the bathroom, while in another family the father (or mother) makes all the decisions and the rest of the family is simply expected to go along.

While you may have one set of rules about what issues should be shared decisions, your partner may have quite a different set. As a result, people need to talk over their expectations where family decisions are concerned. They also need to talk over how decisions get made under emergency conditions, and what constitutes an emergency. Such a discussion reduces the danger that one or the other person will feel betrayed and thus feel compelled to escalate the conflict.

Intimidating with volume and intensity of expression

It is possible, of course, to use volume and the sheer intensity of expression as power. This is a lesson we learn in infancy, when our repertoire of behavior for controlling our environment is limited to our ability to scream at the top of our lungs. As people grow older, some learn to bully with noise or to develop what might be viewed as an adult version of a temper tantrum.

This is tricky territory, however. People who express themselves in quiet or restrained ways may feel intimidated by volume or intensity even when there is no intent to intimidate.

If you are in a relationship with someone whose style of expression is very different from yours, it is important to discuss the issue. If you feel intimidated by your partner's volume and intensity during conflicts, talk about it. Or if you feel your partner is perhaps too sensitive to your "energetic style of delivery," talk about that. (Both people may see the other person's behavior as using power.) Also, share how you feel about your own behavior. Maybe you are aware that you do use volume or intensity as a way of winning or you have wondered whether you are particularly sensitive to intensity because of childhood experiences. This kind of openness will draw you together.

To address this issue, it is essential to express your feelings in a non-accusatory manner: "I feel intimidated when you raise your voice," rather than "You're trying to control me with a temper tantrum." It is a fact that you feel intimidated. It is not a fact that the other person is trying to intimidate or control you. Be very careful about attributing motives to other people since it is virtually impossible to see the world from their point of view.

Withdrawal

One way to exercise power is to walk out, to simply leave the room when the heat is on. Another way is to withdraw emotionally, cutting off communication, possibly even sulking. Most people who withdraw do not see their withdrawal as a use of power. They think they are walking out because they have been hurt or because the other person has intimidated them. They perceive themselves as victims.

The fact is, however, that walking out is a real power play. Complete withdrawal, leaving the scene, cuts off all communication. It is a strong statement of rejection, communicating the message that you refuse to deal with the other person or the issue at hand.

Withdrawal can be a form of punishment. People often time their departures so that the statement they are intending to make with this behavior is quite clear: "You're so bad or you're treating me so terribly, that I'm not even going to talk with you." If your partner has feelings of abandonment and rejection left from childhood, withdrawal can be very powerful and destructive.

Some people withdraw from the scene emotionally. Some people pout; some just will not talk. Both of these behaviors communicate their messages loud and clear. As one man told me, "When my wife goes into her sulk, her silence is like a loudspeaker blaring out what a bad person I am. It freezes all further discussion right then and there, and so it becomes impossible to work out a resolution."

In another form of withdrawal, everybody is polite, and the minimum of courtesies is maintained, but a steely-cold hatred underlies everything that is going on.

Someone who is skilled at withdrawal can quite effectively stymie a person who is more assertive in expressing feelings. Like resistance, withdrawal can be a very powerful strategy, but it is essentially a negative one. We can prevent people from doing things we dislike, but it certainly does not get us the intimacy we desire. Withdrawal is a fear-driven strategy. The very act of building walls to prevent pain also keeps out affection.

The person whose main strategy is withdrawal actually sets themselves up for a kind of half-life. While they may avoid some of the pain and discomfort of a committed relationship, they will most assuredly miss out on the comfort, support, and mutual sharing they might enjoy were they able to be more open.

For some people, it is very threatening to be with a person who withdraws. It may stimulate a fear of losing all closeness and love. If you depend on that closeness and love to feel good about yourself—and many, many people do—then living in fear of the other person's withdrawal can keep you on an emotional roller coaster that is a constant source of anxiety.

Ultimately, the only way to get off this roller coaster is to develop a strong enough sense of your own worth so that you are not dependent on the other person's love to feel good about yourself. When you reach this state, though, you may also feel good enough about yourself that you will also decide not to waste your time in a relationship where the other person cuts you off every time there is a conflict.

If you are someone who uses withdrawal, be aware that you are gambling that the other person will do something to draw you back after you withdraw. But after a while they may not be willing to continue to pay that price. Instead, they will allow you to withdraw until you are completely and permanently out of their life. Most withdrawers have some awareness that this is a danger, and that awareness, which is often unconscious, can be the source of a great deal of anxiety for them.

This discussion leaves one question unanswered: Are there times when walking out or withdrawing emotionally is a perfectly healthy thing to do? Yes, certainly. There are times when both people are so compulsively engaged in the conflict that walking out helps to create a space between them. Even when working as a mediator I try to remain sensitive to when it may be productive to take a break, letting people discharge some of their frustrated energy in other activities. The big difference, of course, is that if I, as a mediator, suggest we take a break, there is no implication that one or the other side is being punished by the disengagement. There is also a clear understanding of when communication will resume. In fact, as a mediator, one of my jobs before taking a break is to define when we will get back together, and how we will resume the discussions. This same strategy can be used by couples by mutual agreement. If you both agree to break off the discussion for a while, with a commitment to a time when you will resume the discussion, then such a break may be very helpful.

There may well be times when mutual agreement is impossible, and one person needs to break off communication because he (or she) is so upset or overwhelmed that they simply cannot continue. What is crucial is that the communication to your partner about why you are withdrawing be nonthreatening. It must be neither accusatory nor punishing, and there must be some commitment to address the issue at a later date.

If you break off with a statement such as, "That does it, I'm leaving!" then there is little hope that the other person will see your withdrawal in a positive light. Your behavior will just come across as a punishing power play. But if you say, "I'm on overload right now, and I just can't cope. I'm willing to talk about this later, but I've just got to get off by myself for a while," then there is some chance that the other person will be able to accept the withdrawal without feeling punished.

Keep in mind, though, that even if you communicate carefully, and in your own mind it is very clear that you are not trying to punish, the other person may still perceive your action as punishing. This is one reason that the commitment to discuss the issue later is important. It clearly tells the other person that the relationship is important to you, and that you definitely want to work to resolve the conflict. There is a communication line still open between you, even if for the moment there is no one on the line. Also, when you have made an agreement to resume at a particular place and time, reestablishing communication does not require a huge concession on either person's part. It is assumed that you will communicate again later, so there is no loss of face involved in reestablishing contact.

Some form of withdrawal may be necessary in an abusive relationship where you feel threatened. If you find yourself in such a situation or know somebody who is, professional help is clearly indicated.

Who is right about when to fight

John has just settled down in front of the television set to enjoy a football game he has been looking forward to for several days. Evelyn, his wife, suddenly enters the room with a huge explosion of emotion, insisting that she must talk to him about their relationship. She says that she has been thinking about it for nearly two weeks now and it is time to sit down and work out some basic issues.

John flies off the handle. "I swear," he says, " You go out of your way to pick fights just when I'm enjoying myself."

Evelyn retorts with, "You're always doing this! Every time I want to talk about something, you're too busy. But when you want to talk, the whole world has to stop for you. You're never satisfied unless you're in total control!"

And now the fight is on. But the fight is no longer about whatever was upsetting Evelyn in the first place. Now it is about who controls the timing for talking about emotionally charged issues.

Certainly it is crazy-making to always have your mate swoop in and pick a fight when you are deeply involved in a completely unrelated activity. But it is equally crazy-making to be rebuffed anytime you want to discuss something that is bothering you. And so it is that timing, when to discuss problems, can easily become the focus of power struggles.

One person can argue that they want to talk about their feelings the moment they have them, not just at the other person's convenience. At the extreme this can mean, "I want you to drop everything you're doing and pay attention to me whenever I want you to." Five-year-old children expect and sometimes require this response, but it is not exactly the basis for a healthy adult relationship.

At the opposite extreme is the person who wants to deal with issues "only when I'm good and ready to deal with them." Emotionally the message in this behavior is, "I'm in charge here, and we will do things according to my timetable," which is also somewhat unrealistic. While struggles over timing are important, there are sometimes deeper issues to consider.

There are always differences in the degree of closeness and intimacy people want. When you want to be close, your partner wants to be left alone. By the time your partner is ready to be close, you have changed your mind, or perhaps are still so resentful from the last rebuff that you only feel like withholding and protecting yourself.

Sometimes, the desire for closeness is expressed as a request (or even a demand) to talk about a problem. Many people try to establish closer contact with their partners by forcing problems to the surface. They feel closer and reassured by talking, even if that talking is a complaint. Although it can be indeed difficult to read between the lines, the hidden message might be, "I've been feeling separate and I'd like to be close." As Evelyn and John's interchange shows, this disguised effort to be close may be perceived by the recipient in exactly the opposite way it was intended. John is likely to feel, "Oh boy, I'm in for it now. Talking about our relationship means she's got a long list of complaints about what's wrong with me." This may only be John's interpretation, or there may be some basis for this interpretation.

Fighting in front of other people

Fighting in front of others is perfectly acceptable for some families. But for others, letting outsiders, even close friends, see them fight is utterly mortifying. Since our "comfort zone" is a perceptual issue, defined by our experience in what family therapists describe as our "family of origin," it is entirely possible for two people to have very different standards for when it is okay to express conflict openly. These standards are rarely conscious; it is just that one person will begin to feel very uncomfortable with the situation, while the other remains quite comfortable.

Both people may feel frustrated or unhappy because of this difference in their comfort levels. People who are comfortable with fighting in public may feel very controlled and constrained by their partner's embarrassment. They may feel that they are having to hold their feelings in, and may argue, "Why should I have to do that just because you're so hung-up?" As the term "hung-up" suggests, they begin to judge their partner's reaction, and are likely to make comments like, "If you'd just join the human race, I wouldn't get so frustrated." Because they feel resentful at being asked to hold their feelings in, when the discussion does take place they often express their feelings with much more intensity than the original issue deserved.

For the person who is uncomfortable with public fights, the feeling of embarrassment or discomfort can indeed be acute. Often they become angry when issues are raised under these circumstances. One man whose wife often got into fights with him in public said, "She knows how uncomfortable this makes me. I always feel like I'm being forced to fight with both my hands tied behind my back." He clearly felt that his wife was doing this to gain a tactical advantage.

Sometimes people do raise issues in public because they know their partner will not fight back. And sometimes embarrassment is used as an excuse for avoiding something unpleasant. Whenever we use these power tactics to manipulate other people, it creates distrust. Then, whenever the same behavior occurs, the distrust may carry over into the new situation even though there is no manipulation or "power trip" intended.

Once again, the preferred solution is to discuss the issue. Set a goal of arriving at a mutual agreement about when you are okay with fighting, and when you are not. Nowhere is there a law which says every time you have a feeling it must be expressed. Nor is there a law which says that just because you are embarrassed by fighting in front of others, you should stop it. But do try to arrive at a balance. There needs to be enough openness so the person who is more comfortable with public fights does not feel unduly controlled, yet the person who does not like them will not be made so uncomfortable that the relationship simply becomes dysfunctional.

Threatening to leave the relationship

In the heat of a battle when the adrenaline is flowing, it is easy for a person to feel that the only solution is to leave the relationship. They may even threaten to leave unless their partner shapes up. A woman in a couples' seminar once put it quite succinctly: "I guess my fantasy is that my threatening to leave is such a great threat that Tom (her husband) will fall apart. Then he will realize the error of his ways." The threat is like some sort of ultimate trump card we use when we are feeling cornered, frustrated or without hope.

Unfortunately, this power play backfires at least as often as it succeeds. The threatened person may reply, "Fine! Go ahead and leave!"

Most marriage and family counselors have heard story after sad story from couples who never wanted a divorce, but once the issue was raised as a threat, both people got so locked in a power struggle that they felt obliged to go through with it.

In most marriages, threatening to leave the relationship is the ultimate weapon in the marital armory. No matter how well you have done at resolving the issue that started the fight, if a breakup is threatened, both people leave the fight unsure of where they stand. The foundation of trust and confidence has been undermined, and this can take a long time to repair.

It helps, of course, if both people understand that threats made in the context of a fight should really be interpreted as, "I'm so upset about this that I'm willing to use my ultimate weapon." It can be heard simply as a measure of how upset the person is, rather than as a genuine desire to abandon the relationship. Since it is a form of bullying that nearly always produces nagging uncertainty when the incident is over, threatening to leave the relationship is a tactic that really does need to be discussed and understood clearly.

Voice tone

You can adopt all the positive behaviors described in this book and undo all of your best efforts with accusatory, belligerent, whining or otherwise offensive voice tones. Early in my own life, I experienced one of those painful insights that you simply never forget. Professionally I had developed a great many skills for resolving conflicts, but whenever I tried to apply them in my marriage, they often failed to get the positive results that my own clients reported. Then one day, during a conflict with my wife, she said to me, "You sound like a done-in little boy!" Regardless of how much intellectual sense I was making, my voice tone absolutely drove her crazy, evoking her feelings of guilt over having wounded me.

As we explored this area, I discovered that I also have a "self-righteous bastard" voice, by which I project an attitude of self-satisfied superiority and moralistic rigidity (especially when I was feeling particularly threatened). I was rarely conscious of these voice tones. I simply slipped into them—and, I must confess, I still occasionally do when I am feeling upset and hurt.

Regardless of the subject we are addressing, voice tone can communicate accusation, close-mindedness, superiority or a desire to dominate. Regulating your voice tone can be tricky. Unless you have had training in this area (as a professional actor might have), you probably will not be aware of slipping into an unproductive tone of voice. If you have a close and caring relationship you can sit down and talk, letting each other know how particular voice tones set you off. Then, whenever the troublesome tones become an issue during a conflict, you can let the other person know, "I'm reacting to your voice tone. It feels like I'm in the hot seat, being accused" or whatever your reaction is at that moment. Having read this particular section, you will be surprised to find that you will become much more aware of voice tone, and begin to find new ways to monitor your tone so that you will get results. If there are voice tones you find difficult to change, you may need to look more deeply at the feelings beneath them.

Physical violence

In recent years, the media have described the terror of physical violence suffered by women with abusive husbands. More recently, there have been reports that men are also sometimes victims of physical abuse. Although many verbal fights can have positive value, there is very little possibility of the positive value emerging if either person knows they are risking physical harm.

The key factor in physical violence is intimidation. You cannot hit someone without making them feel at least somewhat afraid of you, and that effect can last for a very long time. The message communicated through physical violence runs deep. Even when the person on the receiving end is able to say, "I wasn't badly hurt," there is an unconscious response that comes from a deep, almost physiological level, that says, "This person who struck me has no interest whatsoever in my well-being. He (or she) simply does not value my life." Once that message has been transmitted, it is not possible to feel truly safe in expressing your feelings.

If you really value the relationship, both parties need to adopt a non-aggression pact, a fight rule which says "No Physical Violence." If threatening to leave the relationship is comparable to threatening to use nuclear weapons, then the use of physical violence is the equivalent of actually dropping the bomb. It is likely to leave a wasteland where nothing can grow.

In most cities there are support groups and counselors who help people deal with the issue of violence. Physical abuse is a very real danger to be addressed. **Seek professional help if you feel anxiety about getting physically injured in your relationship—or about causing injury to your loved one.**

Pursuers and Distancers

Family therapists use the terms "pursuers" and "distancers" to describe two basic styles of relating. Pursuers respond to emotional problems by engaging; they seek reassurance and emotional comfort by talking about their feelings. Distancers respond to emotional problems by disengaging. Their way of coping is to keep their feelings to themselves until they feel secure. They may prefer to go on long walks or think things over for a long time before expressing themselves.

Pursuers express themselves relatively openly, to a wide variety of people. Distancers are more selective about sharing their feelings. In times of high stress, the pursuer is like to spill anxiety and emotional distress onto anyone who happens to be around. By contrast, in times of high stress, the distancer draws farther into himself, sharing with even fewer people than he usually does.

There are also differences in timing or pacing between pursuers and distancers. Pursuers tend to move through life at extremely high speed, accompanied by sudden stops. Distancers are slower, more deliberate, and steadier. Although everyone has a dominant operating style, a person's style can vary from one relationship to another, and from one issue to another. You may be the pursuer in one relationship and be the distancer in others.

In my own marriage, my wife is the pursuer and I am the distancer. But in my consulting practice it is quite the opposite—I am frequently the pursuer. I am the one who insists that hidden agendas be confronted, emotions be dealt with, and so on.

Because it is so clear to pursuers that solving problems means talking them out, they easily slip into judging distancers as "hung-up" or "emotionally constipated." Pursuers tend to view distancers as being withdrawn, withholding, unavailable, unloving, uncommitted or afraid of closeness. Distancers, knowing it is helpful to think things through, often view the pursuer's need to talk everything over as immature or controlling. Distancers tend to view pursuers as clinging, nagging or demanding.

A problem that arises again and again for pursuer-distancer relationships is that their fights tend to drive them both into more extreme positions. As the pursuer pursues, the distancer feels invaded and threatened and thus withdraws further.

The irony, of course, is that these differences in style may well be why the couples were attracted to each other in the first place. The distancer finds the spontaneous warmth and emotional openness of the pursuer exciting, stimulating, and fun. On the other hand, the pursuer often sees the distancer as very self-possessed, stable, and sure of themselves. But these same positive attributes become negative ones when there is a major conflict or considerable stress. Under these conditions the pursuer's spontaneous nature looks to the distancer as an immature lack of emotional control, and the pursuer thinks the distancer is a cold fish.

That is why conflicts arising from these stylistic differences often focus on timing, that is, on when to talk about issues. The pursuer, feeling anxious until he can discuss what is troubling him, wants to talk right now. The distancer, who approaches problems slowly and deliberately, puts off the pursuer. The pursuer gets even more anxious, and presses even harder to talk about the issue now. The distancer views this response not as an expression of the pursuer's anxiety but as an effort to control. The distancer withdraws even further. Both people feel frustrated and rejected, and the discussion may stop for a while. After some time the distancer may attempt to initiate a discussion, but the pursuer is now feeling so hurt and resentful that this initiative is often rebuffed. Now both people feel separate and alone.

The first challenge in working with different styles is to get over thinking of the differences as character flaws. The first refuge in any fight is to assume that if the other person were just different, we would not have these fights. It helps couples to know that stylistic conflicts are present to a greater or lesser degree in virtually all relationships; that it is not a matter of being unreasonable, insensitive, uncaring or immature. Rather, it results from inevitable variations in the need and the timing of the need for closeness.

The root problem is that both people feel anxious. It is just that the pursuer deals with anxiousness by talking about it, while the distancer handles anxiety by withdrawing and regaining emotional balance. Both the pursuer and the distancer are likely to view each other's behavior as an effort to control. The pursuer feels controlled because the distancer will not deal with the issue when the pursuer has the need to talk, and the distancer feels controlled because the pursuer seems to be demanding that the issue be talked about right now.

If Eve has been stewing about her problems with John for several weeks, there really is not any reason why the discussion has to take place right after John sits down to watch the football game. She has been working on things at a leisurely pace and it is clearly not an emergency. If John does not want to deal with the issues right after the opening kickoff, that right should be respected. But Eve also needs to be given absolute assurance that John will make a definite time to address her problem.

Until we clearly understand each other's stylistic differences, these differences can easily set off power struggles, with the partners wrestling over who is "in charge." To avert such struggles, my wife and I set dates for when we will sit down and talk about the issue; this gives us both some reassurance that our anxieties will be addressed. Unless I acknowledge my wife's need for reassurance, my "I don't want to talk about it now" sounds to her like "I will only talk about things when I'm good and ready." On the opposite side of the coin, I need reassurance that I am not being controlled by her emotional needs; otherwise her "I need to talk about this now" sounds to me like "Whenever I have a problem, you must drop everything you're doing and pay attention to me."

It is interesting to observe how this works. The less pressured I feel, the more likely I am to say, "The heck with it! Let's talk about it now." My fantasies about what the discussion could turn out to be are often more difficult to deal with than the reality. As often as not I would just as soon get it over with now.

While setting dates for discussing problems is a solution for many couples, others find it works better to simply take turns. One time they will open a discussion to satisfy one person's sense of timing; the next time they will go with the other's timing. The obvious hazard here is that it leaves them wide open for arguments about whose timing they honored the last time around.

Emotional emergencies exist. If one person is terribly upset, drop whatever you are doing to give them the attention they need because you care about them. Because you choose to respond to their crisis, though, the issue of control is removed. You made the choice to respond to their need. However, if the person creates crises and emergencies specifically to get attention, this becomes a control issue that needs to be addressed directly.

This problem of pursuing and distancing is an extremely common one; the family therapy literature bears this out. Like most of the crazy-making behaviors, these stylistic issues are greatly eased by open discussion at a time when you are not in conflict. The key seems to be to find ways of shifting from attempting to control the other person to respecting their individuality. When both people feel respected, neither feels compelled to act out extreme versions of the pursuer or the distancer. As a result, the conflicts over styles may occur less frequently and be less extreme.

How to Halt Power Games

One of the simplest and most effective ways to prevent the devastating fights that create emotional wastelands is to establish fight rules. Fight rules set limits on the behaviors you have found to be particularly destructive, to ensure that when the fight is over, you will still have the home base of your relationship.

Fight rules are established by mutual agreement, during times when you both feel good about each other. Setting rules will not prevent all problems, of course. But when your body surges with adrenaline, they can remind you to avoid those actions which experience has shown can threaten the foundations of your relationship. Once we know what these rules are, we can consciously choose whether to honor or to violate them. But we can no longer pretend that we do not understand the consequences.

For many people, the idea of setting rules seems unnatural, even forced. Yet plenty of examples—sporting events, political contests, business transactions—show that anytime people are in a struggle which rouses emotions, chaos reigns unless all participants respect certain guidelines.

The Hidden Rules that Govern Our Fights

When you set fight rules, you will not be creating rules where there are none; rather, you will be replacing old rules (adopted unconsciously) with new rules which you have chosen—consciously and deliberately—together.

Few people are aware that there are already rules that govern their fights. In fact, when I ask people to identify even one of their present fight rules, most cannot imagine why anyone is even asking them such a question. There is the illusion that fights simply do not have rules.

With reflection, however, it is possible to identify them. We all "go by the rules' when we fight; the fact that we draw upon these rules without knowing it does not reduce their powerful influence.

We learn "hidden rules" from our families or from those we are closest to as children. I grew up in a family where any sign of conflict between adults was taboo. When conflict did occur, which it inevitably did, everyone felt acutely embarrassed. My father often responded by disappearing into the bathroom. No one ever challenged his right to stay in there until he was ready to come out.

In the early part of my marriage I was seeing a counselor because I wanted to resolve certain behaviors that limited me from attaining some of my goals. In therapy I discovered some strong unresolved feelings toward my father. Both my wife and my therapist urged me to confront my dad with these feelings in order to clear the air between us. The prospect frightened me. I realized that I had never confronted my father in my life, nor had I ever seen anyone else confront him successfully.

My wife was with me the day I finally decided to share my feelings with him, and the moment I opened my mouth my father got a frightened look on his face and, true to his pattern, retreated to the bathroom and locked himself in. I felt utterly paralyzed by this, and I recognized that the feelings I was having were only too familiar.

My old sense of helplessness in the face of conflict came rushing back from my childhood, sweeping over me in a wave of emotion. My wife, having a very different response to conflicts, got up, went to the bathroom where my father was hiding, and started pounding on the door, demanding that he come out and listen to me.

As this was happening I was experiencing all the old feelings I had had as a child. I was feeling embarrassed, which was predictable. But even more amazing, I was angry at my wife for pounding on the door and yelling at my father, demanding that he come out and confront the conflict. Her behavior was clearly a violation of our family rules; no one had even challenged my father's withdrawal when he was upset. Never mind that my wife was being supportive, that she was on my side, trying to make sure that my father would come out and listen to me. Like other members of my family, I fell into line and started following the unspoken rule of protecting Dad.

Clearly and unmistakably I discovered that there was a part of me, deep inside, that was saying, "Your wife is wrong for treating your father like this." After all, she was breaking the family rules. I was amazed at my own emotional response, wanting to stop her, wanting to control her and tell her that this was not right. In spite of the fact that, as an adult, I thought I had a certain amount of detachment and understanding, my gut response was to demand that my wife honor the old structure—even though I knew how destructive it could be.

After much pounding and yelling, my father—so fearful and embarrassed that at one point he even threatened to call the police—finally unlocked the door and came out. For perhaps the first time in my life, I felt that he really listened to what I had to say. Although it was difficult for us all, the fact remains that important issues got addressed and resolved, healing some old wounds that had previously divided our family.

Situations like this are not as unusual as one might think. Many years after it occurred, I shared this story in a couples workshop. After I related my own story, a woman in the group raised her hand and told a similar story. She said that soon after she was married, her husband got upset with her and she locked herself in the bathroom. She did not come out until he got a screwdriver and took the door off its hinges.

Fortunately for her, her husband very lovingly explained that in a marriage people had to talk things over, even when they were upset with each other. She said that her relationship was turned around by that single incident. Nobody had ever told her that she could sit down and talk a problem through. In her family, the avoidance of conflict was so strong she had never even imagined that such a thing could occur. Through the assurance of her husband's love and compassion she was finally able to discard the old family rule and make a new one that would better serve them in their marriage.

These examples show how powerful family rules can be. Even when we choose to make conscious choices to change them, we may have to wrestle with feelings from the past. Family rules govern when it is okay to fight, whether children may fight with adults, whether or not it is acceptable to fight in front of other people, whether or not it is okay to raise your voice, which issues we confront and which get avoided, what behaviors are "below the belt," and more.

Old family rules continue to govern the ways you handle conflicts unless you actually make the decision to define what these rules are and how they are affecting your behavior. However, even though it can be valuable to have insights into why you act as you do, if the behavior is destructive it is far more important to stop doing it. In the final analysis, it is the change in your behavior—not your insight into why you do it—that will have an impact on your loved one's life and thus on the relationship. Therapists know that when you change a behavior, the feelings stimulated can engender psychological insights, which help make the behavioral changes permanent. But you need not wait for the insight before changing the behavior. Try it the other way around. Change the behavior, and see what insights this brings.

Does Setting Rules Work?

Will both people just forget the new fight rules once the fight gets rolling, and then slip back into old family patterns? Yes, most couples who set rules end up violating them from time to time; but most are completely convinced that having the rules defined keeps their conflicts focused and productive and is one of the most positive techniques they have for minimizing the negative effects of a fight. But because we know what hurts our loved ones, and because we have agreed on behaviors that honor our relationships, we tend to check ourselves whenever we are reverting back to the old family rules. There is an almost automatic reflex to stop ourselves from carrying out destructive behaviors; instead we substitute behaviors that we have previously agreed can be helpful and constructive.

We may not always succeed in honoring out new fight rules. But even when we slip, there is comfort in knowing that we both recognize what we are doing and that we still choose the common goal of preserving the love we share.

If there are so many advantages to having rules for governing our fights, why do so many couples resist setting them? Some people just do not think rules are necessary. They argue that every decent person knows what is fair and that only a very bad person would do something unfair or hurtful. But because each person comes from a different family, with different rules, if you each did what was "fair" in your family, at different times one or both of you would inevitably end up feeling hurt, crying "foul" or accusing the other of "hitting below the belt." Even the best of people with the best of intentions still have very different ideas about what is fair and unfair. By setting rules together you develop a common set of expectations.

Many people like to pretend that they just will not have any fights in the future. Each fight they have is "the last one." Always vowing or at least pretending that there will be no more fights, they keep putting off setting rules for themselves—and the fights continue to drive a wedge between them.

Finally, some people do not set fight rules because they do not believe people are going to change anyway—after all, they argue, "people are what they are." Either put up with things exactly as they are or end the relationship and search for a lover who is free of all personality flaws. It is true that during fights we fall back into familiar behavior, but we really do have other choices. Every personality is capable of a variety of responses to the same situation. Fight rules actually guide us toward discovering new, more satisfying responses. The fight rules we establish with our mates are the road maps for expressing ourselves in ways that deepen our relationships rather than tearing us apart.

Setting Fight Rules

There are nearly as many definitions of what is fair in a fight as there are people. One couple may be most comfortable with no-holds-barred, maximum-decibel conflicts. Others view such behaviors as unfair, hateful, and indecent. So there are few hard and fast rules that apply for everyone. The key to setting effective fight rules is to work together to understand what works best in your relationship.

Here are five steps to follow in setting up rules:

1. Agree on when you are going to discuss fight rules

Fight rules have to be set at some time other than during a fight. Many couples set fight rules in the aftermath of a fight, when they are a little chagrined about their own behavior. Both people are still sufficiently in touch with the pain of the fight that they are willing to accept limits on future fights. The only danger in discussing fight rules during this time is that it may be easy to slip back into accusing or blaming each other for the particular behavior that occurred. There has to be some sense that "neither of us is really happy with our behavior, and it is more important to keep this from happening again than it is to score points about the last fight."

It is extremely important that the time for discussing fight rules be mutually acceptable. If one person is ready to talk about rules but the other is not, you are unlikely to reach agreement. You may need to set dates, rather than try to resolve issues immediately.

2. Agree on the issues of greatest concern

Each couple needs to identify the kinds of things that push their buttons and prompt them to escalate their conflicts. Keep in mind that you may not immediately agree on which behaviors are a problem in your relationship. One person can be deeply hurt by something the other person considers absolutely harmless.

In past chapters we have considered a number of behaviors that drive people crazy, that escalate fights, that undermine our relationships. We have also discussed skills—such as Active Listening—and procedures—such as the Five-Minute Rule—designed to improve communication. All of these behaviors are candidates for rule-making. Following are quick checklists of behaviors to place under control and to bring into play.

BEHAVIORS THAT MAY REQUIRE LIMITS:

❑ Expanding the argument

❑ Using other people or authorities as ammunition

❑ Using "you always" or "you never"

❑ Labeling

❑ Playing shrink ("Pop Psyching")

❑ Hitting below the belt

❑ Bringing up past grievances

❑ Dumping

❑ Resistance

❑ Defensiveness

❑ Blame fixing

❑ Having to be "right"

- ❑ Unilateral decision making
- ❑ Intimidating with volume and intensity
- ❑ Withdrawal
- ❑ Fighting over the right time to fight
- ❑ Fighting in front of other people
- ❑ Threatening to leave the relationship
- ❑ Voice tone
- ❑ Physical violence

SKILLS / BEHAVIORS YOU MAY WANT TO AGREE TO USE:

- ❑ Active Listening
- ❑ Sharing feelings without blame or accusation
- ❑ The Five-Minute Rule
- ❑ Calling a five-minute break
- ❑ Setting dates to discuss issues

Start by identifying which of the behaviors on the first checklist is a problem in your relationship. Not every listed behavior will concern your relationship. You may add other issues to the list that are important to you. Focus on what you and your partner find helpful or harmful in your relationship. You need not limit yourself to what others have done.

Be aware that it is best not to tackle all these issues at once. It may take months before you have considered all the issues that are important. Start with those issues which are most important now, and address the others as they become important.

3. Agree on general rules

Rules may be stated both as a prohibition and as a commitment: what you agree not to do, and what you agree to do. For example, here are some of the rules my wife and I have.

We agree:

- not to expand the issue, and if we do, to return to the original issue once it has been pointed out to us.

- to discuss issues when they begin to bother us, rather than letting them build up until we start dumping on each other.

- to use Active Listening to acknowledge each other's feelings; or when we are too upset to listen, to use the Five-Minute Rule.

- that when one person wants to talk about an issue right now and the other does not, we will set a mutually acceptable time to discuss the issue.

- not to drag in what other people have said to bolster our positions.

Each of these rules has a history. Each is the outgrowth of a problem we were having, and the rule has been set to remind us that we need not engage in painful or destructive behavior.

That is your task. Find those problem areas for the two of you, and agree on behaviors that will either prevent escalation or improve communication.

4. Agree on how the rules will apply

Once you have agreed upon general rules, there is still a good deal of discussion that needs to take place about exactly how they will work. Here are some of the considerations that may come up:

Are there times when it is okay to violate the rules? For example, there may be "emergency" conditions in which it is okay to make unilateral decisions. Are there times when a skill is not to be used? For example, you may not want to use the Five-Minute Rule in front of other people.

How will we let each other know when one of us has broken a rule? Rules are most likely to be broken when we are upset and unreceptive to someone pointing out the violation. How can we signal each other that rule has been broken without becoming accusatory? How do we acknowledge the signal once it is sent?

You may want to agree on a "fallback behavior," in case a rule is broken. For example, my wife and I have learned there are times we are too upset to use Active Listening, so we agreed at these moments to shift to the Five-Minute Rule. Similarly, if one or both of us have expanded the issue, we have agreed in advance to retreat to the original item of conflict once it is pointed out.

5. Agree on how you will evaluate how well your rules are working

How can you tell whether your rules are working? Discuss what your expectations are. Talk about what you think is realistic, and how things will be if the rules are working.

You may also want to set a date to evaluate how well your rules are working. Give yourself time to refine the rules you set, and don't get discouraged if they do not work perfectly at first. Do not be afraid to go back to the drawing board to change the rules or work out more effective and comfortable ways to employ them.

What Happens When Fight Rules Are Broken?

Some of your rules will inevitably be broken. One of you will inevitably cross the line and start evaluating or judging your partner. One of you will inevitably expand the issue, or fall back into using a voice tone that triggers the worst kinds of feelings. The list of possible violations is endless. Since you are already in a fight when it happens, you will probably find yourself escalating the argument by arguing about who broke the rules and why. Such fights are rarely productive.

In a funny way, fight rules have a way of "policing" themselves. In the back of our minds we are both aware that the other person "scores a point" when we break a rule. This is not to say we gloat over that point—this would be as destructive as breaking the rule in the first place. Most of the time the person in violation is only too aware of what she (or he) has done. Any additional comments do not add anything to that awareness; gloating will only distract.

You can create good faith when you both honor the rules you have established together. Violating fight rules is not just a failure to keep a promise; it is also a failure to keep a commitment to yourself. Do not get me wrong. It is bound to happen. If it did not, we would not be human. When violations occur, talk about your feelings, avoiding blame or accusation. Then quickly get back to reaffirming the existing rule or establishing a new rule that fits you better. Remember that just like other couples who have established rules, you are bound to get better at it as you go along.

Putting It All Together

Keep in mind that the rules you make today are not absolutes (the only exception would be the rule against physical violence), so much as they are a road map for keeping your relationship positive, loving, and exciting. As you change, you may also need to change your rules.

As you work with your spouse to create new "conscious rules" to replace old "hidden rules," you are also making a major declaration that you truly care about yourself, the other person, and the relationship you share. Fight rules reduce the discomfort you might otherwise suffer, and that is certainly a worthwhile goal. But the process of working together to establish these rules has its own rewards in deeper sharing and understanding.

In the next chapter we address the issue of the recovery period, the period after fights when we feel so tentative and unsure. The recovery period is necessary not only for clarification and mending but also for discovery and opening up new levels of understanding and intimacy.

Use Constructive Ways of Making Up

How you respond after a fight is as important as how you conduct yourselves during the fight. The period afterward can be absolutely awful, as you experience a deep sense of separation and alienation. Or it can be a very productive time, when you learn a great deal about yourself, the other person, and your relationship. It can even be a time of great intimacy. We experience intimacy, after all, through sharing those thoughts and feelings which are most important to us. Fights often draw out exactly those feelings. So if the manner in which you fought has not been too hurtful, your conflict can lead to very intimate moments. There can be total accessibility, with neither person needing to hide anything, accompanied by a tender, fragile vulnerability with all weapons set aside. It is not surprising, then, that lovemaking follows the fights of some couples.

I often advise people to think of a fight as "complete" only after they have gotten through the recovery period. I have seen far too many cases when the harm inflicted in the aftermath exceeded what had occurred during the fight itself. I have seen couples get into horrendous fights over whether or not to stop the fight or who started the fight in the first place. Some couples get into tremendous power struggles, while others inflict punishment on each other; others require that their partners spend a certain amount of time in the "doghouse" or otherwise do "penance" before they will make up. Still others have so many inappropriate judgments about fighting that they turn even a healthy, relatively benign conflict into something negative, for example, offering the conflict as evidence that "we really don't belong together."

In contrast to the above, I have seen many people use the recovery period for gathering self-knowledge and growth as a couple. Successful couples employ and discuss how they can make the aftermath of every fight constructive, deepening the relationship rather than causing further alienations.

The Value of a Fight

In every fight, we inevitably run some risks. People may come away feeling hurt. There may be resentments or even a desire for revenge. You may feel that you have shaken up what had been a perfectly peaceful relationship. Having paid this price, the challenge of the aftermath is to reap some of the potential benefits inherent in every conflict.

We often forget, or perhaps never learned, that fights have value, that they can clearly be useful. I have learned never to lose sight of the constructive uses of fights. Keep in mind the five most important uses:

Fights help us define issues.

At the very least, a fight should increase your knowledge of the issues. This includes questions such as: Which issues are really important, and which ones are non-issues that quickly dissolve as we confront them openly? What do we each feel about the issue? How do we each see our own lives affected by the issues we have uncovered?

Fights offer new understandings for personal growth.

Fights can prod us toward important personal growth, uncovering self-doubts or fears which, once resolved, can leave us much freer, stronger, more open, and more able to fully participate in a loving and productive relationship. Because fights can bring so much pain, they often motivate us to change our beliefs or attitudes. And if you are careful about your communication skills, you can use the time after a fight to work together, supporting each other in gaining important personal insights.

It is one thing to know that you feel threatened, angry or hurt when the other person says or does a particular thing. But real and permanent growth comes when you can honestly look at the beliefs you hold, and actually see the part you are playing in projecting "meanings" to the actions or words outside you. If I feel very defensive in a particular area, what is it I feel I must defend? Why is this issue so particularly threatening for me? Does the fact that I got my buttons pushed tell me about something going on in me or the relationship that I have not looked at? Are there other areas of my life where the same issue arises?

Immediately following a fight, we often have access to feelings which, in everyday life, we keep hidden. As fights force these feelings out into the open, we can take a fresh look at them and perhaps see the blind spots that up until now have prevented us from seeing how we might resolve them once and for all. In this way, we can eventually come to see that fights really can be our valuable teachers.

Fights help us gain insights into our relationships.

If you build a wall of defense immediately after a fight, it may take a little time before you can freely talk about what you learned from it. On those occasions when you finish a fight feeling good about each other, you have a rare opportunity to share new insights. At these times, you are less defensive, your feelings are on the surface, and you are motivated to find more effective ways of handling conflicts in the future.

Fights can initiate problem-solving.

Fights may not completely resolve conflicts but they do open doors, serving as a natural prelude to a problem-solving session. Through fights we identify the issues. We move past our own resistance to the other person's feelings. We experience some emotional catharsis and we discover the incentives for change. While it is not necessary to have a fight to initiate problem solving, a fight is often the first step in the process.

Sometimes, the really valuable insights fights uncover may have more to do with the ways we fight or communicate than the more obvious subject of the fight.

Fights can help us improve the ways we fight.

The period immediately following a fight often proves to be invaluable for discussing and setting fight rules. As we look back at our actions, we may see behaviors we want to change, and find that we are willing to let go of old ways of coping and start looking for new, more effective ways of relating.

Achieving these benefits has as much to do with how you "make up" as it does with how you fight. So let us take a closer look at this subtle art itself.

What Really Happens

Family therapist Daniel Wile describes a standard sequence for the way most couples make up. Here is how this sequence goes:

STAGE 1: The fight

Gary and Susan get into a fight. It might last just a few minutes or it could go on for hours. They both feel so hurt or threatened by what the other person has said that they lash out with whatever they think will get through.

STAGE 2: An argument over whether to continue the argument

Susan's way of coping with being upset is to go off alone and cool down. But when she tries to do this Gary stops her, arguing that problems are best handled by talking them out. He thinks ending the fight means "running away from problems." So Susan and Gary get into a new argument over ending the fight. This argument can turn into a fight as bad or worse than the original one.

STAGE 3: Sulking

Gary and Susan somehow break off the argument. Then they go off and sulk, refusing to talk to each other.

STAGE 4: Peacemaking attempt (Gary)

Gary expresses his feelings more easily, and gets over his hurt and anger more quickly than Susan does. But he also feels more threatened by the distance between him and Susan, so he initiates a peacemaking attempt. Susan is not ready for this. She rebuffs his efforts. Gary not only feels rejected, but also begins to feel resentment that he is always the one to make the first attempt at patching things up.

STAGE 5: Peacemaking attempt (Susan)

After a little more time has passed, Susan is now ready to make her own peace offering. But now, because Gary is feeling angry at being rejected and is feeling resentful because he feels he is always the one to make the first move, he is not responsive to her efforts.

STAGE 6: Cooling down period

Nothing more is said for a period of time. Both people studiously avoid much contact. If one person enjoys himself or sleeps well while the other person does not, that leads to resentment.

STAGE 7: Sudden end of fight

After an interval—perhaps after a night's sleep—things go on as if the fight never occurred. Neither person says anything for fear that it will start the fight over. They are both just relieved it is over, and do not want to do anything to start it up again.

Most of us will probably recognize some of our own behavior. Although not a description of an ideal fight, it is a fairly accurate depiction of how it is for a great many people. The question is: Does anybody really learn anything from such a fight? So far, I think we can safely say that Gary and Susan have learned little if anything about themselves or their relationship. So how else could we end a fight and use the process to gain self-knowledge and growth as a couple?

Recognizing When the Fight is Over

Some people cut fights off too soon, before there is any resolution. Some just keep slugging away, long after there is any benefit to continuing. If we understand what the end looks like, how it sounds and how it feels, we can better recognize each other's signals for when it is time to stop. We will also have a model for how to wrap things up.

A constructive end of a fight might sound something like this:

FIRST PERSON: *I don't have anything more I need to say. How about you?*

SECOND PERSON: *No. I've said everything I need to say.*

That is not a very witty or dramatic exchange, to be sure. But it does meet two critical standards for determining when a fight is done: (1) both people feel they have had their say, at least for now: and (2) both people have accepted (or are at least resigned to) the fact that the other person feels differently. Both people have stopped trying to convince the other that they ought to feel differently.

By contrast, if the same two people had been in the midst of the fight, and each one was still resisting the other's feelings or the other's sense of what was important, the dialogue between them would be very different. It might go something like this:

FIRST PERSON: *I don't want to fight about this anymore.*

SECOND PERSON: *You're just going to drop it then, as if nothing ever happened?*

FIRST PERSON: *I don't see any point in going on. It's senseless.*

This fight is not over at all. Although the first person says he wants to fight fighting, the underlying message is not one of resolution, temporary or permanent, but of giving up. At the same time, the second person's response, "You're just going to drop it then," carries with it a judgmental tone, with this person clearly not accepting the other person's desire to stop.

As long as one person is upset with, and is trying to change the other, or is not able to accept what the other person is feeling, there is a conflict. The fight may be approaching a resolution but it is not there yet. The underlying message continues to be one of anger toward the other person for taking a particular position.

There are many constructive ways to conclude a fight. One simple, clear message to signal that you are done is, "I'm done. Do you need to say anything else?" This message indicates we have gotten past our resistance. We have accepted the fact that the other person feels as he (or she) does. We may still not like it, but we are through fighting about it.

One minor point of technique: It is better to say, "I don't need to say any more, do you?" than it is to say, "Do you need to say anything more?" The reason for declaring your own position first is that you are taking the risk of being rebuffed, rather than asking the other person to run the risk. Since you have made the first move, the other person can respond without appearing to give in.

An alternative ending is for each person to use Active Listening to summarize what the other person has said. Only when both people feel satisfied that they have been heard can they feel comfortable. Not only does Active Listening ensure that both people have their say, but the verbal summary explicitly acknowledges the right to differ. And there is the additional dimension of both people being able to leave the fight knowing they have been understood.

Emotionally, there is a greater sense of completion with Active Listening than if both people simply agree that neither has any more to say. But it does have one minor drawback: if one or both people are still in a combative mood, they may squabble over the adequacy of the other person's Active Listening responses. Or the responses may trigger further comment, fanning the fires for a new fight.

Some couples go a step further and each write a summary of both people's feelings on a single sheet of paper. When they can agree that their feelings have been adequately summarized by the other, they know they have arrived at the end of the fight.   While all of these techniques can mark the end of a fight, they do not necessarily resolve the issues raised. Many, if not most, conflicts are solved not during the fight itself but in problem-solving sessions afterward. So it would not be unusual for a person to say, "Well, I think we understand each other's feelings pretty well. Right now I need a little time to pull myself together but let us agree to a date for a problem-solving session.'

The Worst Ways to Finish

Many ways of ending a fight are clearly destructive. The most damaging of these can be lumped into three general categories.

• The knockout blow

A knockout blow is administered when one person says something that is so emotionally charged that the person on the receiving end is just devastated and can say no more. People who try for knockout blows are playing with fire. They may win the immediate battle but lose the relationship.

No one can stay in a relationship where they constantly lose. So if you consistently "win" your fights with knockout blows, bear in mind that you are making your partner a "loser." Chances are great that this will breed resentment that will seriously damage or even destroy the relationship.

Some couples get into the strange game of trading "wins." Like television wrestlers, they wage an ongoing battle, with one person scoring the knockout punch one time, the other scoring it the next time around. Both people suffer equally, trading off being winner and loser. But it is a dangerous game, always on the verge of causing so much pain that neither person is willing to stay. In an effort to come up with the winning blow, each person tends to raise the ante just a little bit each round. Over time, this results in a pattern of spiraling escalation. Increasingly, both people start hitting below the belt or picking on vulnerabilities. Each "point" they score breaks down whatever bonds they once shared in their relationship until, more often than not, there is no bond at all.

• The decision about who's right

One sure way to start a fight up again is to discuss who was right. Every time you insist on a decision, you are sounding the bell for the beginning of a brand new fight that can well last for the duration of the relationship.

The person who ends fights by trying to determine who was right has not realized that each person has different emotions, different inner realities, and that they have a right to differ. They may believe that there must be only a single emotional reality or perhaps they feel that their own perceptions are incorrect or threatened when someone else perceives things differently.

• Insisting on a solution "now"

While it is true that solutions to conflicts are sometimes found in the midst of a fight, it would be placing too great a burden on ourselves and our relationships to expect that all fights produce immediate solutions. It is a good idea to think in terms of fights and problem-solving sessions as having two fundamentally different functions. They are related, of course, but in most cases they are related only insofar as the fight forces issues to the surface and allows you to discharge emotional tension; you will resolve the issues that arose in the fight later, through the problem-solving sessions. Insisting that the fight ends with an immediate solution is an unreasonable expectation, and may even get in the way of solving the problem.

Attitudes and Skills for Making Up

For most of us, fighting comes a lot more "naturally" than making up. And yet, there are few people who would not agree that given a choice between the two, they would much rather make up. Like everything else in conflict resolution, making up is a matter of learning skills. Practicing might seem forced or clumsy, but once you have become familiar with them, and have begun applying them on a fairly regular basis, they become second nature. The following are skills and attitudes that have proven to be most helpful and productive among couples with a high success rate for resolving conflicts.

Agreeing that both people contributed to the fight

How many times have you heard or even used the old saying, "It takes two to have a fight"? But if the truth were known, most of us do not really want to believe it. A nagging little voice keeps telling us, "Why should you make up with him (or her)? He started it!"

There has never been a fight in which both people did not contribute something. No matter how nasty, provocative, infuriating, blaming or judgmental the other person may have been, fights do not happen unless a second person buys into them.

When two people finally agree that they have both contributed to every fight they ever had, and that they will contribute to every fight they will have in the future, they liberate themselves and their relationship from the futile and hurtful struggle to attach blame. The attitude that *we* rather than *you* made a fine mess of things reminds us to honor our relationship. By focusing on the relationship, we are more likely to both give and receive help. Making up gets a lot easier when it is clear that both people accept their contribution.

After a fight, focus your attention on how you contributed to it rather than on the other person's contribution. Be very certain that you stay on your side of the line or you are only going to be throwing more fuel on whatever glowing embers still remain.

In the moments immediately following a fight, you are probably hearing a little voice in the back of your mind urging you to tell the other person how much worse his behavior was than yours. But remember, the other person is not so much different than you. They are struggling with that little voice, too, convinced that your behavior was much worse than theirs. If you decide that the little voice is speaking the truth and you act on this perception, you will only be fanning the flames again, and you will find yourself right back in the heat of the battle.

If you must tell your partner how their behavior during the fight affected you, be certain to observe the guidelines for communicating feelings, which we discussed in Tool #4 (Express Feelings, Not Judgments). In particular, be sure you concentrate on how the behavior affected you emotionally—"I felt really put down when you ..."— rather than being judgmental—"You were so nasty to me I could not believe it!" Also be sure you describe the behavior— "...when you brought up the issue of my sister"—rather than judging it—"...when you made that cruel remark about my sister."

Making certain that no one has to lose face

Making up and getting back together have a lot to do with what the Japanese call "face," a term which made its way into our culture as "saving face." In Japan, "face" implies dignity, respect, social standing, the essential qualities needed to have an effective role in society or to participate in a relationship. Losing face can be tantamount to a loss of identity, and this will threaten to end a relationship.

This is a valuable concept. Much of the awkwardness we feel around making up after a fight is an effort to find a way back together without having to give up too much face. It is a struggle that was eloquently captured in the title of a book by Jordan Paul and Margaret Paul, *Do I Have to Give Up Me to Be Loved by You?*

How much should your partner have to give up as a price for being in the relationship with you? There is only one answer to that: If losing face is the price of making up, then the making up has failed.

Requiring that someone "lose" introduces a fundamental instability. The loss of face is like a little death of the self, and if that is the cost, people will avoid addressing issues, even when those issues are essential to the health of the relationship. You will find that when issues finally do get discussed, both partners will feel an added edge of urgency and risk. This urgency will fuel the fires of escalation. It is hard to discuss feelings calmly when you fear that the consequences of what you say could result in another emotional annihilation.

One of the things that kicks off power struggles in the makeup period is the belief that punishing the other person will cause them to change their behavior. But think about your own reactions to this kind of coercion. It is true that if someone uses enough power, you might change your behavior, but usually that change is accompanied by resentment. You will change the behavior, but there is a part of you that will also seek a way to get back at the person who coerced you.

What we really want, instead, is willing change. But what exactly is willing change? The truth is that willing change occurs only when people feel good about themselves. When you are really down on yourself, you do not have the emotional resources for willing change. Any demand for change just feels like added proof of how inadequate you are. Rather than face your inadequacy, you will fight on to try to prove it is not so. When you change because you are unhappy with your own behavior, you do so because your own ego strength allows you to feel safe with that change. In willing change, the price is never a loss of selfhood but a new affirmation of it.

Many of us harbor a secret belief that "if she (or he) really loved me, he would want to change, just to make me happy." In this respect, we measure the other person's love by how much they are willing to comply with our wishes. In effect, this compliance becomes the price for peace, that is, for making up. But there is a bitter irony here that we simply cannot ignore: Is it really possible for a person who constantly faces this kind of humiliation to love the person who does that to them?

"Checking in" to avoid paranoia

Back in my high school days, I did some door-to-door selling to earn extra money. The instructor told the story of a young salesman who was making his first call. As he walked nervously up to the first door, he began remembering all the terrible things he had ever heard about how much people dislike door-to-door salespeople. As he pressed the doorbell, he began anticipating what the person's reaction was going to be when the door opened. When a woman finally answered the door, he blurted out, "Well, I don't like you either!" and stumbled away.

This story captures a fundamental truth. When we are feeling our most anxious, we second-guess what the other person is thinking or feeling, and soon we forget that all the guessing is taking place solely inside our own heads. The making-up period is one of those anxious times. Someone you care about has cut off communication or certainly seems to be making it difficult, and under these circumstances it is all too easy to get into a kind of temporary paranoia about what is going on in his or her head. Keep it up, and soon you will be acting on your fantasies as if they were absolute truths.

Many couples get so locked into their fantasies that even when they do begin to communicate more openly they have great difficulty separating these fantasies from what is actually said. We are probably all guilty of this to some degree. You may have even heard yourself responding to your partner's statement with, "That's what you say, but I know what you're really thinking!" And if you think back to when other people have said this to you, you may also recall how maddening it is having another person insist that he knows your mind better than you do.

Avoid fantasizing or speculating about what the other person is thinking or feeling. If you know from past experience this is a problem, make an agreement that during the making-up period you can have short "check-in" periods designed to minimize these temporary lapses into paranoia. This kind of speculation and second-guessing flourishes when both people are feeling very anxious. Because communication is impaired, the speculations blossom in profusion without the reality checks that more open communication would provide. So even if you are not ready to make up, it may be worthwhile to verbalize what you are thinking and feeling just enough to reduce the space for paranoia. Such a conversation might go something like this:

"I need to check something out with you. I'm beginning to fantasize and I'm wondering what you are thinking and feeling right now."

"Well, I'm feeling pretty discouraged. It seems like we get stuck in this same place over and over and over."

"Yeah, I feel that way too. But the big thing for me is that I still feel really hurt about your comment that I'm not a giving person."

"Yeah, well, I'm still hurting too, but I'm not really ready to talk about it more right now."

For the time being, that concludes the "check-in." Neither person may be thrilled, but at least both people know what is going on. Typically, our fantasies are much worse than anything the other person is really feeling. By reestablishing just a moment of communication, the pain we create for ourselves through our own fantasies can at least be kept to a minimum.

Accepting the inevitability of differences in timing

In the awkward making-up sequence described earlier in this chapter on page 183, Gary made the first attempt at reconciliation and was rebuffed. When Susan later attempted reconciliation, Gary was still so upset at being rebuffed that he rejected her efforts. This may be the result of a power struggle, but just as likely it is the result of a simple fact of life: Because we are individuals, we each have a different pace for handling our feelings.

Some people get over their hurt feelings or anger faster than others. One person may be more upset by a fight and may require more time to recover. Whatever the reason, it is not helpful for couples to expect that they will always agree on the "right time" to make up. It is a bit like the great myth of simultaneous orgasms. It is nice when it happens, but if you get too focused on making it happen, both people can get so uptight that it blocks the natural flow of feelings. For the same reason, the right time for making up is always indicated by our feelings, not by an arbitrary "should" such as the belief that "because I'm ready, you should be ready."

Above all, try to look upon the differences in timing as another example of the differences in your inner realities. By honoring them we leave room for the relationship to flourish, translating individual differences into shared strengths.

Making certain you are ready to make up

Look at another reason that Gary's first attempt may have been rebuffed. He gets very anxious when he and Susan feel bad about each other. Most of us are like this to some degree. It is very easy to respond to anxiety and rush into peacemaking efforts, failing to acknowledge that we are still genuinely upset with the other person. As a result, we might make a move toward reconciliation, but because our upset feelings are still very much present, our comments contain some hidden barbs that perhaps are not quite so hidden as we might want to believe.

In the emotionally charged post-fight state, the other person may be particularly sensitive to these barbs, tuning in on them like a supersensitive radar system. He (or she) is quite likely to react to those barbs rather than to your efforts to make up. If you are in Gary's position, that is, the person making the overture and getting rebuffed, you might conclude that the other person does not really want to make up. However, this might not be the case. Put yourself on the receiving end of the premature peacemaking efforts. You might conclude that the person making the overture could not possibly be serious about reconciliation or he wouldn't have loaded his comments with barbs.

This same phenomenon occurs when people react to beliefs that they "ought to" or "should be" nice, charitable, and loving. They let their "shoulds" override their awareness of their actual feelings of anger, upset or resentment. Their problem is that what you actually feel will get communicated as loudly—probably louder—than your efforts at being nice. It is a little like the times when you were a child and your mother insisted you give poor old Aunt Charlene a kiss, though you really did not like her. It was a pretty dense relative who did not get the message that you were putting on this display of affection against your will. Not only that, it probably made you more resentful of Aunt Charlene, and less able to develop warm, caring feelings.

Be honest with yourself about when you are willing to let go of your feelings. If you move to make up before you are ready, you are more likely to fan the embers into a major blaze than to cool them off. If you sense your partner's attempt at making peace is genuine (no barbs), but you are simply not ready to make up yet, then you can leave the door open but still not rush yourself by: (1) letting your partner know that you realize they are making a peace gesture, and (2) expressing your own need for more time.

INSTEAD OF: *Well, that may be fine for you to be all lovey-dovey, you didn't just have somebody dump all over you.*

TRY: *I hear that you want to make up but I'm still really upset. I just need a little more time to myself. Otherwise, I'm afraid we'll just get back into a fight.*

By explaining, you offer a reason the other person can relate to. She (or he) probably does not want the fight to flare up either. Without an explanation, it is easy to assume that taking more time is just "holding out" and a way of punishing.

If you sense that the other person's effort at peacemaking is also filled with barbs, you may need to send a more explicit message:

"I hear you wanting to make up, but I also felt some barbs. I'm still upset. I need more time, because if I react now, we're going to be right back into a fight."

The good thing about this message is that it acknowledges the peacemaking effort (something the other person needs to hear) and it also acknowledges the barbs (something you need to express). The danger is that when you point out the barbs, the other person may react as if you judged him or her. In truth, you did. "Barbs" is not exactly a non-judgmental term. Keep in mind one important distinction, though. You felt barbs. That is a fact. Leave room for the possibility that the other person did not actually send barbs. The message above does exactly this.

For some people the making-up period extends over several days. Meanwhile, it is a strain on everyone. This uncomfortable period is often described as "walking on eggs" or "walking a tightrope." If you try to keep it up for too long you will start feeling resentful. It is probably not a bad idea to avoid snapping at each other a lot. But you will both be relieved, and you will be able to get back to more genuine feelings, if you do not feel obliged to play a saintly role.

This also applies to peace gestures such as buying flowers and writing poems. The ideal gestures are those which are natural for you. Stay in character. Exaggerated behaviors or complete turnarounds are likely to arouse suspicion rather than create goodwill. If it is in character for you to write poems, do that. If it is in character for you to buy gifts, do that. But keep in mind that for most people extravagant gifts smack of buying your way out of the doghouse or can be interpreted as a kind of emotional blackmail. Whatever the gesture, make it a gesture of love, not penance or bribery. It is the emotion behind the gesture that counts.

Signaling the beginning of the thaw

My wife and I have developed a little signal for when we are not all the way back to feeling okay, but we still want to reassure each other that we care. We hold up a little finger, and if the other one is ready to get a little bit closer, we will entwine little fingers and give a tentative smile. This little gesture evolved out of times when we tried to literally "shake on it" and found that shaking hands was too much of a commitment, not entirely congruent with our feelings. Our entwined little fingers said, in effect, "we're still upset with each other but we acknowledge our essential connectedness, and know that we will make up soon."

There is not a whole lot of risk in holding up your little finger—it is not like saying, "I was wrong." If the other person says, "I'm not ready yet," there is some sense of rejection, but it is not overwhelming.

This gesture is sufficiently intimate, and so much our own creation, that I am not sure we have ever discussed it in public before. But I am sure that other couples have developed similar signals, and you may already have one that you have taken for granted. Developing signals can give couples a way to test the waters when they are still afraid of being rebuffed.

Evaluating the Fight

Any value gained during a conflict can be lost through inappropriate judgments we impose on the act of fighting itself. Right after a fight we are particularly prone to judging according to our old attitudes toward fighting. We may hear an inner voice saying, "See I told you not to be a whiner. You have really made a mess of things now." In order to quell the complaints of this inner voice, we may try to keep a lid on our complaints to avoid fights, but this only ensures that when fights do erupt, they are going to be bad ones. We might hear another little voice telling us, "Don't let them run all over you. Stand up for yourself. Be firm." So after the fight, we engage in posturing to show how tough we really are, sabotaging any potential for intimacy.

If you do not want early childhood influences to dictate what happens after your fights, you need to develop a new, very clear sense of what a "useful" fight is to you as an adult. By establishing a new, adult set of criteria, you will be better able to spot and appreciate the real benefits your fights can have. These new criteria also can help you identify behaviors you want to change, and they show you when you are making progress that is in agreement with your adult choices. Some couples even sit down and evaluate their fights together, sorting out childhood judgments from adult observations. This can be very valuable, although, as I will be discussing later, we take the risk of starting a "fight about the fight."

George Bach, a psychotherapist who was a pioneer in teaching couples how to "fight fair," suggested that couples formally evaluate their fights and identify desired changes. Bach suggested that first you can evaluate fight in terms of the things that were said and done during the fight. Second, you can evaluate them by how you felt afterward.

Here are the key factors to look for in evaluation:

Behaviors during the fight

FIGHT RULES: Did you observe the fight rules you and your partner had agreed upon? If you broke them, did you monitor yourself and get back on track?

LISTENING: Did you accept and acknowledge each other's feelings? Did you use too little or too much Active Listening? Do you both feel that you were understood?

EMOTIONS: Did you concentrate on expressing emotions instead of judgments? Were emotions expressed openly by both you and your partner? Did you express your emotions in ways that minimized blame and accusation?

OWNERSHIP: Did you stay on "your own side of the line"? Did you acknowledge that your emotions were the result of your own interpretations and meanings or did you insist that they were the "truth"? Or instead, did you drag in other people's emotions to justify your own, encouraging further escalation?

ESCALATION: Did you engage in behaviors, such as expanding the issue, which escalated the fight? Did you avoid provocative generalizations such as "you always" or "you never"? When you did engage in behaviors which escalated the fight, did you monitor yourself and make a conscious decision to halt further escalations?

INJURY: Were any of your verbal blows "below the belt"? Did you protect the relationship at the same time you fought?

STAYING CURRENT: Did you address issues in the present or did you bring up past grievances? Did you have a whole accumulation of grievances, instead of just one or two?

EQUALITY: Were you both actively involved in the fight or did one person stay uninvolved, withdrawn? Did either of you try to use power on the other?

VOICE TONE: Did either of you consistently use voice tones which were patronizing, provocative or phony?

Emotional effects of the fight

HURT: As a result of the fight, do you or your partner feel more (or less) hurt, offended, weakened, put down or humiliated?

FEAR: Has the fight increased or decreased your fear of fighting? Has the fight increased or decreased your fear of your partner?

INFORMATION: Do you know more about the issues as a result of the fight? Are you clearer on where you stand, and why; where your partner stands, and why?

HOPE FOR RESOLUTION: Do you feel that your chances of eventually resolving this issue have improved as a result of the fight, or did they get worse?

TRUST: As a result of the fight, do you have more or less trust that your partner will let you know what is bothering him (or her); will listen to what is bothering you; or will fight within agreed-upon limits?

CATHARSIS: Do you both feel better for having expressed your emotions? Does it seem as if the fight helped you "get something off your chest," "unburdened" you, or "purged" you of certain emotions?

INFLUENCE: As a result of this fight, do you feel that you have greater (or less) influence or impact on your partner where this issue is concerned?

REVENGE: Did the fight leave you with a desire to "get even" or to find a way to get back at your partner?

CLOSENESS / INTIMACY: Do you feel that you understand your partner a little better or that you feel he (or she) understands you better or that you feel closer in other ways as a result of the fight?

Scoring the fight

It is not necessary or perhaps even desirable to cover every one of these questions every time you critique a fight. You might cover them all the first two or three times, just to help clarify the kinds of questions that can be important.

Look for connections between the behaviors during the fight and the feelings you later experienced. This way you begin to recognize which behaviors produce trust and confidence, and which are undermining. You may identify key behaviors—such as not listening to the other person, not taking responsibility for escalation as it was occurring or "crossing the line"—that made the fight unpleasant or painful, and then you can work together to change these behaviors.

While these connections between behavior and emotions are very important, fights can trigger feelings which have little if anything to do with how the fight was fought. For example, in a fight one couple had about money, the wife's feelings of panic dated back to when she was only three years old. Her father had become very ill and had lost his job, bringing great financial hardship to the entire family. Only when she clearly saw this link between the present and the past was she able to look at her and her husband's financial difficulties more objectively.

The most emotionally volatile issues that arise in our close relationships tend to be that way because they have long histories, sometimes stretching clear back to birth, and possibly even prior to birth. Early childhood experiences of being unloved, separated, ignored, discounted, abandoned or belittled can be restimulated by present events. So if you feel really devastated by a fight, it may not be because of the way it was fought. Rather, it might be because the conflict brought up emotional issues that have painful roots in your past.

It is important to identify the source of your upset following a fight so that you can prevent such an upset in the future. If the upset came from the way you fought, you may want to discuss setting new fight rules. If the upset linked up with past emotional issues, seek new insights that can help you liberate yourself from the past.

How do you make the distinction between present and past sources of hurt? If a fight was well fought (meaning, openly and directly, and with a concern for the relationship), but you are left feeling very upset, this is usually a pretty good indication that your feelings have more to do with your past than with the present fight.

In nearly all our interactions, we automatically use the other person as a kind of mirror, reflecting back our own inner realities. Thus, one man's extremely emotional reaction to his particularly authoritarian boss mirrored back to him old issues of being intimidated by his overbearing father. Similarly, a woman who was extremely upset by her teenaged daughter's messy room found that it mirrored her own difficulties with self-discipline.

In fights, this mirroring is often expressed by blaming other people for our own feelings. Mirroring is so much a part of the human experience that we can hardly label it abnormal. We become comfortable with this behavior not by eliminating it but by acknowledging and taking responsibility for it.

Taking responsibility for mirroring, which is so often at the core of a fight, starts with getting clear about where our upset feelings really begin. If the problem is that you need to resolve emotional issues inside yourself, then concentrating on how the fight was conducted can be a dead end, leading only to further conflict.

Should You Evaluate a Fight Together?

A tremendous amount of learning can take place when a couple evaluates a fight together, but there is also a genuine risk of getting into a fight about the fight. If you do not evaluate the fight, you are not going to learn from it. But you also want to allow your wounds to heal rather than constantly picking the scabs.

There are certainly advantages to having a trained third party help you evaluate your fights (see Tool #12). But if you do not have such a person in your life, should you risk evaluating your fights on your own? The best way to answer that is for you both to read this material and discuss very honestly and openly how you each feel about taking it on. If either of you feels reluctant to do so, try going through the same evaluation process on your own. Sometimes in the privacy of our own minds we can be more honest about our own behavior than we can when we are faced with the possibility of a second person's criticism.

If you each do a good job of staying on your own side of the line, and are good Active Listeners, the risk of evaluating your fights together are greatly reduced. The key issue, however, is how willing you are to acknowledge and be responsible for your own contribution to the fight, no matter how difficult you feel your partner may have been.

One reason people dread critique sessions is that they tend to concentrate on failings, ignoring the things people have done really well. So I urge you to remember to acknowledge what you have both done well in your fights, even as you are looking at the areas you would like to change. Tell your partner how you feel you have improved in the way you fight, as well as letting them know of areas where you feel they have improved.

While evaluating a fight, talk about your own behavior—"I realized that I was getting on your side of the line when I started analyzing why you were late." When you talk about your partner's behavior, concentrate on how that behavior affected you—"I felt hurt when you…" rather than judging it—"You were really nasty…"

Try fight evaluation as an experiment. For one thing, it forces you to look at your own behaviors more objectively. You begin to see how your behavior influences others. It helps you become aware of "process," that is, how you are fighting instead of only what you are fighting about.

As you increase your own awareness, you will find it easier to modify your behavior when you recognize that it is not constructive. Regardless of how you choose to do it, you will find that evaluating your fights leads to valuable self-knowledge. Doors will open to you, revealing much about your relationship, your partner, and of course, yourself.

Moving Toward Problem Solving

My clients often tell me they discover that fights are not endings but beginnings. Fights open doors to important issues. But once they have surfaced, and after you have discharged the emotional tension you have experienced, what do you do next? We turn now to the development of problem-solving skills.

PART IV

PROBLEM-SOLVING

TOOLS

Identify the Real Issue and Its

Appropriate Problem-Solving Strategy

Before we move on, I would like to offer two cardinal rules about problem solving: (1) Fights and problem solving do not mix; and (2) You must take care of emotional issues first. Let me explain.

Fights and Problem Solving Do Not Mix

During a fight, your body is usually surging with adrenaline as your whole being mobilizes to cope with a threat. In this state, it is extremely difficult to see the other person as a collaborator working on an equal basis to find a solution. During the heat of battle we see the other person as the problem, and this clearly fails to generate the emotional atmosphere we need for problem solving. Instead we need the feeling that we have a problem and we are working together to solve it.

I am not saying that we can or even should try to avoid fights. Sometimes there is just too much emotion invested in an issue to calmly seek a solution. If you do not confront your feelings, they will find their way into the most well-intentioned problem-solving sessions, distorting even your best efforts.

Take Care of Emotional Issues First

I have known all too many couples who, shoving their emotions aside, grit their teeth and push through "calm and rational" problem-solving sessions, only to discover that no matter how sophisticated their problem-solving skills or how rational their approach, their "unexpressed" emotions surface. Suspicion that the other person will not keep his (or her) end of an agreement or an unwillingness to consider the other person's needs can often be the products of repressed emotions and can provoke a major fight. Unresolved feelings of resentment, for example, can bubble up when we least expect them, perhaps causing us to "forget" what we have agreed to do for our part of a solution, thus sabotaging the problem solving we thought we had already accomplished.

In day-to-day problem solving between two people, you need to have some trust that once you have reached an agreement, each of you will hold up your end of the bargain. You cannot bring in the cops or take each other to court every time one of you violates an agreement that you have worked out together. If you feel good about each other after a fight, and have gained an element of trust, you are likely to succeed if you charge right into a problem-solving session. If, however, you still feel antagonistic after a fight, it is best to set up another time for problem solving.

Of course, there will be times when there is a compelling external reason for solving the problem immediately. For example, if you are in the middle of an argument about whose turn it is to take the car and you both have appointments, you may have to solve the problem while your emotions are still quite heated.

If you get together for a problem-solving session and you find that things are still pretty edgy, this is a clue that there is still some emotion that needs to be discharged. Because some time has passed since the original fight that uncovered these feelings, it may be possible to express your feelings openly without blame or accusation or to use Active Listening. If these more moderate alternatives do not work, it may be necessary for the fight to continue before you are both ready to problem-solve. The harsh reality is that when you are ready, you are ready, and when you are not, you are not.

Communicate Problems, Not Solutions

Start out by clarifying your feelings, instead of telling people what you want them to do. This allows them to look at the problem and perhaps collaborate with you to seek a solution.

When my wife and I first married, our marriage created a conglomerate family of five kids, four of them already in their teens. Naturally there was a certain amount of tension as we got used to living together. The kids responded to this difficult period by avoiding dinnertime, the single time in the day when a family naturally comes together.

The children seemed to get an endless string of invitations from friends and relatives. I began to worry that with everyone off in different directions, we would never be able to create a family. I thought about numerous activities we could do together, but finally concluded that having everybody at the dinner table would be the most natural.

One night I announced a new set of rules to regulate how often people could miss dinner. The purpose, of course, was to encourage more interaction, but I explained this only in passing. My emphasis was on the rules. The rules were somewhat elaborate, with different ones applying on weekdays and weekends, and so on. But the emotional message that came through to the kids was, "You must come to dinner!"

Now, having five kids sitting around the table cursing me under their breath was not exactly what I had in mind. I only wanted to create a good family feeling. Instead I managed to produce just the opposite. And then it suddenly dawned on me: I was no longer working on creating a good family feeling; I was working on getting people to the dinner table. Because I told them what to do because of my feelings, rather than describing the feelings themselves, we were locked in a power struggle. I wanted the kids to come to dinner. The kids resisted. The potential existed for a major battle.

Finally, I became wise enough to go back to the original problem and say, "Look, this whole thing about dinner is that I am worried about creating a good family feeling, and I think we are going to have to do some things together to feel comfortable living with each other."

The kids' response was to come up with a number of ideas, many of which I had had on my list of ideas but had not suggested out of fear I would be rushing things. Soon, people being gone at dinner was no longer an issue. On the contrary, our kids started inviting their friends and relatives over for dinner.

I started out by presenting what I thought was the solution—getting everybody to the dinner table at one time. But offering the solution created a power struggle. When I finally got around to offering "the problem," we actually started working together, getting comfortable as a family.

Again and again, I see people making the same mistakes I made— offering solutions instead of problems.

Assuming that everyone perceives the original problem exactly as you do, you just might get everyone to go along with you. However, the other people might not see the problem as you do or even know about the problem. They may simply not agree that a problem even exists.

Unless everyone involved is in complete agreement on the situation, offering solutions creates two brand new problems.

The solution we offer becomes the definition of the problem

When we offer a solution, the problem may never get clearly defined. For example, when I announced my dinner rules, no one else could have known that my goal was to create a good family feeling. The solution I offered led everyone to believe that my purpose was quite singular—to get people to come to dinner. When a wife proposes that she and her husband eat at L'Argent Grosse (the most expensive restaurant in town), he probably does not know she is trying to be close to him. He only knows that dinner at L'Argent Gross will blow the family budget. And that is a brand new conflict to fight about.

The sad thing is that there might have been scores of alternative solutions offered if the people involved were given the opportunity to contribute. However, this can never happen as long as the problem remains obscured by one person's proposed answers. Taking time to clarify the problem may be the most important factor in the process of problem solving.

Offering solutions is particularly exaggerated if you are a person who takes a problem and goes "underground" with it for minutes, hours, days and then emerges with a carefully mapped-out solution.

Offering the solution sets up a power struggle

When we fail to tell another person our feelings, we are robbing them of the opportunity to take a look at the problem and participate in seeking a solution. When I tell you what to do, particularly without giving you a good reason for it, you are faced with an either-or choice. You either accept my solution or you reject it.

By contrast, if I present you with a problem and ask you to help me, it is an invitation to work together. By working together, we are equals, sharing a vested interest. We can feel good about each other and build confidence in our ability to solve problems together. But if I simply notify you one day that I have a solution and I expect you to participate, I am no longer treating you as an equal. In fact, along with the solution I am sending a message that my needs and my answer are more important or better than yours. The first few times I thrust a solution upon you, you may go along with it to please me. But over time this can wear thin. Even if the solutions seemed reasonable every time, there is still the underlying message that I see myself in a superior position, the person with all the answers. For most people this would become a source of resentment, and in time, my announcement of a new solution could become the opening volley for a major power struggle. In addition, just because I have a problem with something in our relationship does not mean that you do or even should.

A young couple came to a counseling session desperate to save their relationship. The problems had started when the husband began working overtime, coming home late at night with no energy left for his wife. She felt abandoned and began wondering if he still loved her. This situation presented a big problem for her. But he was working on a project that he found tremendously exciting and satisfying. At least for the moment his lack of contact with his wife was not a problem for him.

One day she announced her solution, and actually delivered an ultimatum. She said that if he wanted to continue being married to her, he would just have to stop putting in so many hours of overtime. Immediately a power struggle began. He accused her of being jealous of his involvement with his career. He was convinced that she did not want him to enjoy his work quite so much. She counterattacked that he put his work before his marriage.

The escalation stopped only when she withdrew her original proposal for a solution and went back to working with her husband to define the problem.

As soon as the wife told her husband she was feeling abandoned, alone, and in need of reassurance that he still loved her, the young couple was able to see their conflict in a new light. He had been afraid that he was being forced to choose between his wife and his job. She feared she would have to give up their intimacy unless he gave up his job and his overtime.

Working together, they dropped the original solution and stepped back to define the problem. From there, the path to a mutual solution was easy. The young man loved his wife very much and was deeply moved, and even flattered, by her need to feel closer to him. They then agreed that one weekend a month they would get away together to some romantic place, a solution which was satisfying for both.

As we become more familiar with the issues at stake, we can save a huge amount of energy, and possibly pain, by asking ourselves: "Will the way I am communicating my feelings encourage the other person into mutual problem solving? Or will it make it more difficult for us to define the problem and solve it?"

Problems outside the home are often very tangible. They involve property or production schedules or reports to supervisors or meeting with customers or seemingly endless needs and pressures. In closer relationships, however, many of our most difficult problems center on our emotions.

In a marriage, one or both partners may feel unloved, frustrated, separate, worried, left out or even abandoned. These emotions themselves are the problems that need to be addressed. In caring relationships, our partner's feelings matter to us, so we want to respond to those feelings if we can. However, if we feel coerced or controlled, it is difficult to be responsive. Instead, we retreat and wall ourselves off. We take defensive postures rather than share feelings. The alternative, which allows us to remain open to each other, is to communicate the feeling itself: "I'm feeling left out, not as close as I would like to feel," instead of sending the solution: "Next week you've got to stay home and pay attention to family matters."

What Kind of Issue Is This?

There is not just one kind of conflict. Some conflicts are over facts. Others are over issues such as feeling unloved or unneeded or having one's feeling suppressed or discounted. Others involve beliefs about responsibility, fairness, justice, morality, or ethics. Still others are over resources such as money, time, personal space, land or valuable objects.

Although a dispute may seem to focus on just one of these areas, it is rare that only a single issue is involved. An argument over the household budget, for example, may appear to be only over money. But as the argument progresses, we often discover that behind the money issue are strong feelings involving who has the right to control the family resources, and whose needs come first. Beyond this, the same conflict may involve beliefs about what is important in life: security, pleasure, getting ahead, etc.

While a number of general principles apply to all problem-solving situations, different kinds of issues may require different kinds of problem-solving skills. To explore how this works, let us consider the five examples below. In each case a couple is having a disagreement about buying a new car. Although they are all talking about the same thing, each dispute is different, requiring different problem-solving approaches.

EXAMPLE 1: Dispute over information

Paul and Liza are in a heated argument over leasing a car. Liza maintains that by leasing a car for sixty months they can get a more expensive car and still afford the payments. Paul would like the more expensive car, but insists that it is only possible to lease for forty-eight months, at least at reasonable interest rates. This sounds like a simple issue to resolve. But in reality it can become much more difficult. Here is part of their argument:

LIZA: *We could afford it if we put it on a sixty-month lease.*

PAUL: *Don't be silly. They don't make sixty-month leases.*

LIZA: *Of course they do. I saw it in an ad in the newspaper.*

PAUL: *You must have seen some come-on where you get stuck with a giant balloon payment. I remember when we bought the last car, the credit union only offered forty-eight month leases.*

LIZA: *Why do you have to be right about everything? I get so fed up with your sexist attitudes. I bet if I were a man, you'd accept what I said without question.*

PAUL: *Sex hasn't got a damn thing to do with it. You just see some silly ad trying to con the general public, and you don't bother to read the fine print. It's probably Ducky Dan or some other idiot car dealer who knows there are gullible people like you out there who never ask questions. Suddenly it's truth just because you saw it, and I'm not even supposed to ask questions.*

At this point, neither Paul, not Liza knows if it is possible to get a sixty-month lease. Liza might have read the ad wrong. Paul's memory might be wrong, the credit union's policy might have changed, or they might get their loan someplace other than the credit union. When information is challenged, it can turn into a fight about credibility and trust. When Paul does not accept Liza's information (and notice that he does not just question her information, he calls her "silly"),

Liza hears it as questioning her credibility. In no time at all, the fight has moved from a conflict about information into a bitter relationship conflict, with personal attacks lobbed back and forth from both sides. By the time the fight ends, it is difficult to see that the whole thing was touched off by some missing information.

But let us suppose that Paul noticed in the beginning that his conflict with Liza was over information. In that case, he might have said, "You know, I'm not sure what the facts are on leases. Let's call up a couple of lease agencies and find out what we can get."

Similarly, if Liza had noticed that this was a conflict about information, she might have said, "I didn't read all the fine print on that ad I saw so I have to admit that I don't have all the facts. But I'd like to check it out before we make a decision about which car we get."

I recommend the following three steps when you are fighting over each other's credibility:

STEP 1: Determine the kinds of information you each need to be satisfied.

STEP 2: Determine how the information should be gathered so you will both believe the data.

STEP 3: Set a date to get back together and review the information you have gathered.

When you follow these steps, you make it clear it is important that both people feel confidence in the information. By participating in decisions about the information-gathering process, both people have a stake in making certain that the information is credible.

For Paul and Liza this process might go something like this:

LIZA: *I'm willing to go out and get more information before we talk about this more, but can we first talk about the kind of information we need?*

PAUL: *I want to know how long a lease can go, and what the interest rate is for the different lengths of time. I also want to know what the deal is at the end of the lease, so that we don't owe a big balloon payment at the end.*

LIZA: *I know the credit union where we got our last lease has some different options, but maybe we can get a better deal somewhere else. I want to find out if any dealers offer better financing as an incentive.*

PAUL: *I'm afraid that the dealers won't give us all the facts so I want to be sure we also get information from the credit union and maybe a couple of banks or independent leasing companies.*

LIZA: *Okay, I agree with all that. But who's going to get the information? Since you're suspicious of dealers, why don't you talk to a couple of them, and I'll talk to the credit union and a couple of banks.*

PAUL: *That's fair. When should we be ready to talk about this again?*

LIZA: *How about Wednesday?*

PAUL: *That's fine with me.*

The solution to an information conflict centers on an agreement for getting the needed data, whether this is done in a short conversation as Paul and Liza did, or it is compiled in a fifty-page agreement, as is frequently the case with community or business disputes.

EXAMPLE 2: Dispute over a personal issue

Geoff has trouble making up his mind. He thinks he wants to buy a car but he just cannot decide on the model he wants. He has visited numerous dealers, but still is not closer to a decision. His wife, Marcia, has little or no interest in what car he buys since she has a car of her own with which she is quite satisfied. She thinks Geoff worries too much about money anyway, and as far as she is concerned, the difficulty he is having making a decision is his own personal problem. She feels exasperated by Geoff's indecisiveness.

If Marcia could acknowledge that this was Geoff's internal conflict which he has to work out for himself, the dispute would end there. But couples rarely approach this kind of problem that way. So many of the conflicts we face in our relationships start out with one person having a personal problem. The other person gets involved because they want to be helpful, they think they know a way to solve their partner's problem or they get their own issues mixed up with the other person's, and the original problem gets blurred.

Here are a few common examples of personal problems that often precipitate conflicts between couples:

- Choices about personal grooming and what to wear
- Dietary habits
- Committing to an exercise program
- Choosing jobs or careers
- Deciding how to relate to one's own parents

As an adult, you certainly have the right to decide what you are going to wear, what you will eat, how you treat your parents, and so on. If you have problems concerning any of these they are, theoretically, your problems. Yet bloody battles have been fought between couples over every single issue on this list.

Here are four reasons why personal issues become disputes that complicate the problem-solving process.

• Unclear boundaries

Many parents believe they have the right, or perhaps the duty, to control their children's choices concerning dress, eating habits, career direction, school attendance, etc. As children move toward adulthood, however, it hopefully becomes clear that they need to feel confidence about making such decisions on their own. Why, then, do we assume that having attained adulthood we somehow should give up the right to make such decisions on our own when we enter a relationship? Many of us labor under a romantic fantasy that when two people really care about each other there are no barriers or boundaries.

Most family therapists believe that the foundation for healthy re-lationships consists of strong, well-defined boundaries. Yet many of us feel that it is our job to fix any problem a loved one may be having, and do not recognize that this violates the other person's boundaries. Rather than being supportive, it is actually a message that we do not trust that person to solve their problems without our help.

• The belief that others should fix our emotions

In relationships, we may feel embarrassed by the other person's behavior, concerned about them or even tired of their problems. There is a tendency to expect them to change their behavior so that we will not have to experience those emotions anymore. In the effort to get our partners to change for us, there is the message: "If you really loved me, you'd do what I want you to do so that I won't have to feel uncomfortable anymore."

This assumption can create a great deal of conflict. You have the right to tell your husband that you feel embarrassed when he wears his hand-painted tie that looks like a rainbow trout. But he has every right to say, "I feel bad that you find it embarrassing, but I really feel good about wearing it." That leaves you with a problem, but it is your problem, not his.

• Overlapping problems

As an adult, I have a right to eat what I want. If that means I have a weight problem, that is my problem, not my wife's—at least in theory. But in our day-to-day lives, we all know it is not quite that simple. If I get too fat, my wife may find me unattractive and lose interest in me sexually. Then I will have a problem.

We both have problems, but while these may be related they are not the same. And if we are to solve these problems, we must recog-nize their differences and act accordingly. How I regulate my weight is my problem and there is no reason she should get involved in that issue—except if it creates fuss and muss in the kitchen, problems in shopping, and disputes over division of these chores. I may go on a liquid diet, join a weight-loss program, eat only raw carrots and celery for a month or whatever. That is up to me.

But if she does not see me regulating my weight, she often becomes upset and starts commenting on how I am eating. To unravel it, I have to acknowledge that my failure to regulate my weight affects her, and she has to stop trying to control how I accomplish it.

As we will see in later chapters, these apparently subtle distinctions in how problems are defined can have substantial impact on whether problems in relationships can be solved to both people's satisfaction.

• Judgments and values

We violate others' boundaries any time we make judgments about the way they handle a problem or assert that we know a better way. But if you are able to demonstrate to your partner how his or her behavior affects you in a tangible way, your partner should understand why you have a right to comment on (not take control of) what he is doing. If that person's behavior does not affect you tangibly, but simply violates your sense of protocol, then they have every right to set boundaries with you and tell you to "lay off" if you cross them.

For example: If your partner needs to upgrade his wardrobe and does this by cashing in your life savings and buying everything at the most expensive store in town, that solution clearly has a tangible effect on you. But if you think he should see a color consultant to tell him what to choose, your nagging him about it crosses the boundaries of his personal problem.

When other people have problems, your role is best limited to being a listener and, only if requested, a consultant. If your partner is really troubled by something but it does not tangibly affect you, then your most useful asset will be Active Listening. Listen to your partner, serve as a sounding board, offer advice when solicited, but do not make it your job to try to fix his or her feelings. To do so will turn almost any personal problem into a relationship conflict.

EXAMPLE 3: Dispute over relationship issues

Sam and Dawn begin casually talking about buying a new car. They quickly find themselves in an argument over who decides when it is time to buy one. Dawn feels that Sam insists that all decisions have to get made according to his timetable. When he's finally made up his mind it is time to buy a car, then they do it. Sam accuses Dawn of always "pressuring" him to buy a new car, even when they cannot afford it. This issue of timing and feeling pressured comes up nearly every time Sam and Dawn are faced with making a mutual decision.

In the course of their argument, Dawn and Sam start throwing accusations, charges, and countercharges back and forth at each other—"We always have to do things according to your sense of tim-ing!" or "You're always pressuring me!" But the real problem is not cars. Both Dawn and Sam feel that somehow their needs are not being considered by the other person. Dawn feels that Sam does not value her because he "always has to do things according to his time-table." Sam feels that Dawn does not value or love him because she is "always pressuring him" to buy a new car or take a vacation, etc.

It is important to make a distinction between "content" and "re-lationship" disputes. When both people feel loved, valued or accepted, it is possible to have significant disputes about content or subject matter and still feel good about each other. But when you are not sure where you stand in your relationship, there is always a nagging fear that you will not be loved, valued or respected if you truly speak your mind. These doubts are often expressed in unpleasant little squabbles. These squabbles can seem, on the surface, to be about specific subjects, yet there is a sameness about every one of them, which comes from the fact that underlying every disagreement is the same old question: "Am I really important to you?"

If Sam and Dawn can recognize this same relationship issue emerging again and again in virtually every conflict they have, they can stop talking about cars and vacations for a while and start addressing their relationship concerns more openly. Then they can start focusing on the key problem that needs to be resolved, and when that is resolved, their problems about cars and vacations will be easy to handle.

Close relationships constantly undergo redefinition and adjustment. So just because you have been married for twenty years, have been successful in business together or are part of a family, does not mean all your relationship issues are settled once and for all. There are both external and internal influences that force us to reexamine our relationships. As an example of an external influence, the women's movement of the last twenty years has brought about a major redefinition of relationships between men and women. Almost all the issues raised by the women's movement are relationship issues, concerning relationships with spouses, with authority figures, with siblings and offspring. On the surface the issue might be wages or maternity leave, but the consistent underlying issue is equality—being valued as an individual. Where there has been a failure to value women—for example, when lower wages are paid to women than to men performing the same work—then responding to the relationship issues will also require significant behavioral change.

Personal transitions in our lives—such as uncertainties about our careers, challenges raising our children, changes in business demands, mid-life crises, anxieties about getting older, friends moving away or dying—can also bring about shifts in our relationships, raising anxieties about being loved, valued, and accepted.

While relationship issues can reflect what is going on between you and your partner, they may also reflect what is going on inside you or the other person. If you are feeling bad about yourself, you may feel that you are not loved, valued, or accepted by the other person, whether or not it is true. In this case, you need to resolve your own insecurities before you will be able to experience how the other person feels toward you.

There are few people in this world who do not occasionally project their own feelings of inadequacy or worthlessness onto the behavior of their loved ones, rather than dealing with these feelings independently. For example, a man going through a mid-life crisis, questioning whether he has done anything worthwhile in his life, is very likely to blame his family for his feelings. The usual complaint is, "If I hadn't a family to support, I would have..." Nor does it necessarily take a dramatic life event to confuse personal issues with relationship issues.

Inside all of us are old wounds which, when restimulated, can cause us to feel unlovable, valueless or even unacceptable. At those times it is really difficult to sort out what is personal and what is a relationship problem. The solution to a relationship problem might be found in a change of behavior for one or both people. But if personal issues are involved, no immediate behavioral solution is possible, because one or both people will continue to feel unlovable or valueless no matter what behaviors change.

As I have reiterated throughout this book, feelings are the result of the meanings we bring to events. Some people, for example, feel "pressured" any time another person asks them to do something, and no matter how gentle and caring the request, they still experience the sense of being pressured. The person who feels the pressure is the only one who can do anything about changing what he (or she) feels; what is felt comes from inside, not from the other person. As long as we are projecting meaning that really is not there, it is a personal problem.

The resolution of relationship problems, more than any other kind of problem, requires careful use of communication skills. When Dawn comes to Sam with a grievance about timing and decision making, Active Listening can help both of them determine how much of this is Dawn's problem and how much is Sam's.

Relationship problems are always about emotions; thus, their solutions must be responsive to emotions. This often involves changing behaviors in order to meet an emotional need. It can be extremely difficult, however, to determine exactly what change in behavior will satisfy which emotional need. For example, if you feel unloved, what exactly can your loved one do that would allow you to feel loved? Unless you can be specific, it is difficult for your loved one to respond, and it may seem to him or her that this is just another unanswerable grievance.

When someone tells you, "I feel unloved," they fail to define how you can help in working out a solution to that problem. But if they say, "I feel unloved when you spend so much time at the office" or "feel put down when you make decisions without consulting me," they offer some very clear clues about what you can do. If the office is taking up a lot of time during the week, perhaps you can schedule more time to be together on the weekends. If you struggle—as Dawn and Sam did—over whose sense of timing is correct for making decisions, you may be able to mutually agree on criteria such as, "We'll consider buying a car after we have two thousand dollars in our reserve account." Or you might make "assignments": Dawn taking the lead on decisions about cars, Sam taking the lead on decisions about house repairs. Of course, while one person may take the lead, the two will make the final decisions together.

EXAMPLE 4: Dispute over values

Ted and Judith, who are business partners married to each other, are in a dispute about a new car for their small company. Because Ted wants to make sure the car they get impresses potential clients, he proposes buying an expensive, high-status car. Judith has been reading a number of consumer reports and prefers a less expensive and less prestigious car which has an excellent repair record. Ted agrees that Judith's information about repairs and maintenance is probably correct, so this is not a dispute about information. They made a joint decision that it was time to buy a new car, so this is not a relationship dispute. It is simply that Ted thinks status is more important that economy, and Judith thinks economy is more important than status. This is a dispute about values.

The biggest difficulty with value-oriented conflicts is that values usually seem nonnegotiable. If you believe that freedom and human dignity are the highest values, you cannot negotiate with a person who believes that racial segregation or sexual discrimination are okay. In a relationship, if one side compromises in order to settle a dispute, she (or he) may feel that they have just "sold out." They may perceive it not as just a personal loss, but as a violation of moral principles.

The first step toward finding resolutions to value conflicts is to recognize the problem for what it is. Many couples find it difficult to recognize when they are in a conflict over differing values. One reason is that we usually form close relationships with people who share our values. Because their values are so similar to ours, we simply do not develop many skills for recognizing value differences or solving problems that arise because of them. In some cases, however, until our values are put to the test by a conflict, we may not even be aware that we have them. It may be only in the face of a conflict that we clearly confront what really matters to us. So what do we do when someone we care about has different values?

To solve their problem, Ted and Judith have to get past the idea that one of them is right while the other is wrong. They do this by seeking a common ground, focusing on the probable fact that both have equal interest in making certain that their business succeeds. After that, they try to determine which choice of cars will best serve that shared purpose. For example, they may determine that it is most important to have a luxury car to impress potential investors at this time. Or they may decide that the car will be so rarely used for that purpose that economic considerations should determine the selection of the car. On those rare occasions when they need to impress a client, they decide they can rent a luxury car and still be money ahead.

Although buying a car may not be particularly serious moral dilemma, the same strategy holds true for resolving more sensitive conflicts concerning values. Whether the conflict is over children attending religious services, risking the family's financial resources to start a business or even abortion, the principles are the same: Since values are not negotiable, disputes over values require that you stop competing over who is right and start looking for the values which you both share.

EXAMPLE 5: Dispute over resources

Before they go out to buy their new car, Steve and Sarah get into a discussion about who will get to be the main driver of it. They would both like to drive it rather than their old beat-up second car. They both work, and they both admit that there is not compelling reason why one person needs the new car more than the other. But they would both like to drive the new car because it is a lot nicer than the old one. They are arguing over a scarce, valuable resource. Disputes over resources can be about money, property, possessions or other valuable resources which are in limited supply.

Disputes over scarce resources may actually be easier to resolve than the other disputes we have already discussed. Unfortunately, resource disputes often get complicated by an overlay of personal, relationship, and value-oriented issues. For example, Steve and Sarah's dispute about who gets to drive the new car may lead them into relationship issues, such as, "If you really loved me, you'd know that my pleasure in driving the new car is more important than your comfort on your commute to work." All these arguments are attempts to influence the outcome and gain the use of the new car. None of them really directly addresses the issue of determining the use of scarce resources.

Steve and Sarah's problem is really quite simple. They both want the car. While the definition of the problem is straightforward, solving it in a mutually acceptable manner will require the skills we describe in the next two chapters.

Aim at Win-Win Outcomes

Through Collaborative Problem Solving

Imagine football games where both teams go away winners, or courts of law where plaintiffs and defendants are always equally satisfied with the decisions, or political elections where all candidates get exactly the office they want. Adversarial relationships are so much a part of our lives that entertaining these possibilities seems almost laughable.

Most of us assume that wherever there is a winner there must be a loser, and we each spend an inestimable amount of time and energy making certain we stay with the winners. But the whole idea of winners and losers, when applied to intimate relationships, becomes destructive. Indeed, if we are to have constructive, caring relationships, we need to seek an alternative to this way of thinking.

In adversarial relationships there are winners and losers; a person who feels that he (or she) has lost will naturally feel some degree of resentment toward the "winner." That resentment may result in the person withdrawing, becoming more competitive or in any number of behaviors aimed at "getting even." Here are just a few examples:

- Every time Fran tries to talk over a problem with her husband Chip, he belittles, intimidates, and humiliates her. It has happened so many times that Fran now considers it utterly hopeless even to attempt to talk to him. It just is not worth it for her to undergo his emotional outbursts. For weeks after one of these incidents she is not interested in sex with Chip. She has also begun to shift her attention from Chip to her children and friends. She is pleasant with her husband but she does not share any of her real feelings with him.

- When Gene and Sally fight, Gene feels he comes out on the short end of the stick. He has trouble expressing his emotions, and she is so verbal he feels that he just cannot hold his own with her. He also sees Sally as having very fixed ideas about the way things should be, unwilling or unable even to consider his wishes. He is not particularly aware of feeling resentful, but whenever he is out in public, he has a lot of stories to tell about Sally, most of which show her in anything but a good light.

- Early in their marriage, Dave was the only breadwinner in the family while Loretta stayed home and took care of the kids. As the breadwinner, Dave had often insisted that his needs should take priority over the other members of the family. Then as the children grew older and started attending school, Loretta went back to work. She did very well for herself, receiving a number of sizable raises until she now earns more than her husband. She knows that she should not do it, but whenever Dave gets too high and mighty, she cannot resist the urge to remind him that she earns more than he does. Dave, who is extremely upset by this, usually sulks and withdraws from her for several days afterward.

Sometimes the ways in which we get even after "losing" an adversarial confrontation are subtle, such as pouting for a few moments, and sometimes we engage in more aggressive actions to get back on top. When we constantly find ourselves on the short end of the stick, there is a part of us that almost automatically seeks out ways to get even or to protect ourselves emotionally. Over time, resentment can poison the best relationships, tearing apart the foundation of goodwill and love that might otherwise grow.

People who feel it is important to "win at any cost," without concern for what their winning does to the other person, need to be alerted to the fact that there are always two parts to any transaction. The first part is the particular issue that precipitates the initial conflict—such as how to spend this year's Christmas bonus or how to deal with a child coming home late on school nights. The second part is the emotional impact of the manner in which we address the issue.

You can get your way to achieve your goal with regard to a particular issue, but still end up the "loser" if the manner in which you "win" creates so much resentment that the other person withdraws or begins seeking ways to get even. Too many immediate victories can poison even the strongest relationships.

For any close relationship to work well, the partners need to realize that there are alternatives to the adversarial model, that it is possible to choose between immediate but shallow victories and the goals of deeper intimacy and acceptance. The husband who treats his wife's concerns as silly, unreasonable or unimportant may eventually notice that he has ceased to be a very important part of her life.

Win-Win Solutions Require Acceptance of Power

The couples who are most successful in dealing with conflict are those who know how to achieve the win-win outcome, where not only is the conflict resolved to everyone's satisfaction, but the relationship is improved.

There is a popular fallacy that in order to enjoy win-win outcomes, we must avoid using power in our relationships, but that is not the case. On the contrary, we arrive at win-win solutions only when we acknowledge and take responsibility for our use of power. We can create at least as many problems by not using our power as we do by using it. If we shift responsibility for exercising power to the other person, we may end up being resentful for the way things turn out. Of course, both people may choose not to use power, in which case we end up with no solution at all. I can illustrate this through the story of a young couple in a workshop who complained that they had great difficulty making decisions together. When I asked them to demonstrate this through role playing, they responded something like this:

HE: *What would you like to do tonight?*

SHE: *Oh, I don't care; whatever you want to do.*

HE: *Well, I asked you first.*

At this point, one of them often got frustrated and started accusing the other of never wanting to make a decision. As accommodating as they were trying to be, this couple's efforts not to use power usually ended up in a fight.

We must recognize that we all have power in some form, and that we must take responsibility for exercising it. That power may range from manipulating another person into getting our own way to transforming conflicts into deeper understanding for all concerned. Knowing how to handle our own power is the key to transforming adversarial relationships into cooperative ones where everyone wins.

When we think about power, the first thing that pops into mind may be physical power. In this, the most blatant use of power, the perpetrator uses weapons, physical threat or physical restraint. Although this kind of power is usually associated only with police, military or criminal elements, it all too often enters into personal relationships—whether in the form of a slap or a threatening tone of voice. The underlying message in all forms of physical power is that the person who imposes the threat has very little regard for the other person's needs, interests or feelings.

Litigation is a variation of physical force. In the judicial system, decisions based on respect for the courts are ultimately backed up by the police, who can, if required, impose physical force or restraint. The power of the law occasionally intrudes into private relationships in the form of child custody orders, restraining orders or laws governing business arrangements.

In large organizations and in our community relationships, we have another form of power called "legitimate" power. Legitimate power is the authority that a group of people with common interests gives to an elected or appointed leader or leaders to act on their behalf. For example, clubs, co-ops, homeowners, and political groups elect leaders or boards of directors. As a rule, the power is limited by a constitution, bylaws or other statements of purpose. Members accept the right of the appointed leader to act in their behalf, even including the right to place certain limits and controls on the members who appointed them.

While these forms of power may affect our public and private lives, they are generally not the kinds of power that play significant roles in our most intimate relationships. Most couples do not wield guns, do not use physical force, and unless they are suing for divorce, usually do not ask the courts or other institutions to help them solve their problems.

The following are common forms of power that we do find in our relationships:

Belief systems

Power, as well as moral authority, is often defined by our assimilated religious beliefs and social values. In our grandparents' generation, people were taught and pretty well accepted the belief that the wife was to obey the husband. Similarly, moral authority was granted to parents, giving them the power to determine how their children should lead their lives. In many families, of course, these values continue to be influential. In other relationships, these values are no longer considered appropriate or relevant. Wherever these attitudes do exist, they assign power to the person holding a certain role.

Family roles

Traditionally, the main breadwinner was given power over other family members. His needs and desires were given top priority. This power structure has changed in recent years, both because the role of the breadwinner is often shared by two people and because social attitudes have shifted, giving more status and recognition than before to the person who stays home and cares for the family.

Personality differences

Differences in our personalities, skill levels, vulnerabilities, and ability to handle stress can also become the source of power in our relationships. For example, a wife may have a more assertive personality than her husband, and he perceives this as a power that he lacks. On the other hand, the same husband may be better at marshaling facts and logical arguments, and his wife may perceive this as a source of power that she lacks. Some people exert power by knowing which buttons to push to make the other person feel stupid or guilty.

Expertise

Each of us has expertise in some area. A husband, for example, may know a lot about cars and nothing about finances, while his wife may know a lot about finances but nothing about cars. Their expertise becomes the source of power when it is applied to appropriate situations. The husband's expertise about cars becomes a source of power when the family is picking out a new car. The wife's expertise about finances becomes a source of power when the family is working out a budget. As a couple confronts different issues, one person's expertise may be called upon at one moment, the other person's the next; thus power may shift from moment to moment.

Material wealth and earning power

To one degree or another, we may achieve power through the ownership of material resources or our earning power. For example, if one person has ample material resources while the other has little or none, the person with the greater resources tends to have more power than the other. With two-earner families, it is the person with the biggest paycheck who tends to have the most power. Imbalances seem to occur even when the person with the greater resources or earning power does not consciously use that fact to gain leverage over the other person.

To fully appreciate how we use power in our relationships, it is important to understand how our perceptions influence this power. Sometimes, after all, it is not the power the other person wields so much as the power we perceive them as having that determines how much influence they have over us.

The influence of perceived power

If we perceive an individual or institution as having power over us, they will have it. If we do not perceive them as having power, their influence in our lives will be negligible.

A wonderful example of power and perception in our society is found in the reactions most people have when they come face to face with movie stars, famous sports figures or rock stars. Perfectly articulate people may become tongue-tied in their presence. A particularly dedicated fan may adopt belief systems, mannerisms or ways of dress associated with their hero. This kind of power is attributed to a famous person only through the perception of the beholder, who consciously or unconsciously chooses which people influence his or her life.

In most personal relationships, perceived power is nearly always in a state of flux, with both people being on a kind of teeter-totter about who has the greater power at any given moment. In fact, with couples I have worked with, most of the time both partners perceive the other person as having the greater power. Out of our caring for each other there grows a subtle interdependence that makes our perceptions of power increasingly important. For example, we know that if a casual acquaintance criticizes us or withdraws from us, we may be slightly irritated or may not even notice. If a boss is abrupt with us, we may feel hurt or feel insecure about our job for a few moments. But if the person we are closest to acts cold or distant, it can dominate our life, keeping us awake at night or unable to concentrate on our work until we have resolved the conflict. Quite simply, the more we care about another person, the more their thoughts and feelings are likely to influence us.

For our relationships to work well, we must accept that we have power, whether we want it or not. And then we must make a choice about how we are going to use it. We can use it in an adversarial way, getting our needs met at the expense of the other person; or we can use it to deepen our relationships and promote a more complex understanding of each other.

Power that Deepens Intimacy

Where our loved ones are concerned, power is optimized when we use it both skillfully and with love, keeping our concern for the relationship itself high on our list of priorities. This is the essence of the win-win way of relating and is the best way to break out of the trap of adversarial thinking.

There are two clearly constructive uses of power in intimate relationships. The first is to urge the other person to acknowledge our emotions and deal with issues that are of importance to us. The second is to insist that decision-making processes that affect both people are equitable and fair. Let us take a closer look at each of these.

Whenever it becomes necessary, it is entirely appropriate to use your influence or power to insist that your emotions be acknowledged, that important issues be addressed, and that a resolution be sought. Bear in mind that there is a difference between these goals and insisting on a particular resolution that may give you an advantage. To clarify this, consider how this process works in large organizations.

When resolving disputes within communities and corporations, the process of acknowledging each other's needs is called "getting to the table." Both parties have to acknowledge that there is a problem, and both parties have to see each other as having a legitimate right to negotiate. The mediator's first task is to determine if both parties recognize the other. If not, the mediator must figure out a way to create the balance of power that will help bring this about. Sometimes this is done by bringing to bear the power of an external authority, such as the courts, to act in a way that threatens both parties equally. A judge might order both sides to make an effort to reach a settlement, knowing that they may face judicial ire if they do not.

Although "getting to the table" is a lot less formal with personal relationships, it is also true that couples, friends, and roommates go through struggles very similar to the ones that businesses and communities face. For example, Don wants to buy a new car but he cannot get Kristin even to discuss it. Lucy wants to talk about the future of her relationship with her live-in lover, Tom, but he adroitly avoids the issue whenever she brings it up.

As we have previously discussed, there may be legitimate reasons why people do not always agree to negotiate right away. One of these involves timing. One person may be ready to act before another, and there is often no reason that one person's sense of timing should be considered more important than another's. Sometimes, the reason people do not negotiate right away is that they have different priorities.

If you use your power to insist that things be done only according to your timetable, you will be creating a win-lose situation, with all the conditions for triggering the other person's resentment and their desire to "get even." But if you use your power to insist that an issue be addressed at a mutually accepted time, and in a mutually accepted manner, you will have gained a great step forward in achieving a win-win solution.

After considering how your exercise of power might affect the other person in your relationship, it is still important to exercise enough power to make your thoughts and feelings known. Unless you do that, you will end up letting the other person's priority list and timetable dominate, and you will end up being the person who is resentful and looking for ways to get even. Remember, even if you consciously absorb a loss, you can fail to strengthen the relationship.

While it is perfectly legitimate to use your power to insist that certain issues get addressed, you should use that power within certain reasonable constraints. Simply saying, "I don't want to talk about that now" is not enough, unless there is a commitment made to talk about it at another time. Think of this as a two-step process: step one being a mutual agreement to address our issue, step two being a separate follow-up agreement on how to resolve it. Most couples find that the more practice they have at solving their problems by mutual agreement, the less they need to exert power to get their issues addressed. They develop an understanding that both people have the right to raise issues and have them treated with respect.

The other appropriate way to use your power is to insist on a process that is fair to both people. A "fair process" is one in which both people have the same access to information, and have the same opportunity to influence the outcome. A political campaign in which only one candidate gets to use television to reach the public is not a fair process. When a wife or husband is consulted only after the children have been promised something or arrangements have been made with other people, that is not a fair process. When a spouse uses his or her family to gang up on the other person, that is not a fair process.

When you use your power responsibly, you insist on a process which is equitable, not a process which favors you.

Beyond Compromise

Like the fallacy that it is somehow "bad" to use power in our relationships, it is a commonly held belief that we can achieve "win-win" solutions if people will only be a little more willing to compromise "so that everybody can be happy." It brings up mental pictures of those worn-out television sitcom plots of the fifties and early sixties. Mom and Pop would have a disagreement with both of them insisting on getting their own way. The story line consisted of problems piling up as a result of their inability to bend until, in the end, they realized the folly of their stubbornness and agreed to a compromise, Once they did this, everyone lived happily until next week. The message was that life would be rosy if we would not be so stubborn about insisting that thing go our own way.

Compromise is built on an underlying belief in scarcity—that there is just so much to go around. Where relationships are concerned, this often seems to imply that both people have to give something up in order to maintain the relationship. Rather than coming away satisfied, both feel disappointed.

As psychotherapist Daniel Wile suggests, even some of the best compromises are gambles that might produce resentment and undermine the relationship. With the concept of "win-win," it is possible to achieve resolutions without compromise on either side. "Win-win" questions the world view that we are all adversaries or that there is only so much to go around. But how do we achieve a settlement of a conflict that is neither a win-lose situation, a compromise, nor a lose-lose situation? The answer is that we need a process whose goal is to achieve a resolution where both people win.

Process Can Point the Way

Michael, age four, and Jim, age six, are fighting over the last piece of cake. Mom has already announced that they are going to have to share it but Michael and Jim start arguing over who will get the bigger piece. Mom steps in with a process that will ensure that the cake will be divided evenly.

She gives Jim the responsibility for cutting the cake and gives Michael the right to have the first choice between the two pieces. Jim understands that if he cuts one piece bigger, Michael will pick that piece, so he is particularly conscientious about how he divides the cake. The end result is that Jim and Michael participate equally in the process, and both are satisfied with the result.

This story clearly illustrates how process can serve us. Mom's process embodied two key messages: (1) both boys should be treated equally, and (2) both should actively participate in solving the problem. All processes communicate certain values. If the process you use does not communicate equality, as Mom's did, it will be extremely difficult to achieve an equitable solution.

In our most intimate relationships, processes can be too rigid, not permitting room for adjustments or too loose, forcing people to spend the majority of their time arguing about relationship issues. Yet processes help us define what is expected of us and how we ought to behave.

The problem with not making a conscious decision about a process—of just being "natural" or "spontaneous"—is that you can revert to your predetermined, and not always productive, methods for solving conflicts. You may well be defaulting to outdated or irrelevant processes used by your parents, relatives, schools or community which served as models during your childhood. Some of these methods may work; some may not. Only by making a conscious choice about process can you hope to create a win-win outcome.

Win-Win Messages Embedded in the Collaborative Problem-Solving Process

The collaborative problem-solving process we will be recommending contains three messages which help define the relationships of the people using it.

Both people have equal opportunity to participate in the decision-making process

Many decision-making processes permit people to participate only after the issue has been defined or even after decisions have been made about certain options. This is particularly likely to happen in large organizations, where one department or boss may have already spent a lot of time working on an issue. Others are invited into the decision-making process only after most of the work has already been completed. The reality is that other people are being brought in not to participate in the process but to rubber-stamp the work another person has done. Usually this is justified as "saving time," but the danger is that when issues are defined and options are chosen unilaterally, others feel left out and an adversarial climate is established.

The same thing can occur in intimate relationships. Let us say that one person works alone on a mutual issue. Then, after making certain decisions, she (or he) decides to involve the other person. The two people do not have the opportunity to share those parts of the process that include discussing needs and interests, defining the problem or exploring different options. Hence, they leap immediately into talking about the solutions being offered without ever addressing how they arrived at those solutions. This triggers an argument over competing options.

It is very easy to slip into this trap. Collaborative problem solving requires that both people participate in each step of the process from the very beginning. The needs and interests of both people must be considered for a solution to be mutually acceptable.

Both people have comparable access to information

In our earlier discussion of power, we talked briefly about "expertise" as a form of power. This simply means that when someone is an acknowledged expert, he (or she) often exerts considerably more influence on the outcome that the "non-expert," whether or not that person really knows more about the situation.

In long-term relationships there is usually some delegation of responsibility. A husband or wife, for example, may have made decisions (or fallen into a pattern) of one person handling shopping, the other handling the cars; one person handling savings and investments, the other paying bills, and so on. Over time, a certain amount of specialization creeps in, and each person becomes an "expert" in the relationship on a particular topic. Ordinarily this saves time because both people do not have to keep track of every single issue, but if there is a conflict in one person's area of "expertise," there can be problems. Because one person may know more facts about a topic does not mean that both people should not participate in the decision. The hard decisions in life are usually not about facts, but about how important one value is compared to another. Is it more important to save for the future or enjoy ourselves now? Are the needs of the children more important than the needs of the parents? Which is more important, freedom or commitment? It is these kinds of decisions which produce conflict. And while you may need some facts to resolve them, ultimately, no matter how expert you may be, these hard choices have less to do with facts than with who you are as people.

By having both people participate in decision-making processes from beginning to end, adversarial conflicts over expertise can be greatly reduced. There may be stages in the process where the expert may be called upon to present information which the nonexpert would not otherwise have, but both people participate equally in making decisions about how that information will be applied, how options will be evaluated, and so forth. Wherever both people have a stake in the outcome, too much reliance on the "expert" can become the source of much resentment.

Both people have approximately the same ability to influence the outcome

The decision-making process should not in any way give either person an advantage over the other. This is why it is necessary to provide full participation and access to information for both people. Some people have stronger personalities than others and may have more influence on a decision. Also, if one person feels more strongly about an issue than the other, and is willing to exert more energy, that person is likely to have more influence. But for collaborative problem solving to work well, both people must be convinced that there is no inequity built into the process. If they both trust the process, they can cope with the fact that the balance of influence between them can shift from issue to issue.

Clearing the Way for Collaborative Problem-Solving

Preliminary steps:

1. Make sure the fight is over.

2. Agree on the problem-solving process.

If you have been fighting, your body chemistry has to cool down before you will be ready or willing to act in a collaborative manner. If the fight is not over, you will need to schedule your problem-solving session for another time.

How can you tell when a fight is over? When (a) you both feel satisfied that you have had your say, and (b) you have both accepted the right of the other person to differ. You can tell you are still in "fight mode" when you find:

- You are communicating with little digs or barbs.

- You see the other person as trying to take advantage of you while problem solving.

- You do not trust each other to keep agreements.

If any of these begin turning up, you need to stop and express any feelings left over from the fight before you try to process with problem solving.

If you and your partner are reading this book together, you can get started with a quick: "Okay, let's use the problem-solving process described here." However, if you are trying to solve a problem with someone who has not read the book, the first move is to get an agreement on the steps you will be following. Without that agreement, you may both have very different expectations about what is supposed to happen, and end up getting very unhappy with each other because those expectations are not being met.

Because you undoubtedly have years of experience at more adversarial ways of addressing problems, you'll need reminders that you are not playing by the adversarial rules this time around. You will eventually establish an ongoing agreement that you will work together collaboratively to solve any problems that arise. But until those agreements are well established, take a moment to remind each other that you are playing by new rules.

The essence of this process is sharing the emotion that, "WE have a problem to solve." That shared emotion does not always come easily.

There are times when one of you may resist sitting down to seek solutions. You or your partner may be afraid that if you discuss the issue at all, it will just turn into a fight. One of you may not perceive that a problem the other person is having is worth talking about. It may be that you or your partner had past experiences, perhaps even in childhood, that make you distrust that a win-win solution can be found. You and your partner may have different timing for when you are ready to discuss a problem or you may have different styles for working things out. The bottom line is that people will not seek solutions until:

- They agree there is a problem.
- They trust that addressing the problem will make their lives better.
- They are assured that their needs and capacities will be respected.

Sometimes, as with problems such as addictive behaviors, phobias, and unfounded jealousy, collaborative problem solving cannot proceed without outside help such as psychotherapy or other forms of individual counseling.

Sometimes, too, one person may be "crossing over the line" when they request a problem-solving session. An example of this would be the wife who believes that her husband does not demand enough respect at work and so wants to sit down and brainstorm ways that he can demand that respect. Collaborative conflict resolution is rarely effective for "working on the other person's problems" unless, of course, they request it.

If there is a history of adversarial conflict in your relationship, you may want to mutually agree to begin moving toward collaboration, building trust gradually so that both of you can lay down your weapons at the same time. Each new experience of true collaboration builds trust and increases your confidence that it is possible to resolve problems in ways that ensure that both your needs are met.

Steps in the Collaborative Problem-Solving Process

In the 1960s Thomas Gordon put together a simple six-step approach to problem solving. Recent work in this field has not significantly changed the basic thrust of that work, although different people use different wording to describe those steps. Guided by my own professional experience and research, I have modified Gordon's steps while remaining true to the fundamental principles.

Problem-solving process

1. Agree on what you both need for the issue to be resolved.

2. Brainstorm a list of alternative solutions.

3. Agree on which solution(s) best meet both people's needs.

4. Agree on how to implement the solution.

5. Agree on a way to determine if the solution is working.

6. Discuss how the problem-solving process worked.

7. Evaluate how well the process is working.

1. Agree on what you both need for the issue to be resolved.

Instead of beginning with solutions, start by discussing your needs and interests. There is a big difference. For example:

NEED / INTEREST: *I need to know when you're going to get home so that I can plan for dinner. Otherwise, I never know what to fix, and dinner just ends up being overcooked or burned and I get angry at you.*

SOLUTION: *You get home for dinner every night by six or you can forget about dinner!*

This is the single most important step in the entire problem-solving process. In fact, most of the recent developments in conflict resolution have concentrated on how to complete this step satisfactorily, since how you define your needs dictates the course for the rest of the resolution process. Here are points to keep in mind for successfully completing this step:

• Develop a common understanding of the issue before thinking about solutions

Many of us have been told, "Don't complain about the way things are unless you have something better to offer." While this may discourage chronic complainers, offering solutions can be exactly the wrong thing to do in collaborative problem solving.

For example, Rachel and Joe are trying to save money for a down payment on a house. But every month they fall far short of their budgetary goals. Joe thinks the problem is that they are overspending, and his solution is to tighten up on the purse-strings. Rachel thinks the problem is that their budgetary goals are not realistic and they need to review costs and make necessary adjustments, which may mean putting less money in savings than originally planned. Since Rachel and Joe disagree on what the problem is—Joe thinks it's overspending while Rachel thinks the budget is too restrictive—they certainly will not find each other's proposed solutions acceptable. They need to agree on a definition of the problem before the discuss solutions.

Until we can agree on the definition of a problem, there is no way to come up with a solution acceptable to both people. We simply cannot accept a proposed solution until we are convinced it addresses the real problem.

Failure to define the problem not only wastes time, but can also create an adversarial climate. When we start out with a solution, we establish our position and we dig in our heels to defend it. We have all sat through meetings at work, at church, at school, where one group comes in supporting one proposal, while another group comes in supporting another, and soon everybody is choosing sides. Even though everyone wants to solve the problem, the room ends up being divided between those defending one proposal or another, and no matter what happens, there are going to be some people who will go away angry, feeling they have been defeated.

When you start by defining the problem, it gives everyone a chance to participate, to have their say. By the time you are through, both people or sides are working on "our" problem, rather than me trying to sell you on my perspective and you trying to sell me on yours.

• Talk about needs and interests before you talk about solutions

Talk about what each of you would need to feel that the problem was solved. You do this before you talk about possible solutions. Let us look at an example of how this can work:

A family of four decides to take a vacation. When they sit down to discuss where they would like to go, they quickly discover that everyone has a different "solution." The kids want to go to Disneyland; Mom wants to go to San Francisco; Dad wants to go to the mountains. Pretty soon everyone is arguing, trying to convince the others that theirs is the best answer.

But now consider what might happen if instead of immediately looking for solutions, the same family starts looking at needs and interests. We find that the kids want to go to a place where there are "lots of things to do." Mom wants to go to a place where she can shop and attend cultural events. Dad wants to visit a natural setting where he can unwind and maybe do a little fishing.

Having defined the problems in terms of needs and interests, the family then sets to work looking for one place they might go that will most nearly satisfy all concerned. They discover a seaside resort where there is an amusement park for the kids, a musical festival and interesting little shops for Mom, and a wonderful beach and deep-sea fishing for Dad. As impossible as it may have seemed when only solutions were offered, this family indeed finds a place to go where all their needs and interests are satisfied.

If you are trying to problem-solve with people who keep focusing on their own solutions, ask them: "What do you wish to achieve with this solution?" This quickly leads them back into discussing their needs and interests, and from there you can go on to seek ways of meeting them.

It is helpful to write down both people's needs and interests on a single sheet of paper. The list might be entitled "What We Both Need to Have for an Acceptable Solution." These needs will later become the criteria for evaluating your solutions. By writing down both people's needs, rather than having each person develop their own list, you begin by giving each other equal recognition. On less complex issues you may not want to take the time to write out these lists. Instead, use your Active Listening skills so that before you take the next step, you both feel secure that your needs and interests have been heard and are understood.

• Consider establishing problem-solving principles

In their bestselling book, *Getting to Yes,* authors Roger Fisher and William Ury suggest that people develop criteria for objectively measuring when an acceptable solution has been found. The example they give is of the person whose car has just been totaled in an accident. The car is to be replaced by the insurance company, and negotiations have begun with the insurance adjuster. The insurance adjuster's opening comment is, "The most I could offer on that car is $3,500." As Fisher and Ury point out, at this point you have no way of knowing whether that is a horrible offer or a wonderful one. As a result, agreeing on a price will become a simple power struggle. You want to get more; the insurance company wants to give less. Either way, the underlying message is that there is going to be a winner and a loser. "Winning" may be based on who can hold out the longest, on whose personality is the stronger, and so on. But there is really no basis for telling what is fair.

So Fisher and Ury suggest that before you even talk about price, you establish an agreement on the criteria for determining what is fair. Your criterion might be the car dealers' Blue Book or an average of sales prices for similar cars offered in local newspaper ads. The point is, whichever procedure is used, you will then both feel that you have determined a "fair" price.

This approach clearly works well in the kinds of situations we think of as "negotiating," such as buying a car or house, but it is more difficult to come up with objective criteria for relationship problems. If the problem solving is about the equitable distribution of chores, for example, it is worth spending some time agreeing on what constitutes "equitable." Equitable might mean that the division of chores results in both people spending about the same number of hours doing them. Or it might mean that onerous chores are divided equally.

It is possible to go through the motions of defining principles or criteria such as these, making them as objective as possible, and still come up with solutions that fail to satisfy one or both people's emotional needs. Emotions involve perception. As difficult as it may be to establish objective criteria for that realm, it is still helpful to discuss them. In the process of determining what actions would be truly responsive to emotional needs, you will both get clearer on the problem. You will be able to clarify, for example, which parts of the problem are relationship issues, and which parts are emotional issues that can only be resolved by one individual or the other.

- **Define the issue broadly**

In the process of defining needs and interests, it is important to define them as broadly as possible.

If Lesley feels unsupported by Ed, his taking greater responsibility with household chores may allow her to experience more support from him. This change, however, may be more symbolic than substantive. There may be other ways Ed can provide support that will be far more important to Lesley, but for now the chores loom as a powerful symbol. Understanding the broader picture—Lesley's wanting to feel more emotional connection with Ed—helps this couple establish an even more satisfactory solution than his only helping her out with the chores.

Make certain that issues are defined in ways that offer the greatest opportunity for mutually acceptable solutions. When working for win-win solutions, you do not just figure out ways to slice the pie so that everyone will be happy with the piece they get; you also look for ways to increase the size and the quality of the pie.

Take the time to do this step right! Most of us want solutions right now. We get impatient when we are asked to take so much time to define needs and interests. However, rushing through this all-important first step can be a sort of "penny-wise but pound-foolish" approach to conflict resolution. You may quickly rush to a "solution," but you waste time in the long run because the same issue just keeps popping up again and again.

Identifying needs and interests goes a long way toward creating the sense that "we"—not just you and not just me—have a problem. Working toward shared solutions creates the emotional environment which makes it possible to achieve a collaborative solution. Once you have gone through the process a few times, you will be convinced, like me, that it is well worth the time.

2. Brainstorm a list of alternative solutions

Brainstorming means turning on your creativity and letting it flow. But it does not just mean "coming up with a bunch of ideas." It is a process with specific ground rules.

A. Once the problem has been defined, both people list as many possible alternative solutions as they can. All ideas are put on a single list, with one person acting as the "scribe."

B. Write down every idea, without any censorship or editing, and do not identify who came up with which ideas.

C. While the list is being developed, both people should refrain from commenting on the ideas. No negative comments ("that's a dumb idea"), and no positive comments ("that's a great idea") are permitted.

D. The more ideas the better. Push for quantity. Be sure that both people come up with multiple ideas.

E. "Way-out" ideas are welcomed and encouraged, since they serve as springboards to creative thought. Just keep the ideas coming and keep writing them all down.

F. Do not be afraid to elaborate on ideas which either person has already suggested. Be open to combining ideas, coming up with variations or exploring alternatives on the same idea.

G. When you have both run out of ideas, try one more time to see if you can come up with a few more.

H. Only after you have completed steps A through G should you go on to discuss any of the alternative solutions you have listed.

Before applying these brainstorming ground rules, make certain everyone understands the principles behind them. For example, making a single list without identifying who thought of the idea helps prevent people from becoming possessive of them. We tend to resist ideas, no matter how good they might be, when the person proposing them acts as if the idea "belongs" to her or him. But when both people work collaboratively, it breaks down the sense of ownership, and it is easier to concentrate on the merits of the ideas themselves.

The rules to prevent criticizing or judging ideas are based on research showing that creativity is associated with playfulness, a willingness to try out ideas that might be considered unreasonable, silly, impractical or "out of character." The enemy of creativity is our inner "auditor," or "censor," who looks over our shoulder and says, "That idea is ridiculous," or "That doesn't make any sense at all." So-called "reasonable ideas" are part of our fixed ways of viewing the problem, and may themselves contribute to the problem. By definition, a creative idea is one that breaks out of conventional ways of viewing the world.

Ensuring a safe setting is essential to creativity. Zany or way-out ideas may not necessarily be solutions, but they encourage us to think about the problem differently. Most of us approach problems in very fixed ways, and generating farfetched ideas loosens us up, often leading to fresh new solutions.

In brainstorming, the more ideas the merrier. Quantity encourages us to push beyond the obvious. And it is often in this push beyond the obvious, to ideas that really work, that we resolve the conflict and deepen the relationship.

3. Agree on which solution(s) best meet both people's needs

Several problem-solving experts, Thomas Gordon among them, divide this step into two parts: **evaluating alternatives** and **agreeing on solutions**. For example, a couple might want more information on prices, interest rates or child-care options, before trying to reach a particular agreement. Otherwise, where just two people are involved, evaluation and agreement occur more or less simultaneously.

Before evaluating, make certain you are finished brainstorming. Once started, the evaluation process will slow down the creative brainstorming. On the other hand, it is not unusual for new ideas or new combinations of ideas to emerge during the evaluation period. As you share your reactions, you may become even clearer on each other's real needs, and this may suggest a whole new range of possible solutions. So keep an open mind as you go along.

By this point, you have shared your mutual problem, and possible solutions are beginning to emerge. The key word here is "shared." Do not make the mistake now of going off to evaluate possible solutions on your own. If you do, you may become emotionally committed to an idea and you may lose valuable ground in the collaborative feeling you have been building. Then, when you get back together, you risk trying to sell the other person on your own point of view. Soon you are right back in the adversarial soup. The exception to this rule is if, by mutual agreement, you make assignments to do further research: "You check out the bank, and I'll check out the credit union at work." Even when assignments are given, guard against coming back with your information intent on selling it to the other person. Any research is done on behalf of both of you, and your first priority should always be to support the collaborative process rather than to champion a particular solution.

A word of caution: Do not try to work laboriously through every item on your list of alternatives. Instead, pick out those ideas that seem most promising. You might volunteer, "The ideas that I find most interesting are..." Develop a short list of items which just intuitively seem most promising. This short list is still very conditional. You are not making a commitment to any single alternative. Simply respond to those which intrigue you or which give you a little surge of energy. Often the final solution will require a combination of several options from the list or, as you evaluate the list, new possibilities will emerge.

This is also the stage at which your earlier efforts to define criteria begin to pay off. If you have agreed that "the chores should be divided so that both people spend the same amount of time doing them," it is easy to see whether the solution you have chosen does that. Even at this late stage of the game, defensive blaming, accusative words or judgmental behavior can slip back into your negotiations. If you feel this happening, remind yourself to express feelings— *"I'm worried that this idea will not really result in equal sharing of chores"*—not judgments—*"That idea's really unfair."* Be sure to stay on your side of the line—*"I'm uncomfortable with that idea, because I'm afraid I'll be left out of the decision-making process"*—instead of evaluating your partner's behavior or motives—*"I should have known you would like that idea. It puts you in charge, right where you have always wanted to be."* Also, remember to use Active Listening to make sure you get at true feelings about proposed solutions. Active Listening will help both of you find out which parts of proposed solutions are acceptable and which parts are not.

If one or more options meet the criteria, agreement comes quickly and easily. But it is not always that easy. Here are few guidelines to follow if you have trouble.

- **Remind each other that you are after a mutually acceptable solution**

We are all so used to win-lose situations that it is easy to slip back into that mentality. If you feel that things are getting adversarial, say, "I'm worried we're forgetting that we're trying to come up with a solution acceptable to us both." This can help refocus what you are trying to do, and help break up the adversarial mindset.

- **Identify areas of agreement**

If you find yourselves focusing on points of disagreement, do not miss the forest for the trees. Stop and summarize: "Okay, let me check. We're in agreement that we'll do such-and-so, but we're not in agreement on how to do thus-and-so. Your concern is that such-and-such will happen and I'm worried that so-and-so will happen." This gives a sense of progress, that you really have accomplished a lot already; gets a lot of issues "off the table," so that you are not overwhelmed or confused by a proliferation; and creates a sense of momentum, a feeling that you are almost there, which encourages both people to be more conciliatory on the remaining few points.

In effect, your summary is a little reminder that if you get too hung up on a few points, you may lose the mutual benefits you can both enjoy from a satisfactory, resolution.

- **Agree on an interim process**

Sometimes you just are not ready for a final solution. You may feel you do not have enough information. You may still be exploring your feelings about why the issue is so important in your relationship. It may be wise to come up with an interim process that will take you one step closer to getting the information you will require for your final agreement.

Suppose you are trying to work out an equitable distribution of chores, and you are really stuck. You might agree to keep records of the time spent on chores and then get back together in two weeks to talk again. That would be an interim process. You have not really resolved the issue but you have created a sense of progress toward a resolution, and you have provided for a period of experimentation and discovery. You both have a sense that something is happening, and you are not just stuck in a painful impasse.

• Use a trial period

Sometimes you will come up with a solution you think might work, but it is scary to agree to it on a long-term basis. You do not have to. You can agree to it on a trial basis, with an agreement to renegotiate if, after the trial, it is not working for both people. After the trial you may have learned something which causes you to modify the agreement or you may both feel sufficient confidence in the agreement that you are willing to commit to the agreement on a long-standing basis.

• Defer to the person who is most deeply affected

Many issues are of greater concern to one person than another. To continue with our example of unequal chores: One person may be convinced that the chore distribution is grossly unfair, while the other has simply never thought about the problem. Under these conditions, it is entirely appropriate for the person who is most concerned to carry a little more weight in choosing the solution, so long as it is done collaboratively and is acceptable to the other person. Instead of arguing about which one is better, the person who is less involved might say, "I'm comfortable with any of these three alternatives. Why don't you just pick the one which you like best?"

• Give it a little more time

With problems that have been around for a long time, there may be no compelling reason to resolve them instantly. But you may still want to get the ball rolling. If, after getting things started, you run into an impasse, relax. Unless there are external reasons the problem has to be solved right then, such as meeting a deadline or avoiding a price increase, it is often helpful to give yourself a little breather, and come back to the issue at a later time. If either of you is afraid that the issue will just get dropped, make a date for when you will work on the problem together again. New ideas often come up in the interim, and with a little distance, our early objections may fade, giving us more room for negotiation.

• Keep on talking and trust the process

Many times when I listened to a couple discussing their positions, I despaired that any resolution could possibly emerge. The only positive sign was that nobody had walked out. So we would just keep talking and talking, and eventually, almost as if by a miracle, a solution would arise from the mist. As a result, I have learned to trust the process, even when I can find little or no evidence that the ingredients for a solution are present. As long as the stalemate is not intensifying antagonism between the two of you, just keep talking, trusting that somewhere, somehow, an answer will emerge. "Hanging-in" and trusting the process is often the very best way to break a stalemate.

If a stalemate pushes you back into an adversarial way of relating, stop and make a date for a future session. Sometimes it is better to back away rather than forcing something to happen and risking new resentments.

Sometimes, in spite of our best efforts at collaborative problem solving, compromise seems to be the only choice, with each person giving up something important to achieve an agreement. Just remember, compromise is always a gamble, possibly leading to resentment. So do not settle for compromise too quickly.

Sometimes it is our own expectations that create the feelings of giving something up. For example, suppose you want to sell your house and your real estate agent says you ought to expect to sell it for $295,000. Thanks to the real estate agent's statement, you have pegged your expectation at that figure. Now suppose a buyer comes along and offers you $280,000. To accept such an offer feels like a real comedown, at best a compromise. It will seem like a loss even though you bought the house for only $230,000 four years ago.

The issue really is not so much one of compromise as it is of your expectation level, and that is a perceptual problem. This kind of situation occurs all the time in business. You expect a transaction to produce a certain level of income, and once this expectation is established, anything less seems like a loss even though you have made a reasonable profit on the deal.

One way to handle a compromise is to treat it as an interim solution. (You cannot do this when selling a house, but it works for many relationship issues). Accept the compromise for a defined period of time and find out what feelings emerge. You may experience much less or much more resentment than you anticipated. Either way you have gained valuable information that you can use when it is time to discuss the problem again. Today's compromise may be only a stepping-stone to a solution that feels good to everyone. All too often we get caught in a trap of thinking that we will have to live for the rest of our lives with whatever we decide today.

4. Agree on how to implement the solution

Many perfectly good agreements are shipwrecked by hidden expectations and misunderstandings about how they are going to be put into action. This can easily happen when a couple, with great relief, achieves an agreement and simply stops right there. Then, a few weeks later, they are both accusing each other of breaking the agreement or adding things they had not previously agreed to. What is happening is that both people have their own expectations about how the agreement is to be carried out, but they have not clearly expressed these during their collaborative problem-solving session. They made assumptions that the other person never even suspected. Those expectations may have been about who was going to do what, when they were going to do it or the manner in which they would do it. Now that their expectations have not been met—never mind that they never expressed them!—they both feel resentful.

Once you have a solution, make certain you define who is going to do what, where, and when. It is a way of making sure that both of you know what is expected. When expectations are expressed, everyone knows their part in working toward a solution, and has made a commitment to making it work.

The word "commitment" is crucial here. If both people agreed to a solution, but only one person is putting effort into carrying out the plan, then it is time to take another look at whether or not there really is a mutually acceptable agreement. If this happens, start right at the beginning, using collaborative problem solving to define the problem, identify needs and interests, and so forth.

Interestingly, this problem usually occurs because one or both of you were trying to be "nice," rather than sharing your genuine feelings in the first steps of the process. Then when you got down to Step 4, you found yourself unwilling to make a commitment. Being "nice" is not right when it creates this kind of divisiveness. More resentment is created when you go all the way through the process and then reveal your hidden feeling than if you express those feelings right up front.

Sometimes the problem is a "sub-issue," which can quickly be resolved. At other times you simply have to start all over again, and that can be maddening indeed. Remember, whenever strong emotions are involved, deal with those first. If necessary, express your feelings about reaching this impasse before you try another round of problem solving.

Be very certain that you have clearly articulated what you expect of the other person in your joint agreement. Do not make assumptions. And remember: Just because the other person does not handle their end of the agreement with the same style as you does not mean they are not satisfactorily fulfilling the agreement. Compare the outcome of their behavior with the fundamental agreement, rather than insisting that your way is the only way. Style does not matter; performance does.

Occasionally a situation does arise where, by mutual consent, one person is going to implement the agreement on behalf of both people, e.g., one person may be negotiating with the auto dealer to buy a car. In such a situation, discuss expectations about how the agreement is to be implemented. If you have specific expectations for how the other person will handle a situation on your behalf, be very careful to tell them exactly what you expect; do not wait until they have carried out their mission to let them know your expectations. Having shared these expectations, you need to discuss and agree upon which of these are to be included in the final agreement and which can be ignored.

5. Agree on a way to determine if the solution is working

Establish a way to evaluate the solutions you have worked out together. Most couples find it helpful to establish checkpoints, that is, specific dates when they discuss how well their agreement is working. Without checkpoints, there is a tendency to let things slide, then resentments build up until someone explodes. Checkpoints provide opportunities for making minor corrections or adjustments, thus avoiding the necessity for a new problem-solving session. Use checkpoints to reflect on your progress and congratulate each other for the positive aspects of your agreement.

Objective criteria are helpful here. You can evaluate how your agreement is satisfying the criteria you set up. If it is not satisfying, schedule time for another collaborative problem-solving session so that you can get back on track. If it is meeting your criteria, share the satisfaction of knowing you are successful.

Over time you will become increasingly comfortable and confident with the collaborative problem-solving process. It will seem more and more natural. When a new problem arises, it will simply seem like another issue to be addressed, not a signal that your relationship is failing.

6. Discuss how the problem-solving process worked

After you have gone through the steps of problem solving, spend a few minutes discussing how the whole session worked for you. Remember, these are new skills for both of you, and every confirmation will help you both build confidence.

Remember to use your communication skills even in this sharing. Stick with your feelings, not your judgments. Discuss how you were affected by the process. Avoid "crossing the line" by evaluating your partner's behavior. Tell your partner how his or her behavior made you feel, but do not judge it.

Also, share the good feelings! Positive reinforcement is usually far more powerful than negative criticism. Make it your goal to build a shared sense of success, of competence and confidence.

7. Evaluate how well the process is working

The signs that a solution is not working, and that it is time for a new collaborative problem-solving session, are that one or both people are not living up to their end of the bargain or one or both people are nagging, prodding or reminding the other to carry out the agreement.

If there is not enough commitment to motivate you or your partner without nagging, it is time to work on a new solution. Initiate new problem solving quickly. Do not nag; problem-solve. Avoid letting your resentments or disappointments build up until they are standing in the way of finding new solutions.

Solutions will not last forever. Give both yourself and your partner room to change your minds, though you should always let the other person know you have done so or are planning to do so, by initiating a new problem-solving session.

What to Do When Agreements Break Down

Sometimes, regardless of how sincere your efforts are, agreements break down and you end up with compounded resentments: not only are you upset about the breakdown of the agreement, but you are still upset about the original problem

How do you get out of an agreement that is not working? You start by seeking the consent of the other person. You say, "This isn't working for me. I'd like to come up with another answer that we can both feel good about." Ideally, you can reopen the problem solving, discuss why it is not working, and agree on a better solution. The new agreement releases you from the old one.

When agreements are broken, there are often intense feelings of resentment or disappointment, and the chances of a fight are high. Ultimately, the solution is to reengage in problem solving. In the meantime, use the communication skills you have been learning to prevent these intense feelings from escalating into a bad fight.

The Payoff

Thousands have discovered that the spirit of collaboration strengthens their relationships and brings a whole new level of trust and pleasure. With each successful use of collaborative problem solving, your confidence will increase and you will pull together as a team. As this confidence grows, fears of conflict fade. If you know how to handle conflict, it is not so scary anymore. You find yourself quickly moving past defensiveness and on to solutions that make your life together lighter, easier, and much more secure.

Tool #12

Seek Outside Help When Appropriate

Some years ago after writing his bestselling book *"Parent Effectiveness Training,"* Thomas Gordon suggested that he and I develop a "Marriage Effectiveness Training" course. Although I was convinced of the project's value, I was uncomfortable because I felt that I would have to hold up my own marriage as a model of perfection before I could be so presumptuous as to teach others.

Over the years, my wife and I have worked very hard at developing conflict resolution skills, and I am sure that we would neither still be together without them nor enjoy the deepened intimacy that has become such an important part of our life together. Love alone is seldom enough. It is the skills we learn along the way, either through long, arduous trial and error or more quickly and easily through books, workshops or the help of counselors, that can make the difference between joy and grief.

No matter how skilled a couple, and no matter how strong the bond of their relationship, periodically couples seem to hit issues that turn their relationship into an emotional merry-go-round, going in circles with no apparent resolution in sight. And when that happens, they may start looking outside their relationship for help.

Many people turn to friends to discuss their problems. While friends can offer great support in time of need, they can also reinforce many of the same attitudes and habits which triggered the problem in the first place. When couples are in danger of getting a divorce, for example, it is not unusual for friends to take sides, even pointing out the worst "faults" of the other person. Good friends are rarely neutral. They have a vested interest in our lives.

Having supportive friends is essential, of course. But if you want to resolve conflicts in your marriage, friends cannot always give you what you need. You need someone who can step outside what is happening and bring fresh insights.

How can you tell if your friend can do this for you? Ask yourself the following questions, and if your answer to more than two of them is "yes," rest assured that, as important as this friend may be to you in your time of need, she (or he) is anything but neutral.

1. Does the friend judge or evaluate your behavior or the behavior of the other person in the relationship?

2. Does your friend tell you what you should do about your problem or feelings?

3. Does your friend takes sides?

4. Does your friend have his or her own agenda for how you should act in the situation?

Far more people use friends rather than therapists when they need help. So how can you tell your friend how to help you and your partner out during a conflict, rather than reinforcing the problems that got you there? If this person is a close and trusted friend, you might want to discuss with them how to help each other whenever one of you is in need by employing some of the skills we have discussed in this book. You might share what you have learned or have them read the book, practicing some of the skills together. At the very least, you can make a pact with your friend to use Active Listening whenever either one of you requests help in the midst of a conflict. Your pact with each other might include a promise to respect each other's need to make his or her own decisions and to be cautious about judging or evaluating the behavior of anyone involved in the conflict. It might include a promise to refrain from telling each other how to resolve your problems.

What is the alternative other than the emotional support your friend can give? This help will usually come in the form of a counselor or therapist. Counselors and therapists are trained to stay neutral, outside the emotional heat, while helping you make decisions about what is good for you in terms that hold true to your own values, needs, and interests. When they listen, they do not judge you. Instead, they listen in order to help you discover positive attitudes, feelings and skills that you already have and which you can build on. They may also assist you in identifying beliefs and misunderstandings that might be blocking you from carrying out the solution that will work best for you.

Most therapists are careful about telling you what to do about your feelings. If they do advise you in a directive way, it would only be after getting to know you quite well. One of the goals of counseling and therapy is to help you strengthen your own abilities, not to have you blindly follow your helper's advice.

Unlike a close friend, a therapist is not a part of your "inner circle." In their private lives they have their own beliefs and feelings, their own friends, and their own conflicts. But as professionals, their job is to help you focus on your own thoughts and feelings, and make the kinds of choices we have been describing throughout this book. The subject of every good counseling session is you—or your relationship if you have come as a couple.

One of the great barriers to getting any form of outside help is that it involves admitting "we have a problem." For many people, this barrier is even greater because they judge people who need psychological help or counseling as "sick" or "emotionally disturbed" or "really messed up." Since few people want to accept that sort of judgment about themselves or their intimate relationships, they avoid getting help which could improve the relationship.

In the 1960s a great change occurred in the fields of psychology and counseling. Until that time, psychology was viewed primarily as a way of assisting people with severe emotional disturbances. But from the 1960s onward, there has been a growing trend toward providing counseling services that focus on helping healthy people become more effective and happier in every area of their lives. Much counseling is now skill-oriented, that is, aimed at helping people build their own capacities for dealing with everyday life.

Many different kinds of professional helpers are available in most communities. To help choose the right one for you, here are some of the categories of problems, and the kinds of resources that are available in each case.

Skill Development

A number of skills have been described in this book—skills for listening, communicating feelings, problem solving, etc. It's often hard to use these skills in real life because you are so emotionally involved in what is being said that it is hard to think also about how you are saying it. Some readers may want to join a group to fine-tune their skills in a safe setting. The skills in this book can be further strengthened by attending a training program. Going through a training program together as a couple is one way to create closeness as well as acquire skills. As you listen to the trainer and the other trainees, you will find it is natural to discuss how you communicate in your own relationship. But because it is not being discussed in the context of a fight, and there is no blame attached, it is easier to talk about the issues without feeling "put on the spot" or blamed for problems.

There are many courses already available in local communities which teach communication skills similar to the one I have described. These courses are available through community colleges, mental health centers, parent-teacher organizations, and churches or other places of worship. Look for words in the course descriptions such as "communications training," "active listening," "congruent sending," and "win-win conflict resolution."

Private counselors and consultants will help you and your mate as you practice these skills. My wife and I go to a therapist who helps us by allowing us to practice new skills while working on real life issues, with the security that there is someone to help keep us on track if we get defensive or reactive.

Process, Relationship, and Personal Issues

Let us take a look at the meaning of "process," "relationship," and "personal," as they apply to counseling.

PROCESS ISSUES: Many of the factors leading to conflict have to do with the manner—the "process"—by which couples go about addressing issues, quite independent of the actual subject of the conflict. Because process is so often a matter of habit or is so conditioned we do not even think about it, couples sometimes need help identifying how the manner in which they are trying to solve problems is setting them up for bitter fights. An objective person is often able to see process flaws in a way that someone who is used to them cannot. Sometimes these problems can be resolved fairly quickly once both people can see how the manner in which they are relating is contributing to the problem.

RELATIONSHIP ISSUES: Conflicts in intimate relationships can bring up all kinds of issues: unresolved feelings about parents, intimacy, commitment, responsibility, unrealistic expectations—the list could go on and on. Even couples who are doing well with "process" can still run into emotional issues which just do not seem to have resolutions. While it is not necessary to change one's personality to resolve conflicts, personality can contribute to conflict. Many couples discover that as their two personalities interact to create a relationship, that relationship, like a third person, can take on aspects of both people's personalities. In relationship counseling, both people who helped create the relationship are usually present, and the focus is less on individual personality than it is on finding ways to make the relationship more satisfying.

PERSONAL ISSUES: You might seek counseling for personal issues because you feel inhibited in expressing your feelings, because you have unresolved anger or pain left over from your childhood or because you are frequently depressed. All these problems can put pressure on your relationships, and can even dictate how you cope with conflict. But they are still essentially your own personal issues and are best deal with in that context.

In many cases you can talk with a prospective counselor over the phone before making a commitment to working with them. During the phone call (which in most cases will be limited to ten or fifteen minutes) or during your first session together, clearly describe what you want. Agree to work with that person only if you feel good about them. As with choosing any professional help, personal trust is at least as important as credentials. So above all, honor your own feelings when picking out a counselor. The following are different kinds of counselors you might consider:

Ministers, rabbis, pastoral counselors

Couples may be more comfortable going to a minister or rabbi because they are confident that such a person will share their own values. Many ministers and rabbis have received extensive training in pastoral counseling and are well qualified. But becoming a minister does not automatically mean the person has trained as a counselor. If you are considering going to your minister or rabbi, ask first about his or her training and experience, and assess the degree to which counseling is a strength. In particular, if you want to work on process or relationship issues, you will want to ask if the minister, rabbi or pastoral counselor has a good background in these.

Marriage and family counselors

Therapists with training in marriage and family therapy are usually well qualified for dealing with process and relationship issues. This usually includes background and experience with teaching communication skills and working through process issues. Increasingly, marriage and family counselors are willing to work with short-term crises, that is, to help people address issues that are immediately pressing. In most states, marriage and family counselors have credentials in social work, psychology or marriage and family counseling.

Clinical social workers

Clinical social workers are normally trained in family therapy, as are marriage and family counselors, but look not only at what is going on in the relationship or even in the family, but how the broader community might be impacting or provide resources to the couple. Clinical social workers would be particularly aware of community resources if relationship problems are compounded by problems such as substance abuse, physical abuse or child abuse.

Clinical psychologists

Some psychologists are psychotherapists, and some are not. The type of psychologist who does therapy is usually identified as a clinical psychologist or psychotherapist. Some clinical psychologists work primarily on personal issues, while others are highly qualified to work on process and relationship issues as well. Tell any prospective psychologist what kinds of issues you want to work on, and feel free to ask about what kind of work they normally do.

Psychoanalysts

Psychoanalysts do a form of depth therapy (analyzing dreams, early childhood traumas, etc.) which can be extremely valuable for resolving personal issues. Psychoanalysis can involve a commitment to attend sessions at least once a week, even daily in some cases, for a period of several months or even years. As helpful as it may be personally, it is not specifically designed to resolve process or relationship issues so much as to bring insight and resolution to personal problems.

Psychiatrists

Psychiatrists are medical doctors with a specialty in treating emotional problems. A few are also psychoanalysts. Most work primarily with emotional illness. If you are dealing with a major emotional problem which can be controlled through use of prescribed drugs, then you will probably see a psychiatrist. Psychiatrists, because they are physicians, are the only mental health professionals permitted to prescribe drugs. Psychiatrists may be helpful in addressing personal issues. Their ability to help with process or relationship issues depends on their interests and training outside their medical training in psychiatry.

Mediators

If you are trying to resolve a major issue, and your primary emphasis is on getting it resolved, and less on gaining insight or skills, you may want to consider a mediator. Mediators are increasingly used by family courts to resolve issues such as custody of children and financial support agreements. Mediation is also used to resolve landlord-tenant issues and some large community and environmental disputes. Essentially mediators provide the "process skills" so that you can work together to effectively resolve your dispute. They can structure meetings, guide the various participants along, and teach communication skills to aid in the problem-solving process. A mediator's skills are primarily in the realm of process, and to date, few people are using mediators to help them resolve issues which are primarily emotional.

Although there are differences in professional training, the individual differences between people within these professions makes many of the distinctions blur. As a result, you need to actually meet counselors and interview them before you make a commitment to work with them. The most important points are: (1) know what kind of help you want, and specify this as you talk with prospective counselors; (2) feel free to ask about a counselor's background—do not be intimidated, just ask the questions you need to be comfortable; and (3) know that how you feel about a potential counselor as a person— whether you feel comfortable and satisfied they can help you—is quite possibly the most important criterion for selecting a helpful professional.

In our busy lives, counselors are becoming more and more important. We can resolve important issues that might otherwise spread out over years. In the process, we gain access to knowledge and expertise that can vastly improve the quality of our relationships and the quality of our lives.

Conclusion

There is no such thing as a conflict-free relationship. Conflict is simply an essential part of the human experience. Peace is not the absence of conflict but a continuing process of resolving conflicts so that, rather than threatening our relationships, they teach us more about ourselves and each other. Once we can accept this definition of peace, it is easier to make the commitments to use the tools for becoming truly effective at resolving conflicts. These tools are:

Tool #1   Take Responsibility for the Outcome of Conflicts

Tool #2   Accept Conflict as a Normal Part of Human Relationships

Tool #3   Understand the Reality and Importance of Feelings

Tool #4   Express Feelings, Not Judgments

Tool #5   Listen So that People Feel Understood

Tool #6   Recognize and Break the Spiral of Escalation

Tool #7   Identify and Set Limits on Crazy-Making Behavior

Tool #8   Replace Power Games with Fight Rules

Tool #9   Use Constructive Ways of Making Up

Tool #10   Identify the Real Issue and Its Appropriate
              Problem-Solving Strategy

Tool #11   Aim at Win-Win Outcomes Through Collaborative
              Problem Solving

Tool #12   Seek Outside Help When Appropriate

As I have tried to emphasize throughout the book, all the skills will become easier, more effective, and more natural, with practice. Be patient. Recognize that the skills we have explored do not always come quickly. As you begin to apply these skills regularly, you will find that they require less and less conscious effort, while actually producing increasingly better results.

In taking on the responsibility for the outcome of your conflicts, you are reclaiming decisions which until now may have been made only by default. The kinds of skills we have been exploring hold the blueprints for gaining freedom from these unconscious habits, permitting us to make more conscious decisions about the ways we approach conflict.

In the beginning, it may seem that these new skills take more time and seem more complicated than the ways you have dealt with conflict in the past. Rest assured that it will get much easier as you go along. In the long run, you and your loved ones will be building a body of agreements which will greatly simplify decision making and conflict resolution.

The first few times you use collaborative problem solving, each step can seem gigantic and may also feel mechanical and unnatural. But as you both get better at applying these skills, and you gain understanding about the processes for resolving conflicts, you will find that you have much more time for life's greater rewards. Fears and anxieties that you once thought were a normal part of life will begin to fade. Increasingly, you will find yourself enjoying the special comforts of mutual caring and understanding as you learn to move beyond the secret hurts and angry words.

Together you will discover a sense of shared adventure, a common purpose, which grows deeper and deeper as you work together in these new ways. It is an adventure with immeasurable dividends in personal growth.

I have done my best to pass on to you a road map for the adventure, but only you can make the journey. As you start on your way, the skills and concepts will help enhance and enrich every relationship you establish, whether it is at home, on the job or in leisure hours with your friends.

Have a wonderful journey!

Bibliography

BACH, GEORGE R., and PETER WYDEN, *The Intimate Enemy,* New York: William Morrow, 1970.

BECK, AARON, *Love is Never Enough: How Couples Can Overcome Misunderstandings, Resolve Conflicts, and Solve Relationship Problems Through Cognitive Therapy,* New York: Harper & Row, 1988.

BILLINGS, ANDREW, "Conflict Resolution in Distressed and Nondistressed Married Couples," *Journal of Consulting and Clinical Psychology,* 46 (1979), 368–76.

BOLTON, ROBERT, *People Skills: How to Assert Yourself, Listen to Others, and Resolve Conflicts,* New York: Simon & Schuster, 1979.

COSER, L., *The Function of Social Conflict,* Glencoe, Ill.: Free Press, 1956.

DEUTSCH, MORTON, *The Resolution of Conflict: Constructive & Destructive Processes,* New Haven, Conn.: Yale University Press, 1973.

EMMELKAMP, PAUL, et al., "Marital Therapy with Clinically Dis-

tressed Couples: A Comparative Evaluation of System-Theoretic, Contingency Contracting, and Communication Skills Approaches," in Hahlweb, Kurt, and Neil S. Jacobson (Eds), *Marital Interaction Analysis and Modification,* New York: Guilford Press, 1984.

FISHER, ROGER, and WILLIAM URY, *Getting to Yes: Negotiating Agreement Without Giving In,* New York: Penguin Books, 1983.

FOGARTY, T.F., "The Distancer and the Pursuer" *The Family,* 7 (1979) 11–16.

GORDON, THOMAS, *P.E.T.: Parent Effectiveness Training,* New York: New American Library, 1975.

GORDON, THOMAS, *P.E.T. in Action,* New York: Bantam, 1978.

GORDON, THOMAS, *Leader Effectiveness Training: The No-Lose Way to Release the Productive Potential in People,* New York: Bantam, 1980.

GORDON, WILLIAM J.J., *Synectics: The Development of Creative Capacity,* New York: Harper & Row, 1961.

GOTTMAN, J.M. and Lowell Krokoff, "Marital Interaction and Satisfaction: A Longitudinal View," *Journal of Consulting and Clinical Psychology,* 57 (1989), 47–52.

GOTTMAN, John, *Why Marriages Succeed or Fail: How You Can Make Yours Last,* New York: Fireside, 1995.

HEITLER, SUSAN M., *From Conflict to Resolution: Skills and Strategies for Individual, Couple, and Family Therapy,* New York: W.W. Norton, 1990.

KOTTLER, JEFFREY A., *Beyond Blame: A New Way of Resolving Conflicts in Relationships,* San Francisco: Jossey-Bass, 1994.

MARKMAN, HOWARD, SCOTT STANLEY and SUSAN BLUMBERG, *Fighting for Your Marriage,* San Francisco: Jossey-Bass, 1994.

NOTARIUS, CLIFFORD and HOWARD MARKMAN, *We Can Work It Out: How to Solve Conflicts, Save Your Marriage, and Strengthen Your Love for Each Other,* New York: Berkeley Publishing Group, 1991.

PARNES, S.J., *Creative Behavior Guidebook,* New York: Scribner's, 1967.

RUBIN, JEFFREY and CAROL RUBIN, *When Families Fight: How to Handle Conflict With Those You Love,* New York: Ballantine Books, 1988.

SIMMEL, GEORGE, *Conflict and the Web of Group Affiliations,* Glencoe, Ill.: Free Press, 1955.

TANNEN, DEBORAH, *That's Not What I Meant!: How Conversational Style Makes or Breaks Relationships,* New York: Ballantine Books, 1988.

TANNEN, DEBORAH, *You Just Don't Understand!: Women and Men in Conversation,* New York: Ballantine, 1990.

TAVRIS, CAROL, *Anger: The Misunderstood Emotion,* New York: Simon & Schuster, 1982.

WEHR, PAUL, *Conflict Regulation,* Boulder, Colo.: Westview Press, 1979.

WEINGARTEN, HELEN, "Conflict Essential in a Healthy, Intimate Relationship," *Marriage and Divorce Today,* 10 (1985): 1–2.

WEINGARTEN, HELEN and SPEED LEAS, "Levels of Marital Conflict Model: A Guide to Assessment and Intervention in Troubled Marriages," *American Journal of Orthopsychiatry,* 57 (1987), 407–17.

WILE, DANIEL, *After the Honeymoon: How Conflict Can Improve Your Relationship,* New York: Wiley, 1988.

Titles Published by Aslan

Argument With An Angel. A modern day parable about finding the good within each of us by Jan Cooper $11.95; ISBN 0-944031-63-3

Coffee Crazy—A Guide To The 100 Best Coffee Houses In America by Mary Beth Bizjak $12.95; ISBN 0-944031-64-1

Gentle Roads To Survival: Making Self-Healing Choices in Difficult Circumstances by Andre Auw Ph.D. $10.95; ISBN 0-944031-18-8

Intuition Workout: A Practical Guide To Discovering & Developing Your Inner Knowing by Nancy Rosanoff $12.95; ISBN 0-944031-14-5

Lovers For Life: Creating Lasting Passion, Trust and True Partnership by Daniel Ellenberg Ph.D. & Judith Bell M.S., MFCC, $15.95; ISBN 0-944031-61-7

Mind, Music & Imagery: Unlocking the Treasures of Your Mind by Stephanie Merritt $13.95; ISBN 0-944031-62-5

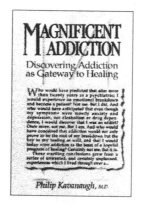

The Joyful Child:
A Sourcebook of
Activities and Ideas for
Releasing Children's
Natural Joy by Peggy
Jenkins Ph.D., $16.95
ISBN 0-944031-66-8

Magnificent Addiction:
Discovering Addiction
as Gateway to Healing
by Philip R. Kavanaugh,
M.D. $12.95;
ISBN 0-944031-36-6

More Than Just Sex:
A Committed Couples
Guide to Keeping
Relationships Lively,
Intimate & Gratifying
by Daniel Beaver M.S.,
MFCC, $12.95;
ISBN0-944031-35-8

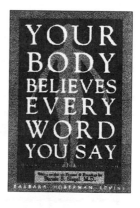

New Woman Manager:
50 Fast & Savvy
Solutions for
Executive Excellence
by Sharon Lamhut
Willen $14.95
ISBN 0-944031-11-0

The Motion Picture
Prescription Watch This
Movie and Call Me in
The Morning: 200
movies to help you heal
life's problems by Gary
Solomon Ph.D. "The
Movie Doctor " $12.95;
ISBN 0-944031-27-7

Your Body Believes
Every Word You Say:
The Language of the
Body Mind
Connection
by Barbara Hoberman
Levine $13.95;
ISBN 0-944031-07-2

More Aslan Titles

The Candida Control Cookbook What You Should Know And What You Should Eat To Manage Yeast Infections by Gail Burton $13.95; ISBN 0-944031-67-6

Facing Death, Finding Love: The Healing Power Of Grief & Loss in One Family's Life by Dawson Church, $10.95; ISBN 0-944031-31-5

How Loving Couples Fight:12 Essential Tools for Working Through the Hurt by James L Creighton Ph.D $16.95; ISBN 0-944031-71-4

If You Want To Be Rich & Happy, Don't Go to School Ensuring Lifetime Security for Yourself & Your Children by Robert Kiyosaki $14.95; ISBN 0-944031-59-5

Lynn Andrews in Conversation with Michael Toms edited by Hal Zina Bennett, $8.95; ISBN 0-944031-42-0

Solstice Evergreen: The History, Folklore & Origins of the Christmas Tree 2nd ed by Sheryl Karas $14.95; ISBN 0-944031-75-7

Upcoming Titles

The Gift of Wounding: Finding Hope & Heart in Challenging Circumstances by Andre Auw Ph.D, $15.95; hardcover ISBN 0-944031-77-3 Jan 1999

What Happened to the Prince I Married: Spiritual Healing for a Wounded Relationship by Sirah Vettese Ph.D $14.95 ; ISBN 0-944031-76-5

To order any of Aslan's titles send a check or money order for the price of the book plus Shipping & Handling

> **Book Rate** $3 for 1st book.; $1.00 for each additional book
> **First Class** 4 for 1st book; $1.50 for each additional book

Send to   ***Aslan Publishing***
           2490 Black Rock Turnpike # 342
           Fairfield CT 06432

To receive a current catalog: please call (800) 786–5427 or (203) 372–0300
E-mail us at: **info@aslanpublishing.com**
Visit our website at **www.aslanpublishing.com**

Our authors are available for seminars, workshops, and lectures. For further information or to reach a specific author, please call or email Aslan Publishing.